LEGACIES OF
THE AMERICAN
REVOLUTION

LEGACIES OF
THE AMERICAN
REVOLUTION

Copyright © 1978 Utah State University

Library of Congress Cataloging in Publication Data

Main entry under title:

Legacies of the American Revolution.

Includes bibliographical references.
1. United States--History--Revolution, 1775-
1783--Influence--Addresses, essays, lectures.
2. United States--History--Revolution, 1775-1783--
Addresses, essays, lectures. I. Gerlach, Larry R.
II. Dolph, James A. III. Nicholls, Michael L.
E209.L44   973.3   78-5888
ISBN 0-87421-097-6

CONTENTS

v

LEGACIES OF THE AMERICAN REVOLUTION

PREFACE

Because the discovery and dissemination of knowledge remain the primary functions of the academy, a series of scholarly lectures devoted to an assessment of America's Revolutionary heritage seemed an appropriate way for the largest public institutions of higher education in the state of Utah to observe the nation's 200th anniversary. This volume is the outgrowth of such a series held during the academic year 1975-1976 at the University of Utah, Utah State University, and Weber State College. Ten prominent historians were asked to prepare a public lecture on selected topics relating to the theme, "Legacies of the American Revolution." Michael Kammen inaugurated the lecture series with addresses at each of the sponsoring institutions. Richard D. Brown, Joseph A. Ernst, Sung Bok Kim, and Bernard W. Sheehan visited the University of Utah and Utah State University in Logan. Richard L. Bushman, Jerald A. Combs, Willie Lee Rose, and John W. Shy appeared at the University of Utah and Weber State College in Ogden. Linda Grant De Pauw, Distinguished Bicentennial Professor at the University of Utah, spoke only in Salt Lake City.

In these Bicentennial Times "a decent respect to the opinion of mankind," as Thomas Jefferson would have it, necessitates an explanation as to the reason for yet another commemorative book about the American Revolution. The intrinsic value of the volume lies, of course, in presenting the views of ten historians concerning the significance of the Revolution. In addition, this collection differs in one or more important respects from other compilations of conference papers, public lectures, or commissioned essays. In contrast to similar anthologies, the volume is comprised of essays linked by a central theme rather than being a melange of eclectic offerings, directed to a general audience instead of a professional readership, concerned more with tracing legacies of the Revolution than with examining the event itself, and written (with one exception) by Revolutionary specialists charged with projecting *from* 1776 instead of by non-specialists reflecting *upon* the Revolutionary era.[1] Moreover, it is hoped that publication of a set of essays which transmits the traditions and legacies of the past to present and future generations will serve as a partial antidote to the vulgar hucksterism and vapid chauvinism of a Bicentennial celebration that often overlooked the thoughts and deeds of the Revolutionary generation.

Although assigned a general topic (e.g., the social legacies of the Revolution), each contributor was permitted to fashion a presentation that reflected individual interests and inclinations. Consequently, as indicated by the title of the volume, the essays herein constitute neither a comprehensive catalogue of Revolutionary legacies, nor form chapters of an integrated treatment of the subject, nor promulgate a single interpretation of the causes or consequences of the Revolution. Some pieces offer a sweeping survey of a given topic, while others are a detailed excursus of an aspect of a larger problem; some consist of syntheses of previous scholarship, while others present the findings of new research; some take a long-range view of the meaning of the Revolution for the course of American history, while others focus closely on happenings during the Revolutionary era as a prelude to subsequent developments; some appear here essentially in lecture form, while others are expanded and refined versions of informal presentations. For all the diversity and distinctiveness of the individual contributions, they form a coherent whole through a common purpose — an assessment of legacies of the American Revolution. "E pluribus unum" applies equally to this volume and the nation about which it is concerned.

---

[1]See, for example, Jack P. Greene, Richard L. Bushman, and Michael Kammen, *Society, Freedom, and Conscience: The American Revolution in Virginia, Massachusetts, and New York* (New York, 1976); *Contrast and Connection: Bicentennial Essays in Anglo-American History* (Athens, Ohio, 1976); *Freedom in America: A 200-Year Perspective* (University Park, Pa., 1976); Sam Bass Warner, Jr., *The American Experiment: Perspectives on 200 Years* (Boston, 1976); *The American Revolution: Explorations in the History of American Radicalism,* Alfred F. Young, ed. (De Kalb, 1976); American Enterprise Institute for Public Policy Research, *America's Continuing Revolution* (New York, 1976); *The American Revolution: A Heritage of Change,* John Parker and Carol Urness, eds. (Minneapolis, 1975); *Essays on the American Revolution,* Stephen Kurtz and James H. Hutson, eds. (Chapel Hill, 1973); and the volumes produced to date by the Library of Congress Symposia on the American Revolution — *The Development of a Revolutionary Mentality* (1972), *Fundamental Testaments of the American Revolution* (1973), *Leadership in the American Revolution* (1974), and *The Impact of the American Revolution Abroad* (1975).

It is not possible to thank formally everyone involved in promoting the lecture series and producing this book. But several persons deserve special recognition. Without the assistance and encouragement of J. Boyer Jarvis, Associate Vice-President for Academic Affairs at the University of Utah, Richard Swenson, Vice-Provost of Utah State University, and Daniel L. Martino, Coordinator of Cultural Affairs for Weber State College, the unique interinstitutional enterprise would not have been possible. And were it not for the support of Gail, Joan, and Linda, everything would have been much more difficult.

L. R. G.
J. A. D.
M. L. N.

INTRODUCTION

BY LARRY R. GERLACH

"The American war is over," Benjamin Rush remarked in 1787, "but this is far from being the case with the American revolution. On the contrary, nothing but the first act of the great drama is closed." To Philadelphia's gadfly physician, "it remains yet to establish and perfect our new forms of government; and to prepare the principles, morals, and manners of our citizens, for these forms of government, after they are established and brought to perfection."[1] Rush and his compeers knew that theirs was a continuing revolution; that the audacious experiment in republicanism required a radical transformation of principles, perceptions, and practices; and that the dynamics of the new political and social order would profoundly effect subsequent generations.

Two centuries have passed since representatives of twelve British colonies from New Hampshire to Georgia (and the three Pennsylvania counties known as "Delaware") assembled in Philadelphia and brought forth a new nation. The drama staged in the Pennsylvania State House in the early summer of 1776 remains the single most important chapter in the annals of American history. The Declaration of Independence has, as John Adams predicted, been "celebrated, by succeeding Generations . . . by solemn Acts of Devotion to God Almighty . . . Pomp and Parade, with Shews, Games, Sports, Guns, Bells, Bonfires and Illuminations from one End of this Continent to the other."[2] But few Americans today truly know its import. Over the years many of the thoughts and deeds, hopes and fears of the Revolutionary generation have faded from public memory. Most of the men

---

[1]Rush, "An Address to the People of the United States . . . on the Defects of the Confederation" [May 1787], quoted in Alden T. Vaughan, ed., *Chronicles of the American Revolution* (New York, 1965), p. 334.

[2]Adams to Abigail Adams, July 3, 1776, *The Book of Abigail and John: Selected Letters of the Adams Family, 1762-1784*, Lyman H. Butterfield, *et al.*, eds. (Cambridge, 1975), p. 142.

who pledged their lives, fortunes, and sacred honors to the quest for nationhood are now known only as quaint signatures on a piece of parchment; the Declaration they endorsed is often discussed but only infrequently read and imperfectly understood.

It should be an evident truth that one cannot comprehend the history of the United States without understanding the causes, course, and consequences of the Revolution. The Revolutionary era witnessed not only the creation of the republic, but also the formulation of the nation's fundamental political and social creeds.[3] In the Declaration of Independence, the Constitution, and the Bill of Rights are found those Revolutionary principles — among them republicanism, popular sovereignty, personal liberty, federalism, and egalitarianism — that have given unique shape to the American historical experience. And from nearly three decades of rebellion, war, and nation-building emerged basic attitudes, assumptions, and perceptions about persons and institutions — ranging from politicians and racial minorities to the military and the press — that profoundly influenced the course of events for the next 200 years.

It is appropriate that an inscription on the facade of the National Archives in Washington, D.C., wherein is a permanent display of the Declaration of Independence and Constitution, proclaims: "What is Past is Prologue." The United States is essentially what it is in 1976 because of what happened in 1776. The legacies of the Revolution are as integral a part of the history of Utah and Nebraska as of Connecticut and New Jersey; as relevant to native-born citizens irrespective of sex, race, or religion, as to newly arrived immigrants. The Founders knew as much. Rush was right: "The Revolution Is Not Over."[4] Or, more accurately, many of its legacies have not yet run their course.

I

Whatever the merit of John Adams' contention that a "radical change in the principles, opinions, sentiments, and affections of the

---

[3]In general, see Paul K. Conkin, *Self-Evident Truths. Being a discourse on the Origins & Development of the First Principles of American Government — Popular Sovereignty, Natural Rights,* and *Balance & Separation of Powers* (Bloomington, 1974), and Gordon S. Wood, *The Creation of the American Republic, 1776-1787* (Chapel Hill, 1969).

[4]Rush, "An Address . . . on the Defects of the Confederation," *Chronicles of the American Revolution,* p. 338.

people" constituted "the real American Revolution," there is no question that the Revolution lives today in "the Minds and Hearts of the People."⁵ A nation, like an individual, needs roots — a sense of heritage, of place, of continuum. For the past 200 years the Revolution has been the center of our national historical consciousness, providing a link with the past and constituting a principal cultural means of welding a pluralistic society into a nation indivisible. Because the Declaration of Independence and the Constitution contain the fundamental testaments of America's National Faith, the "Founding Fathers" are Alexander Hamilton, Thomas Jefferson, and George Washington instead of William Bradford, John Smith, and John Winthrop. The Revolutionary generation is the personification of the American political tradition: Jefferson and Hamilton remain the exemplars of political liberalism and conservatism; Nathan Hale, who under the hangman's noose regretted only that he had but one life to give for his country, is the premier patriot, while Benedict Arnold, because of his perfidious defection to the British, made his name synonymous with treason. The Revolution is indeed "the most memorable Epocha" in American history;⁶ no other event more readily and more pervasively evokes a sense of the past and national identity.

The ways of transmitting the traditions of the Revolution to the American people are varied and numerous. Historic sites and shrines ranging from Lexington Green and Monticello to Independence Hall and the Yorktown battlefield create empathy with the men and women of '76; so, too, do national holidays, monuments, rituals, and symbols — every schoolchild learns about the Revolution through Washington's birthday, the Jefferson Memorial, the Fourth of July and the Liberty Bell. Histories of the Revolution abound; surely more books and articles have been written about the birth of the republic than any other event in American history except, perhaps, the Civil War.⁷ The arts also disseminate the Spirit of Seventy-six. Well known paintings and portraits by such artists as Charles Willson Peale and

⁵Adams to Hezekiah Niles, February 3, 1818, *The Works of John Adams,* Charles Francis Adams, ed., 10 vols. (Boston, 1850-56), 10:282-83.
⁶The phrase is from John to Abigail Adams, July 3, 1776, *Book of Abigail and John,* p. 142.
⁷The most comprehensive catalogue of writings on the Revolution is Ronald M. Gephart, *Revolutionary America, 1763-1789: A Bibliography* (Washington, D.C., forthcoming).

Jonathan Trumbull,[8] imposing statuary like Cyrus E. Dallin's equestrian Paul Revere,[9] the buoyant melody of "Yankee Doodle," and the stirring stanzas of Henry Wadsworth Longfellow's epic poem "Paul Revere's Ride" evoke the Revolution. And through the novel, whether the "juvenile literature" of an Everett T. Tomlinson or the "adult fiction" of a Kenneth L. Roberts, generations of Americans have thrilled to and learned from larger-than-life adventure stores with a Revolutionary setting.[10]

Michael Kammen's examination of the major American novels treating the Revolution demonstrates that the axiom "each generation writes its own history" is as applicable to novelists as to historians. In delineating the three historical periods in which novels with a Revolutionary setting were especially popular, Kammen traces the changing attitudes of "imaginative writers" toward academic historians and reveals the ways in which novels mirror both the cultural climate of the day and the shifts in Anglo-American relations. He also describes an enduring theme that pervades nearly all fictional writing about the formative years: the Revolution as a rite of passage. This provocative excursus raises numerous important questions about the meaning of tradition in culture and the role of literature in creating an historical consciousness. Could it be, for example, that the novelists' penchant for depicting the Revolution as a rite of passage — since most people derive notions of the past from historical novels rather than from scholarly volumes — has contributed significantly to the popular view of the Revolution as a completed success story rather than as an ongoing process of political and social evolution?

---

[8]See Charles Coleman Sellers, *Charles Willson Peale* (New York, 1969); Theodore Sizer, *The Works of Colonel John Trumbull: Artist of the American Revolution*, (New Haven, 1967); and Irma B. Jaffe, *John Trumbull: Patriot-Artist of the American Revolution* (Boston, 1976). A recent, penetrating discussion is Michael Kammen, "From Liberty to Prosperity: Reflections upon the Role of Revolutionary Iconography in National Tradition," *American Antiquarian Society, Proceedings*, 86, pt. 2 (1976): 237-72.

[9]For an account of Dallin's struggle with the city of Boston to erect the statue, see Rell G. Francis, "Cyrus E. Dallin and His Paul Revere Statue," *Utah Historical Quarterly*, 44 (1976): 4-29.

[10]See the comments about Tomlinson's work by Whitfield J. Bell, Jr., "Everett T. Tomlinson, New Jersey Novelist of the American Revolution" in William C. Wright, ed., *New Jersey in the American Revolution: Political and Social Conflict* (Trenton, 1974), pp. 76-88. For a general discussion of novelists' conceptions of history, see Harry B. Henderson III, *Versions of the Past: The Historical Imagination in American Fiction* (New York, 1974).

II

Although novelists have conceived of the Revolution as the culmination of the maturation process (explicitly for individuals but implicitly for the nation as well), the revolutionaries considered themselves to be engaged in an act of creation not completion. They experienced first-hand the wrenching dislocations attendant to rebellion and warfare as well as the tribulations concomitant to fashioning a new political order. And they hoped that their bold scheme of republican self-government would carry far beyond the Revolutionary era. Because the American Revolution, unlike most subsequent revolutions, experienced no "Thermidorian reaction," no counter-revolution to destroy nascent republican principles and institutions, Thomas Paine's bold declaration of 1776 proved prophetic. "The cause of America," he proclaimed in *Common Sense,* "is in great measure the cause of all mankind. . . . 'Tis not the concern of a day, a year, or an age; posterity are virtually involved in the contest, and will be more or less affected even to the end of time by the proceedings now."[11]

From the initial skirmish between Massachussetts militia and royal troops at Lexington and Concord on April 19, 1775, until well after the British surrender at Yorktown on October 19, 1781, war was the central fact of life in America.[12] (Appropriately, the soldier has become in the public mind a primary symbol of the Revolution: the Redcoat mercilessly massacring Bostonians is the personification of the British threat to American liberty, while the "embattled farmer" standing defiantly at the "rude bridge" in Concord is the embodiment of the courage and conviction that won independence.) The War of Independence, simultaneously a clash of regular armies and an internecine struggle between partisan irregulars, touched in some manner virtually every community; in all, eight years of warfare produced some 1,546 military and naval engagements which claimed directly or indirectly an estimated 33,769 casualties.[13] Although much has been

---

[11]Paine, *Common Sense,* reprinted in Merrill Jensen, ed., *Tracts of the American Revolution, 1763-1776* (Indianapolis, 1967), pp. 402, 419.

[12]The most serviceable one-volume surveys of the war are Don Higginbotham, *The War of American Independence: Military Attitudes, Policies, and Practice, 1763-1789* (New York, 1971) and Marshall Smelser, *The Winning of Independence* (Chicago, 1972).

[13]Howard H. Peckham, ed., *The Toll of Independence: Engagements and Battle Casualties of the American Revolution* (Chicago, 1974), p. 130.

written about the military dimension of the Revolution, the literature until recently consisted largely of drum-and-bugle chronicles of battles, generals, and campaigns. In increasing numbers historians are now viewing the Revolutionary War from broader vistas, recognizing that the significance of the conflict reached far beyond the battlefields. Some are studying the creation of a military establishment and peacetime military policy after the conclusion of hostilities.[14] Others are focusing on the broad impact of the war on society.

John W. Shy treats the struggle for independence as a chapter in the history of war rather than military history. Appreciating the difficulty modern Americans have in comparing the Revolutionary War with the world-wide holocausts of the twentieth century, he takes care to place wartime statistics relating to service and casualties in the perspective of the day. He also assesses the immediate as well as the long-range political, social, economic, and even psychological legacies of the war. In his suggestive essay, the war becomes something of a prism which refracts the spectrum of factors that influenced both the outbreak of hostilities and the nature of post-war America. War, Shy reminds us, involves more than the stark tragedy of death and destruction; it also produces subtle transformations of thought that affect society as a whole.

The American Revolution was accompanied by significant social change. But because of the frequent discrepancies between theory and practice, inconsistencies in defining terms, and the problems posed by an especially heterogeneous populace, there is considerable disagreement about the Revolution as a social movement.[15] At first glance, independence appears to have brought about little change in social institutions and class structure. On the eve of the Revolution there was no American aristocracy with privileges prescribed by law, no class

---

[14]For the debate over "national security" in the new nation, see Richard H. Kohn, *Eagle and Sword: The Federalists and the Creation of the Military Establishment in America, 1783-1802* (New York, 1975).

[15]For the general points of contention, see the classic statement by J. Franklin Jameson, *The American Revolution Considered as a Social Movement* (Princeton, 1926), and the subsequent studies by Frederick B. Tolles, "The American Revolution Considered as a Social Movement: A Re-evaluation," *American Historical Review*, 60 (1954): 1-12; Jackson Turner Main, *The Social Structure of Revolutionary America* (Princeton, 1965); and Jack P. Greene, "The Social Origins of the American Revolution: An Evaluation and An Interpretation," *Political Science Quarterly*, 88 (1973): 1-22.

consciousness beyond recognition of social standing and economic interest, no established church in the sense of a state ecclesiastical hierarchy; moreover, various pre-modern, Old-World practices such as primogeniture and entail had generally passed into disuse. Close scrutiny, however, reveals a sweeping societal transformation. Nearly two decades of protest and armed rebellion disrupted established patterns of activity and behavior. Social forces unleashed by the Revolution found expression in, among other things, the separation of church and state and the rise of denominationalism, a proliferation of public schools, the advent of humanitarian reforms ranging from abolitionism to revision of penal codes, and the development of an American system of law and jurisprudence coupled with the rise of a professional bench and bar. But the most enduring social legacy of the Revolution was attitudinal. With a stroke of Jefferson's pen Americans philosophically loosed themselves from the sins and systems of their fathers: the tyranny of tradition, class, ignorance, churches, armies, and monarchs was gone. The new political order based upon egalitarianism and democratic self-government had brought about a radical transformation of time-honored assumptions and values.

Political and societal values, Richard L. Bushman points out, were necessarily interwoven in a republic based on popular sovereignty. The political success of the experiment in independence depended upon a citizenry actuated by a sense of public virtue (self-sacrifice for the common welfare) as well as motivated by those traits of personal industry (ambition) calculated by "Poor Richard" to ensure material success. But as Bushman points out, the value systems are mutually contradictory: although one cannot be free (independent) without being prosperous (wealthy), prosperity logically leads to inequality and ultimately tyranny. His observations about the dilemma of the Revolutionary generation in attempting to balance the two contradictory impulses has a decidedly modern ring, for throughout the past two centuries Americans have simultaneously embraced republican simplicity and the pursuit of wealth, just as they have tried to be both free and equal.

The most immediate and far-reaching consequences of the Revolution were political. The transition from dependent colonies to independent states carried with it the responsibilities as well as the rights of political autonomy. The Constitution of 1787 that forged a nation from thirteen confederated commonwealths not only established a national constitutional-legal environment and governmental structure, but also codified such innovative theories as popular sovereignty, separation of powers, checks and balances, and federalism. Most important, the experiment in republican self-government gave rise to new attitudes and assumptions about the nature of political authority, of the role of the citizenry in government and politics, of the relationship between elected officials and the people, and of the characteristics of both good rulers and good citizens; in turn these Revolutionary principles and precepts found expression in such practices and procedures as expanded suffrage, frequent and regular election of public officials, formation of popular political parties, and reliance upon specially constituted conventions for partisan and non-partisan political purposes.[16] In short, the Federal Constitution and the appended Bill of Rights in which are contained the basic political ideas and ideals of the Revolution still provide the foundation for an extraordinary number of institutions, practices and philosophies associated with government today.

In contrast to the usual preoccupation with democratic institutions and republican ideologies, Richard D. Brown focuses upon the concept of a written constitution. To the Revolutionary generation a formal charter was more than a blueprint for government: it was a "higher law" which would protect fundamental political liberties from transitory majoritarian fancy. His timely discussion of the Founding Fathers' concept of a constitution as higher law in light of the modern tendency to regard constitutions as "super-statutes" which codify policies and procedures raises important questions concerning the future of government in America. The moral of the story of constitution-making in the states is clear: should the ideal of the Federal Constitution be similarly repudiated, what then of the polity and principles it has sustained for the past two centuries?

Despite the fact that there were important economic ramifications

---

[16]In general, see Wood, *Creation of the American Republic;* Chilton Williamson, *American Suffrage from Property to Democracy, 1760-1860* (Princeton, 1960); William Nisbet Chambers, *Political Parties in a New Nation: The American Experience, 1776-1809* (New York, 1963); Richard Hofstadter, *The Ideas of a Party System: The Rise of Legitimate Opposition in the United States, 1780-1840* (Berkeley and Los Angeles, 1969); and Richard Buel, Jr., *Securing the Revolution: Ideology in American Politics, 1789-1815* (Ithaca, 1972).

to almost every political, social, and military development during the Revolutionary era, knowledge of the economic dimension of the Revolution remains fragmentary and episodic. Moreover, the story is still told generally in traditional fashion. The economic "causes" of the Revolution are seen largely in terms of colonial discontent over imperial taxes, monetary policies, commercial codes, manufacturing regulations and control of western expansion. During the war years the discussion turns mainly on the destruction of property, the disruption of routine business activity, profiteering, price-fixing, wartime production and troop supply, confiscation of loyalist estates, and chronic inflation and indebtedness. Postwar America is viewed largely from the perspective of the state governments and the confederation congress wrestling with such thorny problems as taxation, regulation of commerce, creation and settlement of the national domain, establishment of a stable monetary system, and payment of wartime debts. After the adoption of the Federal Constitution — itself the subject of diverse economic interpretation — attention focuses on the assumption of state debts by the central government, the funding of foreign and domestic obligations at par, Hamilton's reports on manufactures and the national bank, and the expansion of international trade.[17] Although in recent years scholars in increasing numbers have responded to Clarence L. Ver Steeg's invitation to consider the American Revolution as an economic movement, there is still no comprehensive, integrated economic history of the Revolutionary era.[18]

This sorry state of historiographical affairs exists in part because, as Joseph A. Ernst suggests, there were few enduring economic legacies of the Revolution. To be sure, the fact of national independence itself necessitated numerous changes in economic procedure, practice, and policy.[19] But, Ernst contends, the Revolutionary era produced

---

[17]See, generally, Curtis P. Nettels, *The Emergence of a National Economy, 1775-1815* (New York, 1962); Stuart Bruchey, *The Roots of American Economic Growth, 1607-1861* (New York, 1965); and Douglas C. North, *The Economic Growth of the United States, 1790-1860* (Englewood Cliffs, N.J., 1961). See also E. James Ferguson, *The Power of the Purse: A History of American Public Finance, 1776-1790* (Chapel Hill, 1961) and Forrest McDonald, *E Pluribus Unum: The Formation of the American Republic, 1776-1790* (Boston, 1965).

[18]"The American Revolution Considered as an Economic Movement," *Huntington Library Quarterly,* 20 (1957): 361-72.

[19]See ibid for a suggestive assessment of the economic consequences of independence.

no structural transformation of the economy, no fundamental alteration of economic life, no new economic theories. That, of course,
is implicit in Hamilton's economic messages of the 1790s. Yet as Ernst
argues, the economic factor did loom large in late eighteenth-century
America. Indeed, he contends, adverse short-run fluctuations in the
economy combined with long-term swings to set the stage for significant
economic reform — reform that was temporarily side-tracked because
of the quest for independence. In analyzing the economic tensions and
trends during the decade before independence, in suggesting a new
way of viewing postwar economic developments, and in discussing
the political economy of the Revolution in such a way as to differenti-
ate between the pre-1776 revolutionary movement (economic) and the
independence movement (political), Ernst sharpens our perspectives
on the American economy during the era of the Revolution.

By definition the American Revolution — at base an anticolonial
struggle for political independence — was a significant international
event. For Great Britain the American rebellion posed a threat to a
world-wide empire and raised the prospect of a general imperial war.
For monarchist Europe republican America was seen as undermining
both the power of Britain and the political stability of the continent.
For the American rebels diplomacy was considered from the outset a
key to the winning of independence. As befits the significance of the
subject, the diplomacy of the American Revolution has been studied
in great detail.[20] Worthy of study in its own right, Revolutionary
diplomacy takes on added importance because of its pervasive influence
upon the formulation and execution of American foreign policy for
the next two centuries.

American diplomacy began with the Revolution. There was
no American foreign policy prior to 1776, and during the war there
was no agreement on any international objective other than achiev-

[20]Surveys of the diplomacy of the Revolution include Lawrence S. Kaplan,
Colonies into Nation: American Diplomacy, 1763-1801 (New York, 1972) ; Richard
W. Van Alstyne, *Empire and Independence: The International History of the
American Revolution* (New York, 1965) ; Paul A. Varg, *Foreign Policies of the
Founding Fathers* (East Lansing, 1963) ; and Samuel Flagg Bemis, *The Diplomacy
of the American Revolution* (New York, 1935). Much valuable information and
insight are offered by two specialized studies: Richard B. Morris, *The Peacemakers:
The Great Powers and American Independence* (New York, 1965), a study of the
negotiations leading to the Treaty of Paris, and William C. Stinchcombe, *The
American Revolution and the French Alliance* (Syracuse, 1969).

ing independence. For global perspective and guidance, Americans embraced the diplomatic, as well as the political, theories of the Opposition Whigs in England. As explained by Thomas Paine in *Common Sense* (the diplomatic charter of the new nation), the Revolutionaries held that America was the world's best hope to show the way toward progress, that the nation should pursue commercial intercourse with all countries but enter into political alliances with none, and that prosperity was the primary source of both power and liberty. In attempting to implement their utopian vision, American diplomats at first were truly innocents abroad. Save for Benjamin Franklin, none had had any meaningful experience in foreign affairs; not surprisingly, their behavior was idealistic, if not naive, at the same time it was realistic, if not cynical. Yet they were extraordinarily successful. Due in large measure to unique circumstances, the United States first secured considerable wartime assistance from France without giving anything substantive in return and then obtained a peace settlement from Britain that was far more favorable than could have been expected. The rhetoric and reality of Revolutionary diplomacy would later find consistent expression in a confident, even cocky United States pursuing a foreign policy that turns on pragmatic means designed to achieve ideological ends.

Jerald A. Combs points to the ideals of the Revolution as the principal source of continuity in American diplomacy during the past 200 years. In both domestic and foreign affairs, he points out, the Founding Fathers attempted to achieve the mutually reinforcing — yet potentially incompatible — goals of liberty and prosperity through policies that were both realistic and idealistic. The continental expansion, international mercantilism, and diplomatic neutrality that marked United States foreign policy in the nineteenth century must be viewed, he suggests, primarily from the perspective of a genuine desire to promote liberty and prosperity. The rise of the United States to great power status in the twentieth century, Combs notes, poses grave questions concerning the traditional conduct of foreign affairs. Do the principles of Revolutionary diplomacy — the voice of a new nation struggling for a place in the international community — have relevance today for the foreign policy of the most powerful nation in the world?

III

From Thomas Jefferson's facile pen flowed the most moving and momentous words ever written by an American. "We hold these truths to be self-evident," he wrote, "that all men are created equal, that they are endowed by their Creator with certain unalienable Rights, that among these, are Life, Liberty, and the pursuit of Happiness." With that declaration, and the observation that government properly derived its "just Powers from the consent of the governed," Jefferson voiced the philosophical tenets underlying the American Revolution. In so doing, he simultaneously bespoke the noblest hopes and aspirations of generations yet to come.

But for approximately two-thirds of the American people the Declaration of Independence was more rhetoric than reality, the Revolution more a promise deferred than an expectation fulfilled. Afro-Americans, Indians, and women were generally outside the experiment in republican self-government. Although an integral part of society, they were persons apart whose activity was constrained by law and tradition. Legal codes as well as social customs placed women, especially married women, in a position of subordination to men; persons of red or back skin faced the formidable obstacles of racism and ethnocentrism. Yet the future of America's most conspicuous "minorities" had not been finally determined on the eve of the Revolution. Legal restrictions notwithstanding, it was possible, primarily because of economic considerations, for females to function as equals in what was predominantly a "man's world." Despite the debased condition of Negroes and Native Americans, it was not clear whether they were Insiders or Outsiders — that is, whether they were primitive peoples who might eventually be brought within the fellowship of Western culture or barbarians who were permanently beyond the pale of civilization.

The Revolutionary experience determined to a considerable degree the immediate future of Indians, blacks, and women in the new nation. For the Redman, the Revolution meant additional loss of territory and acceleration of westward removal. It also, as Bernard Sheehan demonstrates, confirmed for whites the notion that the Indian was indeed an Ignoble rather than a Noble Savage and thus made the first Americans objects of both scorn and paternalism. For blacks, the Revolution brought consolidation of their lot as either slaves or second-class citizens. Although the Founding Fathers, in what was perhaps the period of the most intensive social self-scrutiny in American history, placed the creation of the national union above the abolition of human bondage, the Revolution, Willie Lee Rose contends, set in motion a process that would ultimately result in freedom and first-class status for black people. For women, the Spirit of '76 wrought few changes in either condition or outlook. American women, Linda Grant DePauw suggests, were far more concerned with challenging their legal subordination to men and emulating the social position of European women than with the right to vote or feminist ideology. Generally speaking, then, in the aftermath of the Revolution freedom and opportunity for Afro-Americans, Indians, and women actually decreased in America.

It would, however, be a mistake to lose sight of the long-range significance of the Revolution for all disadvantaged or oppressed groups in America. Notwithstanding embarrassing discrepancies between profession and practice, the United States has traditionally been the land of freedom, equality, and opportunity. And without question it is the Revolution in general and Thomas Jefferson's Declaration in particular that have provided both the dynamic (the pursuit of happiness) and the rationale (the creed of equality) for the continuing quest for civil liberty, social justice, political democracy, and human dignity that is the most conspicuous feature of the American historical experience.

IV

The Founding Fathers would have thought Ralph Waldo Emerson guilty of only slight poetic license when he wrote in the "Concord Hymn" (1847) of the "shot heard round the world." Those responsible for the creation of the republic were convinced that the Spirit of '76 would spread over the globe and inaugurate a new era in the history of mankind marked by liberty and justice for all. Convinced that "all eyes are opened, or opening, to the rights of man," Thomas Jefferson from his deathbed shortly before the fiftieth anniversary of the adoption of the Declaration of Independence, expressed the hope of the Revolutionary generation for the Declaration and the Revolution of which it was a symbol: "May it be to the world, what I believe it will be (to some parts sooner, to others later, but finally to all), the signal of arousing men to burst the chains under which monkish ignorance and superstition had persuaded them to bind themselves, and to assume the blessings and security of self-government."[21]

At first it appeared as if the Revolution was indeed the harbinger of things to come. During the late eighteenth and early nineteenth centuries a series of revolts against colonialism and privilege erupted throughout the Old and New World in what has been labeled "the age of the Democratic Revolution."[22] But then the democratic revolutions took an undemocratic turn, and eventually gave way to a new kind of revolution that reflected the imperatives of an industrial and imperial world. Disturbed by the reactionary developments in Europe that "cast a gloomy cloud" over the "hopes of seeing improvement in the moral and intellectual condition of man," Jefferson nonetheless remained undaunted in his belief that "light and liberty are on steady advance."[23]

However, as Sung Bok Kim indicates, a comparison of the salient features of the American Revolution with those of subsequent world revolutions reveals that the Revolution has had slight impact on modern history. Indeed, it would appear as if the greater portion of mankind has either rejected the principles of 1776 or found them anachronistic. Where the Revolutionary generation, already enjoying unprecedented material prosperity and personal liberty, commenced a war for political autonomy in 1776, peoples elsewhere in the world have launched class struggles aimed not at self-government but the alleviation of economic want and social misery. Thus it is the authoritarian Jacobin phase of the French Revolution, not the libertarian American Revolution with its unique experiment in democratic republicanism, that has served as the working model for modern revolutionaries.

[21]Jefferson to Roger Weightman, June 24, 1826, *The Writings of Thomas Jefferson,* Andrew A. Lipscomb and Albert E. Bergh, eds., 20 vols. (Washington, D.C., 1903), 16:159-60.
[22]Robert R. Palmer, *The Age of the Democratic Revolution: A Political History of Europe and America, 1760-1800,* 2 vols. (Princeton, 1959, 1964). See also Arthur P. Whitaker, *The United States and the Independence of Latin America, 1800-1830* (Baltimore, 1941), and the several essays in *The Impact of the American Revolution Abroad* (Washington, D.C., 1975).
[23]Jefferson to John Adams, September 12, 1821, *The Adams-Jefferson Letters,* Lester Cappon, ed., 2 vols. (Chapel Hill, 1959), 2:574-75.

Still, as Kim notes, the ideals expressed in the Declaration of Independence have ever stirred the hearts and minds of progressive reformers everywhere. It is at least partial vindication for the American Revolutionaries who considered the spirit of the independence movement to be far more significant than the structure of the new nation. "The flames kindled on the 4th of July, 1776," said Jefferson, "have spread over too much of the globe to be extinguished by the feeble engines of depotism; on the contrary, they will consume these engines and all who work them."[24] Perhaps someday mankind will overcome the pernicious problem of scarcity; if so, mankind might be able to afford the luxuries of political liberty and social equality, and Jefferson's dream might yet come true.

As I finish writing this Introduction to a volume of essays assessing legacies of the American Revolution, it is 200 years to the day that Richard Henry Lee moved in the Continental Congress that "these United Colonies are, and of right ought to be free, and independent States." On July 2 the congressmen adopted Lee's resolution; two days later they endorsed Jefferson's Declaration of Independence, less a bill of particulars against America's last monarch than the creed of the new republic. It is important for us, the then unborn generation for whom the men and women of the Revolution risked their all, to be aware of our Revolutionary heritage in order to appreciate not only what we have been, but also to determine what shall we be as a nation. The satisfaction Thomas Jefferson and his compatriots derived from the Revolution arose from the conviction that "a just and solid republican government maintained here will be a standing monument and example for the aim and imitation of the people of other countries."[25] Today the United States remains, as Jefferson proclaimed, "the world's best hope." Whether it continues to be so depends upon the extent to which the American people continue to embrace the Spirit of Seventy-six as "the creed of our political faith — the text of civil instruction — the touchstone . . . which alone leads to peace, liberty, and safety."[26] Therein lies the challenge of the Third Century.

---

[24]Ibid, p. 575.

[25]Jefferson to John Dickinson, March 6, 1801, *Writings of Thomas Jefferson,* 10:217-18.

[26]First Inaugural Address, March 4, 1801.

THE AMERICAN REVOLUTION AND THE HISTORICAL IMAGINATION

BY MICHAEL KAMMEN

The title of this essay might very well conceal a multitude of sins, convolutions, and flights of fancy. Therefore I must begin by explaining what mischief I am into, and by clarifying my terms.

My current research is directed at uncovering the meaning of tradition in American culture. The concept of tradition has received very little attention from scholars in the United States, in part, perhaps, because the country appeared for so long to be so new. Because it looked to be lacking in tradition, serious study of the Americans' sense of their own past scarcely seemed worthy of attention. As George Chalmers, the Loyalist historian, wrote back in 1780: "Of these colonies it cannot be asserted, as it is of European nations, that their origin is uncertain or unknown. . . . Here, there is as little room for the dreams of conjecture or the obscurities of tradition. . . ."[1]

Lamentations for the loss of national memory have been far more common in the American experience than confident assertions or uses of tradition. For every William Gilmore Simms, who in 1851 began a novel about the American Revolution in South Carolina with these words: "I summon to my aid the muse of local History — the traditions of our own home," there have been half a dozen like William Caruthers, an exhausted Virginia novelist who pleaded from Savannah in 1846 that someone "furnish me with some old tradition upon which I can weave a story."[2] Michael Paul Rogin has summed up the situation quite simply in his new book concerning *Andrew Jackson and the Subjugation of the American Indian:* "Liberalism insisted on

---

[1]Chalmers, *Political Annals* (1780), quoted in Wesley Frank Craven, *The Legend of the Founding Fathers* (New York, 1956), p. 63.

[2]Both Simms and Caruthers are quoted in William R. Taylor, *Cavalier and Yankee. The Old South and American National Character* (New York, 1963), pp. 185, 249.

the independence of men, each from the other, and from cultural, traditional, and communal attachments."[3]

Nevertheless, as our country celebrates the 200th anniversary of its independence, and as we near the completion of four centuries of settlement, one finds both an abundance of national tradition as well as growing interest in it. Therefore it is high time for an historian of American culture to turn his hand to the same sort of study which engrossed Lucien Febvre in his last years. Febvre apparently finished his book in 1956, the year of his death, after which the manuscript mysteriously disappeared. It was entitled "Honor and Fatherland," and according to Fernand Braudel "it explored a field where little has yet been done, that of collective states of mind, being a study of the transition from fidelity to a person—the prince (that is, honor) to fidelity to the nation (patriotism). The history, in short, of the birth of the idea of fatherland."[4] If Lucien Febvre's approach was a fresh one in Europe so recently as the 1950s, you may imagine how little this sort of thing has been done in the United States.

I cannot, however, embrace it all in a single presentation. Consequently I propose to examine one major segment of that larger project: I mean the impact of the American Revolution upon national tradition. Even that, though, is a huge and complex phenomenon; therefore, I shall focus here upon the responses of some imaginative authors to the American Revolution. By imaginative authors I mean the writers of romances and novels, rather than professional historians. And I do so without apology. As Samuel Eliot Morison once wrote, "the great public, when it reads history at all, takes it in the painless form of the historical novel or, at best, biography."[5]

---

[3]Rogin, *Fathers and Children: Andrew Jackson and the Subjugation of the American Indian* (New York, 1975), p. 8. See also Alexis de Tocqueville, *Democracy in America,* J. P. Mayer, ed. (New York, 1969), p. 507: "The woof of time is ever being broken and the track of past generations lost. Those who have gone before are easily forgotten, and no one gives a thought to those who will follow."

[4]Braudel, "Personal Testimony," *Journal of Modern History,* 44 (1972): 466-67.

[5]Morison, *Vistas of History* (New York, 1964), p. 23. See also George V. Taylor, "History, Literature and the Public at Large," *North Carolina Historical Review,* 42 (1965): 180-91; R. Gordon Kelly, "Literature and the Historian," *American Quarterly,* 26 (1974): 141-59; and Murray Krieger, "Fiction and Historical Reality: The Hourglass and the Sands of Time," in Ralph Cohen and Murray Krieger, eds., *Literature and History* (Los Angeles, 1974), pp. 43-77.

If my quarry is the Revolution's impact upon popular culture, then by what conveyance will our safari proceed? The trek we take will be by means of the historical imagination of American authors from James Fenimore Cooper to Kenneth Roberts.

I am well aware that the phrase "historical imagination" means different things to different people. It is an elusive expression, to be sure; but nevertheless it has palpable meaning in an evocative way. Here, for example, is an excerpt from the autobiography of G. M. Trevelyan, written when he was 72 years of age, and published in 1949:

> I saw my first play (apart from London pantomimes) in the old Stratford theatre; it was Frank Benson in *Richard III*. Small as I was, historical imagination was already the keenest pleasure of my life. I knew the *Lays of Ancient Rome* by heart (and have never forgotten them, turn me on where you like); and my father was my playmate, with his entrancing talk and familiar jokes about historical scenes and persons. . . . And now, for two blissful hours in Stratford theatre, I actually lived in the past, seeing real people walking about in gorgeous Fifteenth Century clothes.[6]

We must proceed very carefully, however, because the aspiring historian has often been warned against the danger of flights of fancy taken to excess. Here is that same Samuel Eliot Morison, whom I cited a moment ago, complaining in a different essay about the fact that Everyman seems indeed to prefer historical fiction to historical reality. "What is the place of imagination in history?" asks Morison. His answer seems designed to explain why the historian, even one so gifted with literary grace and narrative power as the Admiral himself, cannot hope to achieve the audience and popularity of a good novelist.

> An historian or biographer is under restrictions unknown to a novelist. He has no right to override facts by his own imagination. If he is writing on a remote or obscure subject about which few facts are available, his imagination may legitimately weave them into a pattern. But to be honest he must make clear what is fact and what is hypothesis. The quality of imagination, if properly restrained by the conditions of historical discipline is of great assistance in enabling one to

---

[6]Trevelyan, *An Autobiography & Other Essays* (London, 1949), p. 3.

discover problems to be solved, to grasp the significance of facts, to form hypotheses, to discern causes in their first beginnings, and, above all, to relate the past creatively to the present.[7]

Morison is hardly the first, however, to caution the historian about abusing his own imagination or becoming overly dependent upon that of others. Nor is he even the first authority on the American Revolution to express such misgivings. That tradition began at the start of the nineteenth century when distinguished participants in the Revolution began to wonder themselves whether novelists would tell their tale before historians could do so properly. As John Adams wrote to Thomas Jefferson on July 30th, 1815, "Who shall write the history of the American Revolution? Who can write it? Who will ever be able to write it? . . . Some future Miss Porter, may hereafter, make as shining a romance, of what passed in Congress, while in Conclave, as her *Scottish Chiefs.*"[8]

What on earth is Mr. Adams being so nervous about? Well, Miss Jane Porter was a British woman, a contemporary of Sir Walter Scott, who wrote historical romances which enjoyed great vogue. Her *Scottish Chiefs*, published in 1810, may have been as popular in the young republic as it was in Britain. Hence John Adams' apprehension that her American counterpart might put the Continental Congress, and George Washington, and Thomas Jefferson, and *himself* into a potboiler of some sort before scrupulous scholars could come along to set the story straight.

Nor was Adams alone. Most of his contemporaries, especially among the participants in our struggle for independence, shared these fears and expressed them vocally.[9] Moreover, there is a sense in which they had good reason to be concerned because the authors of romances

---

[7]"History as a Literary Art" (1946) in Morison, *By Land and by Sea* (New York, 1953), pp. 289, 297. For Morison's concern about the treatment of John Paul Jones in imaginative literature, see his *John Paul Jones: A Sailor's Biography* (Boston, 1959), p. xi.

[8]Adams to Jefferson and Thomas McKean, *The Adams-Jefferson Letters,* Lester J. Cappon, ed., 2 vols. (Chapel Hill, 1959), 2: 451.

[9]See, for example, John Jay to Jedediah Morse, February 28, 1797, in *The American Revolution: New York as a Case Study,* Larry R. Gerlach, ed., (Belmont, Calif., 1972), pp. 181-82; John Randolph of Roanoke to Josiah Quincy, May 23, 1813, in Edmund Quincy, *Life of Josiah Quincy of Massachusetts* (Boston, 1868), p. 331; John Adams to William Wirt [1818?], in John P. Kennedy, *Memoirs of the Life of William Wirt,* 2 vols. (Philadelphia, 1850) 2: 51.

did, in fact, get there first. In 1826, on the occasion of the fiftieth anniversary of the Declaration of Independence, Jared Sparks complained that no complete history of the Revolution had yet appeared; and two years later Chancellor James Kent blithely (and perhaps ruefully) told the New-York Historical Society that "our origin is within the limits of well-attested history. This at once dissipates the enchantments of fiction. . . ."[10]

But ever since 1821, when James Fenimore Cooper published *The Spy* to instantaneous success, the Revolution had become *the* favorite subject of American fiction. Cooper followed it with other romances about the later eighteenth century, such as *The Pioneers* and *The Pilot,* both in 1823, *The Last of the Mohicans* (1826), and eventually *Wyandotté* (1843) and *Satanstoe* (1845). An older friend, James Kirke Paulding, contributed such volumes as *The Dutchman's Fireside* (1831) and *The Old Continental* (1846). Down in Maryland John Pendleton Kennedy produced the likes of *Horse-Shoe Robinson: A Tale of the Tory Ascendancy* (1835); and William Gilmore Simms eventually brought out a cycle of seven romances about the Revolution in South Carolina.[11]

Most of these (and many other) fictional treatments of the Revolution appeared in the quarter century between 1821 and 1846. Those few which emerged during the 1850s, however, such as the last in Simms' series, had more to do with the sectional crisis and slavery than with the Revolution. Thereafter, for nearly half a century, the American Revolution ceased to be a particularly popular topic in national literature. A few interesting items appeared, notably Herman Melville's *Israel Potter* (1855) and Edward Bellamy's *The Duke of Stockbridge* (serialized in 1879). But basically American fiction took "other" turns from 1845 until about 1895; and those who wanted history got it straight from the romantic, narrative historians of the day: George Bancroft, Francis Parkman, William H. Prescott and

---

[10]Sparks, "Materials for American History," *North American Review,* 23 (1826): 276; Kent, "An Anniversary Discourse," *Collections of the New York Historical Society,* Second Series, (New York, 1841), 1: 12.

[11]Simms, *The Partisan* (New York, 1835); *Mellichampe* (New York, 1836); *The Kinsmen* (Philadelphia, 1841); *Katharine Walton* (Philadelphia, 1851); *The Sword and the Distaff* (Philadelphia, 1853); *The Forayers* (New York, 1855); *Eutaw* (New York, 1856); and *Joscelyn, A Tale of the Revolution* (New York, 1857), which was not considered a part of the cycle.

those authors of state histories which began to emerge during the 1850s. To some degree they seem to have rendered the historical novel superfluous.

During the mid and later 1890s, however, it made a vigorous comeback, with the result that *Hugh Wynne, Free Quaker* (1897) by S. Weir Mitchell, and *Richard Carvel* (1899) by Winston Churchill, and *Janice Meredith* (1899) by Paul Leicester Ford, and a continuum of novels by Robert W. Chambers, dominated the literary landscape and became the most extraordinary best-sellers in American literary history up to that time. Stephen Crane's untimely death in 1900 interrupted his work on a major novel about the American Revolution — a book he hoped would provide him with fame and fortune far beyond *The Red Badge of Courage*, which had come out in 1895.[12]

This burst of patriotism and nostalgia waned after about 1906 or so; but within two decades it revived once again. First came *Drums* (1925) by James Boyd, with wistful illustrations by the popular N. C. Wyeth; and *Lord Timothy Dexter* (also 1925) by John P. Marquand. But the really popular figure during the next twenty years would be Kenneth Roberts, a journalist-turned-historian who discovered the Revolution and eventually looked at it from nearly every angle: in *Arundel* (1929), *Rabble in Arms* (1933), *Northwest Passage* (1937), *Oliver Wiswell* (1940), and other works. Alongside Roberts's output there was also *Drums Along the Mohawk* (1936) by Walter Edmonds; *The City in the Dawn* (1943-48), a trilogy by Hervey Allen; *Johnny Tremain* (1943) by Esther Forbes; numerous novels and stories by Howard Fast; and many, many others who made the Revolution immensely popular fare for American families during the 1930s, 1940s, and into the early 1950s. Such names as F. van Wyck Mason, Inglis Fletcher, Bruce Lancaster, and Elswyth Thane are not usually sighted in the galaxy of American literary stars; but if I had in the bank what any one of them earned from novels about the Revolution, I would promptly retire to Tahiti.

You will not be surprised to learn that we are just now entering a fourth period in which fiction about the Revolution is once again

---

[12]For Crane's interest in his family's roots in revolutionary New Jersey, see *Stephen Crane: Letters,* R. W. Stallman and Lillian Gilkes, eds., (New York, 1960), p. 94, 124; see also "The Battle of Bunker Hill," in *The Works of Stephen Crane,* Fredson Bowers, ed., 9 vols. (Charlottesville, Va., 1969-71), 9: 303-312.

in vogue. Perhaps it all began in 1973-74 when Gore Vidal's *Burr* became a runaway best-seller and topped the fiction list for months. But there is also *The Hessian* (1972) by Howard Fast; *American Primitive* (1972), a drama by William Gibson; *The Kentucky Trace. A Novel of the American Revolution* (1974) by Harriette Simpson Arnow; most recently *Valley Forge* (1975) by MacKinlay Kantor; and a trilogy — *The Bastard, The Rebels,* and *The Seekers* — by one John Jakes, a 45-year old television adman from Dayton, Ohio, who seems to know exactly what the mass culture wants and is ready to provide it. His paperback pulp, in red, white and blue, can be purchased at the check-out counter of every American supermarket — along with cigarettes, chocolates, and Tums for the tummy.

Because I am a historian, and therefore qualified only to speak about past phenomena which have run their course, I shall say no more here about the likes of *Burr, Valley Forge,* and *The Bastard.* But I shall have my hands full with those three major periods in which fiction about the Revolution was popular; for the very existence of three such discrete periods is a boon to the cultural historian. He can look for discontinuities in order to use the novels as a litmus test for social change. And he can look for fundamental patterns of persistence in order to pose the question: what enduring impact has the Revolution had upon American culture?

I shall try to perform both of these functions, and perhaps as a result will be in a better position to assess whether Adams and Jefferson and Jay had so much cause for anxiety. Did Fenimore Cooper and Winston Churchill and Kenneth Roberts really do such a terrible disservice to revolutionary historiography and the national ideology? Are *Satanstoe* and *Richard Carvel* and *Rabble in Arms* no improvement at all upon poor Miss Porter's *Scottish Chiefs?* I shall reserve judgment until the end.

II

In order to look for discontinuities as a measure of cultural change, it is necessary to establish some categories (or themes) to use as bases for comparison. There are many one might draw upon, but I have selected three: first, the historical novelist's attitude toward his counterpart, the historian; second, the reasons why these imaginative writers chose to write about the Revolution in particular; and third, the Anglo-American relationship as it is reflected in their works of fiction.[13]

As for the first of these themes, its elucidation in the earliest period, 1821-1845, is fairly straightforward. Fenimore Cooper and his contemporaries felt empathy and rapport with the historian's craft. Cooper was fond of this quotation from Joseph Fielding, for example: "I am a true historian, a describer of society as it exists, and of men as they are." He insisted that *The Last of the Mohicans* was neither a novel nor a romance, but a history. To be sure, Cooper acknowledged that "the privileges of the Historian and of the writer of Romances are very different, and it behooves them equally to respect each other's rights. The latter is permitted to garnish a probable fiction, while he is sternly prohibited from dwelling on improbable truths; but it is the duty of the former to record facts as they have occurred, without a reference to consequences, resting his reputation on a firm foundation of realities, and vindicating his integrity by his authorities."[14] What emerges as the predominant attitude, however, is *respect* and a sense of being participants in sister disciplines whose goals were similar though their "privileges" might vary. This empathy will begin to dissipate when we come to our second period, and will disintegrate entirely when we reach the 1930s and 1940s.

What about my second category for comparison: the reasons why these authors chose the Revolution as their subject matter? The answer here is well-known in this first period, and will occasion little surprise. As Cooper stated in 1831, "mental independence is my object," or, as we might put it: literary nationalism. Aspiring authors in the young republic had been stung by that condescending quip of one British essayist, "who reads an American book?" Consequently they

---

[13]In order to delineate and clarify the shifts which occurred between 1821-45, 1895-1909, and 1925-50 I am going to be gross rather than subtle in my emphases. There are, however, exceptions and variations upon the patterns I describe. One finds, for example, ambivalence about the Anglo-American relationship in works from all three periods; and one finds some novels in each period which depict the Revolution primarily as a civil war. What I have attempted within the limited space of this lecture is a broad overview of the larger configuration which these books make. I cannot here account for all the aberrations and idiosyncratic points of view, though I hope to do so in the longer study of which this is a part.

[14]Cooper, *The Pilot,* preface; for William Gilmore Simms, see "The Epochs and Events of American History," in his *Views and Reviews in American Literature, History and Fiction,* First Series, C. Hugh Holman, ed. (1845: Cambridge, Mass., 1962), pp. 34, 36-37.

were determined to demonstrate not only that there might be American books worth reading, but that their subject matter might be indigenous American materials as well. The Revolution, which seemed to be the predestined culmination of colonial development, as well as the crucible of American nationality, was quite obviously *the* determinative event for imaginative writers to use in order to achieve "mental independence."[15]

And what of my third category: the delineation of Anglo-American relationships? Here, again, their emphasis in this early period will hardly come as a surprise — strong Anglophobia. It had, after all, been a bitter war for American independence from Britain. More recently, moreover, there had been the War of 1812, in which the British hardly won endearment by burning the Executive Mansion in Washington. And in 1823 the Monroe Doctrine had been proclaimed because of a desire in the United States to keep the western hemisphere free from Old World influence. Then the Canadian boundary question heated up in 1837-40, aggravating old sores and opening new ones. The result, in sum, was that public opinion tended to be anti-British, that *both* sides in American party politics expressed their hostility accordingly, and that such writers as Washington Irving and James Kirke Paulding cut their literary teeth, so to speak, by biting John Bull in various and sundry fleshy places. This tendency would begin to alter, as well, especially in the 1890s; and would then undergo a stunning reversal during the 1930s and 1940s.

Even as our attention shifts from period number one to period two, however, we get a preview of coming attractions from Walt

---

[15]Cooper to Samuel Carter Hall, May 21, 1831, in *The Letters and Journals of James Fenimore Cooper,* James Franklin Beard, ed., II (Cambridge, Mass., 1960), p. 84; see also *The American Literary Revolution, 1783-1837,* Robert E. Spiller, ed., (New York, 1967); Marcus Cunliffe, *The Literature of the United States* (Harmondsworth, England, 1954), chaps. 2 and 3; Cunliffe, *The Nation Takes Shape 1789-1837* (Chicago, 1959), chap. 8; and see also James Kirke Paulding's letter to Thomas W. White of Richmond, quoted in the preface to the second edition of *The Dutchman's Fireside,* William I. Paulding, ed. (New York, 1868), p. ix: "It has always been one of my first objects, to which a great portion of my life has been devoted, to incite and encourage the genius of this country, and, most especially, to draw its attention and its efforts toward our own history, traditions, scenery, and manners, instead of foraging in the barren and exhausted fields of the Old World. I have lived to see this object in a great measure accomplished, and one of the most gratifying of all my reflexions is, that possibly I may have had some little agency in bringing it about."

Whitman. In the preface to his *Leaves of Grass,* first published in 1855, Whitman offered these two declarative sentences: "Great genius and the people of these states must never be demeaned to romances. As soon as histories are properly told there is no more need of romances."

By the 1890s, novelists who wrote about the American Revolution no longer shared Cooper's respect for the practicing historian. Instead, echoing Whitman, they lamented that the histories haven't been properly told because historians are guilty of neglect. Writing about General Sullivan's march through the Iroquois country in 1779, for example, one novelist, William E. Griffis, asked "why is the whole subject so slurred over or ignored by the average historian?"[16] What's more, insist the imaginative writers, fiction is more uplifting than history anyway! As Robert W. Chambers declared in his preface to *The Maid-at-Arms. A Novel* (1902): "Romance alone can justify a theme inspired by truth; for romance is more vital than history, which after all, is but the fleshless skeleton of romance." (p. vii)[17]

If respect has given way to criticism and even disdain, what has happened over half a century to our second measure of change: the rationale for writing about the Revolution in particular? Achieving "mental independence" has slipped into the background as a bumptious people acquired some measure of self-confidence, so that literary nationalism is now supplanted by yet another stimulus — in a word, nostalgia. One can see it, for instance, in the fact that so many novels from the turn of the century take the form of spurious memoirs. *Richard Carvel* is offered as Daniel Clapsaddle Carvel's reminiscence of his grandfather, symbolically dated December 21, 1876. *Hugh Wynne, Free Quaker* is supposed to be "a memoir meant for my

---

[16]William E. Griffis, *The Pathfinders of the Revolution* (Boston, 1900), p. 5; see also William O. Stoddard, *The Fight for the Valley* (New York, 1904), pp. v-vi.

[17]Historians, for their part — even the best of them — seem to have been ambivalent about historical fiction and sometimes critical of their own discipline as well. Worthington C. Ford reviewed *The Youth of Washington,* for example, an incredible concoction by S. Weir Mitchell, and blandly volunteered that the book "may be judged as history or as fiction, according to the taste of the reader, and possesses high merit in either aspect." (*American Historical Review,* 10 [1905]: 444.) Looking back to the 1870s, Henry Adams wrote in *The Education* that history as a discipline "had lost even the sense of shame. It was a hundred years behind the experimental sciences. For all serious purposes it was less instructive than Walter Scott and Alexandre Dumas." (Modern Library edition, p. 301.)

descendants" (p. 2); and the narrator of *Maid of the Mohawk*, reminded that his "span of life is drawing toward its close," seeks to "go back through the halls of memory and open up the past. . . ."[18]

The causes of this nostalgia, both in the writers and their readers, are not at all hard to find. First, they sought to recapture the physical details of an age slipping rapidly beyond the blur of hazy reminiscence. When Cooper and Simms wrote, the quality of life had not changed very much from what it was in revolutionary times. Overland travel still meant a carriage or venture on horseback. People still made their butter and various essentials at home. By the 1890s, however, technology had altered the routine pace and pattern of existence. Men and women were more likely to take a train than a carriage, and were more likely to purchase their butter at the neighborhood grocery. In part, therefore, their nostalgia required (and received) the re-creation of physical minutiae in loving detail. The reading public that adored *Janice Meredith* immersed itself in trivia and trivets — what one author would call *The Quest of the Quaint*.[19]

Even more than household gods and goods, however, this audience sought escape from the painful realities of industrialized America, from the class conflict which threatened to rend the very fabric of a society — most especially during the depression years, 1893-96. Then, too, there were all those awful immigrants, those strange-looking, strange-sounding folk who printed newspapers in their own languages and wore the costumes of their native lands on feast days and other moments dedicated to the preservation of special ethnic identities. Why, they were "un-American," perhaps even "un-Americanizable." Consequently those true Americans who could link their ancestry to colonial times, or wished that they could, sought solace in the Revolution, the Founding Fathers, and a simpler, more homogenous America that was comparatively free (they thought) of class conflict, social protest, and industrial violence. Wistful nostalgia, then, was paramount in the historical fiction of the late nineteenth century.

---

[18]Frederick A. Ray, *Maid of the Mohawk* (Boston 1906), 1-2; see also Robert W. Chambers, *America, or the Sacrifice: A Romance of the American Revolution* (New York, 1924), published simultaneously with a D. W. Griffith film of the same title and ostensibly based upon the "memoirs" of Nathan Holden.

[19]Virginia Robie, *The Quest of the Quaint* (Boston, 1916, 1927). See also Robert and Elizabeth Shackleton, *The Quest of the Colonial* (New York, 1908).

And what of the Anglo-American relationship? It too was changing, and in ways one can correlate rather precisely with the romances
of that period. There remained a strong residue of Anglophobia, most
especially in eastern Massachusetts and in the Middle West. Samuel
Eliot Morison's delectable reminiscence of his childhood during the
1890s informs us that

> one of my boyhood friends from New York, a girl who married
> a Bostonian, told me that the one thing that struck her on
> coming here was that Boston was still fighting the War of
> Independence. The traditions of the American Revolution
> were central to my upbringing; memorials and landmarks of
> it were all about us. Popular extracurricular reading was
> Charles Carleton Coffin's *Boys of '76* — Philip Weld told me
> that I must read it, or fight him! I was proud of Faneuil Hall
> and the Adamses, highly approved the Cleveland-Olney dip-
> lomatic sock-in-the-jaw to Lord Salisbury, firmly believed
> America to be the best country and Boston the finest city on
> earth; and that the United States Navy, having "licked
> England twice," could do so again, if necessary. It was only
> *after* growing up that I began to entertain feelings of kindness
> and admiration toward our mother country.[20]

And yet, for most Americans a turning point occurred between
1895 and 1898. First, Great Britain got out of a territory claimed by
Venezuela, which we desperately wished her to do. Then Britain
stood aside when we became involved in Cuba, and after that helped
to neutralize the rest of Europe while we picked upon pathetic Spain
for a "splendid little war." The result was a perceptible shift in which
Anglophobia gave way to ambiguity, to luke-warm affection, and
eventually to detente and alliance.[21] That shift was mirrored explicitly
in most of the historical fiction about revolutionary America which
became *à la mode* in 1899 and 1900. Here are the very last lines of
Richard Carvel, for example:

---

[20]Morison, *One Boy's Boston, 1887-1901* (Boston, 1962), pp. 66-67. See also
S. Weir Mitchell to Amelia G. Mason, August 27, 1912, in Anna Robeson Burr,
Weir Mitchell: His Life and Letters (New York, 1929), p. 281.

[21]See Edward P. Crapol, *America for Americans: Economic Nationalism and
Anglophobia in the Late Nineteenth Century* (Westport, Conn., 1973); Bradford
Perkins, *The Great Rapprochment: England and the United States, 1895-1914*
(New York, 1968). For earlier anticipations at mid-century, see Frank W.
Thistlethwaite, *The Anglo-American Connection in the Early Nineteenth Century*
(Philadelphia, 1959), pp. 173-74; and Ralph Waldo Emerson, *English Traits*
(Boston, 1860).

Ere I had regained my health, the war for Independence was won. I pray God that time may soften the bitterness it caused, and heal the breach in that noble race whose motto is Freedom. That the Stars and Stripes and the Union Jack may one day float together to cleanse this world of tyranny! (p. 534).[22]

And that leads us to the third period, principally the later 1920s, the 1930s and well into the '40s, a period which saw a "general preoccupation with the American past generated by the superheated nationalism which followed World War I."[23] It is symptomatic as well as symbolic that Gutzon Borglum began to carve those colossal heads on Mt. Rushmore in 1927. During the two decades which followed that date, residual touches of Menckenesque cynicism and an ancillary penchant for historical debunking, were slowly but steadily supplanted by a powerful mood of patriotism and reaffirmation. One visible measure of that may be found in a search for authenticity which took many forms: the restoration of Colonial Williamsburg, the increasing popularity of early American antiques as home furnishings, the gathering in of Henry Francis DuPont's great collection at Winterthur, the creation of Cooperstown, New York, as a living museum *par excellence,* and so forth.

What happened under these circumstances to the novelists' feelings about historians? Well, the answer would be funny if the feelings expressed weren't quite so fierce — and contemptuous. Kenneth Roberts, for example, did a great deal of serious research for his lengthy novels; but he was terribly disappointed that the secondary sources simply did not provide him with the basic story line he wanted to build upon. He became quite engrossed in the American campaign for Quebec during the winter of 1775-76, for example, and utterly frustrated by the fact that no historian had ever done his homework for him — at least, not in the form that Roberts needed it. He wrote to a friend in 1935:

---

[22]See also the last lines of Ford, *Janice Meredith,* p. 536; Harold Frederic, *In the Valley* (New York, 1890), p. 280; and also James K. Hosmer, "The American Evolution: Dependence, Independence, Interdependence," *The Atlantic Monthly,* 82 (1898), especially pp. 34-35: "The work of our fathers, then, was to sever the English-speaking world, — a work one hundred years ago most noble and necessary to be done for only so, in that day, could freedom be saved. At the present time, however, may it not be the case that the work to be done is not of severance, but of union?"

[23]Douglass Adair, "The New Thomas Jefferson" (1946) in Adair, *Fame and the Founding Fathers,* Trevor Colbourn, ed. (New York, 1974), p. 238.

As soon as I got the broad picture of what had happened, it dawned on me that nobody had ever written it — nobody: not even historians: Nobody had pieced the mosaic together and got a picture that made sense. You could find out what happened when Arnold's troops marched to Quebec, but you couldn't get the relation of the march to the war, or to the country, or to the people. . . . It took me two years of the hardest sort of study to understand the 1776-1777 campaigns in their entirety. All you've got to do is read the histories yourself and see what you get out of them. . . . If it's properly presented, I believe the experiences of the Northern Army are almost without parallel in the history of War; but out of what history can you get an understanding of it? Not out of one damned history. Or out of ten. And if that isn't a show-up of our historians, I don't know what is.[24]

So Roberts and his fellow writers criticized historians — publicly as well as in private correspondence — for losing the drama, ignoring the little people, and failing to get the story straight.[25] In addition, the impact of Relativism suggested to some novelists that fiction was a superior form of historical knowledge anyway, because information about the past which had been endowed with imagination easily surpassed mere facts strung together without meaning. Here is Hervey Allen writing about "History and the Novel" in 1944 after two volumes of his trilogy, *The City in the Dawn,* had been completed.

It is in this capacity to produce an illusion of reliving the past that the chief justification for the historical novel exists. Since no one, neither historian nor novelist, can reproduce the real past, one may infer that, if supremely well done, the historical novel, by presenting the past dramatically, actually gives the reader, a more vivid, adequate, and significant apprehension of past epochs than does the historian, who conveys facts about them.[26]

---

[24]Roberts to Chilson Leonard, November 27, 1935, Kenneth Roberts MSS, The Library, Phillips Exeter Academy, Exeter, New Hampshire.

[25]See Walter Edmonds, "How You Begin a Novel," *The Atlantic Monthly,* 158 (Aug. 1936): 189, 190, 192.

[26]Allen, "History and the Novel," *The Atlantic Monthly,* 173 (Feb. 1944): 120. There is also Dos Passos, writing in 1929 that the true role of the novelist was to be a historian of his own age because he is "able to build reality more clearly out of his factual experience that a plain historian or biographer can." See John P. Diggins, "Visions of Chaos and Visions of Order: Dos Passos as Historian," *American Literature,* 46 (1974): 330; and also the observations by Inglis Fletcher quoted in Richard Walser, *Inglis Fletcher of Bandon Plantation* (Chapel Hill, 1952), pp. 68, 69, 74.

Thus the novelists have now persuaded themselves not merely that their task is quite different from that of the historians, but that they do a vastly superior job to boot. The respect of a century earlier, in Cooper's day, has vanished.

And what of their reasons for choosing to write about the Revolution? Neither nationalism nor nostalgia has disappeared entirely, but both become far less important than a new rationale: the search for America's national character, and especially its origins. Imaginative authors now stress the development of those qualities which would one day make the nation great: courage, individualism, endurance, self-reliance, pioneering hardihood, and particularly *leadership*. There are long paeans to leadership in Roberts's *Northwest Passage,* for instance, and little homilies like this one, from John Paul Jones, in James Boyd's *Drums:* "jest ye remember this: to lead men in a fight, the great thing is this — to show them the way yourself and yet to keep your wits and eyes about ye and observe how matters stand." (p. 362).

Then, too, there is the notion of American nationality as a mosaic of ethnic fragments — the whole being much greater than the sum of its parts. So in *Drums Along the Mohawk* one finds key characters of English, Dutch, Irish, Scots-Irish, and Palatine German origin, each one acting according to the characterological imperatives of his or her native bent. Or in *Raleigh's Eden,* by Inglis Fletcher, there are French Huguenots, Highland and Lowland Scots, Dutch, English, Welsh Quakers, even a Moorish architect who designs Governor Tryon's fabulous palace at New Bern, and an unspecified Oriental who sells his wares at the wharves in Edenton. In James Boyd's *Drums,* when that famous encounter between the *Bonhomme Richard* and the *Serapis* occurs, we find that the crew of the *Bonhomme Richard* is a a kind of all-American team. In the heat of battle a tall Vermonter mutters gloomily, a stocky Pennsylvania Dutchman nods his head with cheerful vigor, and a red-haired Georgian oozes laconic common sense (pp. 364-65).

There is a related phenomenon at work in these novels, but one the authors seem to be somewhat ambivalent about: and that is much greater emphasis than ever before upon the lives of *ordinary* people. This is true of Edmonds and Fletcher, who have already been mentioned, but even more of Esther Forbes in *Johnny Tremain,* say, or Edward Stanley in *Thomas Forty* (1947), or even of Kenneth Roberts in *Oliver Wiswell* — both in his treatment of the Leighton family as well as the back-country Loyalists in South Carolina. And the point being made about these ordinary people involves their independence and freedom — a freedom scarcely possible anywhere else in the eighteenth-century world. As Bruce Lancaster said about his purpose in writing *Guns of Burgoyne*, "I wanted to show free men — the free men of the colonies — and it seemed to me that the best way to do that was to let them be discovered by a man who never had been free, who had, when he came here, no conception of freedom."[27]

And yet, although the *menu peuple* are often treated with sympathy and understanding by these authors, there is also an underlying strand of skepticism toward them. They are frequently referred to as "rabble," and pejoratively as the "rag-tag and bob-tail democracy." Even Johnny Fraser of North Carolina (the young hero of *Drums*), although disillusioned in London by English fatuousness and decadence, observes that "maybe the government here is not as good as the American loyalists think it is, but it's better than an American Revolutionary mob." (p. 309). A fair number of these novelists, and a goodly part of their audience, I believe, were elitists whose mood during the later 1920s and 1930s was hostile to the excesses of democracy. There are clear signs that the democracy they preferred was a deferential one; or at least, that democratic government worked best in a quasi-democratic society where status had its perquisites and the elite provided real leadership.[28]

Finally, what became of the Anglo-American relationship in this third period? Well, what happened involves a marvelous, and often amusing, inversion of the Anglophobia from a century before. To be sure, it by no means disappeared entirely, least of all wherever the *Chicago Tribune* enjoyed circulation. Mayor William Hale (Big Bill) Thompson vowed that if King George V ever so much as set foot in

---

[27]Lancaster (1896-1963) is quoted in his obituary, The *New York Times,* June 21, 1963, p. 29. See also Conrad Richter, *The Free Man* (New York, 1943), the story of an indentured servant from Germany who arrives in Philadelphia just before the Revolution.

[28]See Roberts, *Oliver Wiswell* (New York, 1940), pp. 202, 258, 381. The implicit argument of these novelists is not at all unlike the explicit argument of their contemporary, historian Charles S. Sydnor, in *Gentlemen Freeholders: Political Practices in Washington's Virginia* (Chapel Hill, 1952), especially chaps. 1, 8, and 9.

Chicago, "I'll crack him in the snoot."[29] A struggle also occurred over lend-lease, and the Anglo-American alliance was not without some strains. Nevertheless, Great Britain now had a very positive "image" in most of the United States, and that created problems for would-be authors of books about the War for Independence.

It seemed less appropriate than it once had to cast as the custo-

---

[29]Felix Frankfurter relates a marvelous conversation derived from a social incident in 1940 (when Secretary Stimson announced that the American fleet would protect allied shipping against German submarines). Justice Frankfurter attended a dinner at the Norwegian Embassy in Washington, and recalls:

> There was present that night Senator Gerry of Rhode Island, a direct descendent of Elbridge P. Gerry. He was very nice but not profoundly intellectual, the generous donor to the Supreme Court of the finest, perhaps the finest law collection in private hands, coming down from all the Gerrys, a beautiful collection. He was one of the guests, and as the speech of Stimson's went on about why we were giving this help to England — the menace to freedom — I could see Gerry's face. He was an isolationist, and I could see great disapproval on his face. I'd had pleasant relations with him because he was a friend of Justice Roberts, and I'd seen him at Justice Roberts' so that it was a prefectly easy, pleasant, non-intimate relation. When the speech was over, and as we started to go in to join the ladies I said, "Senator Gerry, one of these days I'd like to ask you a question."
>
> He said, "Why don't you ask it now?"
>
> I said, "It's likely to lead to some discussion. There isn't time, but if I can put it to you quickly, it was plain enough that you didn't approve of this speech of the Secretary of War. You don't like it, and so that leads me to put to you this question: How is it that I who, as far as I know, haven't remotely a drop of English blood in me, who never heard the English language spoken, certainly never spoke a word of it until I was twelve, who never saw England until I was past thirty, have such a deep feeling about the essential importance of the maintenance of England, have such a sense of kinship professionally speaking with English institutions and feel that ours are so deeply related to their history and therefore am profoundly engaged in this cause with Englishmen, whereas you who I believe have nothing but English ancestry would on the whole view with equanimity the destruction of England?"
>
> He said, "The difference is that I have something you haven't got."
>
> I said laughingly — he was a very rich man — "I suspect that you have a great many things I haven't got." I wanted to say how I envied his wine cellar. He had a famous wine cellar, "But what in particular is there that bears on the question that I put to you?"
>
> "You see, you haven't got what I have — a memory of the red coats."

Felix Frankfurter Reminisces. Recorded in Talks with Dr. Harlan B. Phillips (New York, 1960), pp. 275-76. See also Charles Grant Miller, *The Poisoned Loving-Cup. United States School Histories Falsified Through Pro-British Propaganda in Sweet Name of Amity* (Chicago, 1928).

mary villains George III, Lord North, Charles Townshend, and all those political myrmidons in Parliament; and so an alteration does, in fact, occur. We hear much less about them, all of sudden, and the Revolution becomes less of an imperial conflict and more of a civil war *within* the colonies. The villains are more likely to be indigenous Loyalists, or certain apolitical dolts who lacked the native wit to see on which side the future of a great republic lay, or else nasty and brutish Indians, like Joseph Brant, who ran around the countryside massacring innocent patriots. Moreover, if one wanted "bad guys" from Europe, one didn't need to specify George III and Lord North in particular because there were always those vicious Hessians, obvious forerunners of Hitler and his twentieth-century Huns. And if one was still determined to pin the rap on George III, then one carefully pointed out that he wasn't really English anyway, but a *Hanoverian* with totalitarian tendencies who hired Hessian storm troopers to do his bidding.[30]

What's also fascinating about this period is that particular people who logically *should* have written fiction about the Revolution did not, apparently because psychologically they *could* not; whereas certain sorts of people who traditionally had *not* been associated with the genre, now got involved. It became possible, perhaps even acceptable, for Englishmen to do so; and in 1940 Robert Graves — poet, mythographer, and polymath — produced *Sergeant Lamb's America,* a bizarre narrative adaptation of his "campaign experiences in the American War of 1775-83." That book was sufficiently successful that Graves followed it with a sequel, called *Proceed, Sergeant Lamb.*[31]

Meanwhile, someone like Howard Swiggett ought to have written historical fiction about the Revolution. He had, after all, written

---

[30]See, e.g., the works of Inglis Fletcher, as well as Robert Graves', *Sergeant Lamb's America* (New York, 1940), pp. 261-62, 318, and *Proceed, Sergeant Lamb* (New York, 1941) pp. 302, 304.

[31]It is also significant that in 1940, for the first time, a major novel about the Revolution appeared in which the Loyalist position is portrayed with great sympathy: Kenneth Roberts's *Oliver Wiswell.* A few years earlier Honoré Willsie Morrow had written *Let the King Beware* (New York, 1936), in which the hero is a Massachusetts Tory who returns to England; a few years later Robert Gessner sought to make Benedict Arnold's defection understandable in *Treason* (New York, 1944); and Kenneth Roberts treated Arnold with great sympathy on several occasions.

about it at great length in non-fiction,[32] and he was one of the most popular American novelists of the day. Yet *none* of his fiction touches the Revolutionary era, and I think I know why. What do you suppose Mr. Swiggett did during World War II? From 1940 until 1945 he served in New York as Deputy Director General of the British Ministry of Supply Mission, for which he eventually received the O.B.E. He was a strong Anglophile, and my suspicion is that he, and some others like him in this period, didn't want to cope with the problem of writing imaginative literature about a time when the United States and Britain were enemies. There simply were too many complexities in setting up the "good guys" and the "bad guys," not to mention the dramatic imperative of eliciting sufficient hatred of the enemy.[33]

There was, finally, one other episode which ought to be mentioned in this context — an episode which helped to prepare the way for a more favorable treatment of England and the English during our third period. In 1917 a film entitled *The Spirit of '76* had been made in the United States. It concerned the Revolution, and depicted certain well-known events, such as Patrick Henry's most famous speech, Paul Revere's ride, and the Wyoming Valley (Pennsylvania) massacre, among other scenes. A federal judge, however, directed that the movie be seized. His reason? We had just entered World War I as England's ally; and, under the terms of a recently passed Espionage Act, in the court's opinion this film was "calculated reasonably so to excite or inflame the passions of our people or some of them as that they will be deterred from giving that full measure of co-operation, sympathy, assistance, and sacrifice which is due to Great Britain, as an ally of ours" and "to make us a little bit slack in our loyalty to Great Britain in this great catastrophe."[34] The producer went to prison, believe it or not, for three years; and the movie was destroyed. The court case

---

[32]Swiggett (1891-1957), *War Out of Niagara. Walter Butler and the Tory Rangers* (1933); *The Extraordinary Mr. [Gouverneur] Morris* (1952); *The Forgotten Leaders of the Revolution* (1955), and others.

[33]For an obituary biography of Swiggett, see the *New York Times,* March 8, 1957, p. 25. James Boyd died in 1944 at Princeton, New Jersey, where he had gone to participate in a special course given for members of the armed services of the British Commonwealth. Every summer between 1928 and 1939 Elswyth Thane did historical research at the British Museum, and *The Light Heart* (1947) is dedicated "To My Friends in England."

[34]See Zechariah Chafee, Jr., *Free Speech in the United States* (Cambridge, Mass., 1941), pp. 10, 55, 487, 522.

itself surely has the most wonderful title in all of our constitutional history: *United States* v. *The Spirit of '76!*

III

There is much more to be done, by way of cultural explication and evaluation, with these three periods and the vast corpus of historical fiction about the Revolution. I have only skimmed off a bit of the cream for this essay; and I have confined myself to citations from well known novels. In the larger study of which this is a part, for example, I intend to distinguish between those works in which the *setting* is historical but the plot itself is historically inconsequential (such as *The Spy*), and those where the actual narrative is self-consciously historical (such as Cooper's *Lionel Lincoln*).[35]

I also intend to devote considerable attention to particularities of the periodization sketched out in this essay: what contact, for example, do these three periods make with the larger rhythms of American culture? and how do they relate to certain contemporaneous, and really more famous episodes, in American literary history? I have in mind, needless to say, the emergence of Transcendentalism in the later 1830s, Naturalism at the close of the nineteenth century, and Modernism in the late 1930s and 1940s. There are, I believe some interesting antiphonal relationships between Cooper and Emerson, between Weir Mitchell and Theodore Dreiser, Kenneth Roberts and William Faulkner. The word *antiphonal*, in fact, is exquisitely appropriate here, so much so that I really do not mind using it in lieu of "contrapuntal."

But for now I must move on to some sort of dénouement, which really means turning the issue over and asking whether there is any underlying angle of vision which has persisted irrespective of period? For if there is, then surely such an enduring theme would be central to the Revolution's meaning in American thought and culture.

I am persuaded that there is, indeed, just such a persistent theme, and that it is pervasively and powerfully important. Yet it is also elusive and a bit problematic. It is almost easier to illustrate than to define or explicate. Therefore I am first going to give one example

---

[35]See John P. McWilliams Jr., *Political Justice In a Republic. James Fenimore Cooper's America* (Berkeley, Calif., 1972), pp. 4, 74.

from each of the three periods, and *then* move on to a brief concluding discussion of its meaning and implications.

My first illustration comes from *The Dutchman's Fireside* (1831) by Paulding, the story of Sybrandt Westbrook, who is introduced to us as "a bashful young gentlemen." The time is a few years prior to the Revolution, and because Sybrandt seems to be too bookish and lacking in aggressive self-confidence, he is sent to spend some time with William Johnson, Superintendent of Indian Affairs in the northern part of Britain's continental empire.

> Every day when the weather permitted, and indeed often when a dandy sportsman would have shrunk from the war of the elements, they pursued the manly, exciting sport of hunting. The image of war, most especially in this empire of savages and beasts of prey — this course of life gradually awakened the sleeping energies of Sybrandt's nature that had been so long dozing under the scholastic rubbish of the good Dominie Stettinius, . . . He acquired an active vigor of body, together with a quickness of perception and keen attention to what was passing before him, that by degrees encroached deeply on his habit of indolent abstraction. He caught from the stranger something of his fearless, independent carriage, lofty bearing, and impatience of idleness or inaction. In short, he acquired a confidence in himself, a self-possession, and self-respect, such as he had never felt before, and which freed him from the leaden fetters of that awkward restraint which had hitherto been the bane of his life. (pp. 115-116)

My second illustration is to be found in Harold Frederic's *In the Valley* (1890). I will eschew another long quotation, and simply point out that chapter seven is entitled, "Through Happy Youth to Man's Estate." In it young Douw Mauverensen has to make a long trip from his secure home in the Mohawk Valley to the "far Lake Country." The year is 1772, and the ordeal is what we today might call a survival trip. Douw must encounter a great amount of grave danger — unfriendly Indians presumably, fierce bears, and perhaps even some poison ivy — and he passes the test. In sum, he goes away from home a boy and returns, five months later, a man. We are left in no doubt that this means a man prepared to defend American rights in the Revolution.[36]

---

[36]See especially pp. 112-13, 126, 129, 132-35.

My third illustration is taken from *Drums Along the Mohawk,* which was published in 1936. The entire book, of course, deals with the maturation to full manhood of Gil Martin, who gets married on July 10, 1776, the very day that New York accepts independence; but the same process is dealt with in briefer compass for some lesser characters, such as John Weaver. Toward the end of this very long book, the local militia has gone out to fight one last, bitter skirmish against Tory rangers and their Indian allies. The bedraggled and exhausted militia return at war's end, and Walter Edmonds tells us that

> John Weaver returned with them. He did not look at all like the boy who had started out. He was like a stranger to Mary. She felt even younger than on her bridal night; and when they went to bed in the Herter house, she was shy and half frightened. He seemed so much stronger — even in his happiness with her she was aware that he had been with men and become a man. Though she had never thought of him otherwise, she knew that the John she had married was a boy; and proud as she was of him, now his touch conveyed to her a strange sense of warning that she would never be as close to him again in all their lives. (pp. 478-79)

Well, what does it all mean? What is to be made of these passages, and literally many hundreds more just like them?[37] What it means, almost to the point of unbearable monotony, is that imaginative writers have consistently perceived the American Revolution as a national *rite de passage,* and have relentlessly projected that vision to an ever-widening readership.

It all begins in *The Spy,* when Cooper has Dr. Sitgreaves say — referring to America — that "The child was of age, and was entitled to the privileges of majority." (ch. xiii). And it culminates, for the moment at least, in an editorial by James Michener which appeared during 1975 in The *New York Times.* Michener, one of America's

---

[37]See, for example, James Fenimore Cooper, *Satanstoe* (Lincoln, Nebr., 1962), pp. 33, 42n., 75, 78, 80, 92-93, 118, 122, 368-69; Wayne Whipple, *The Story of Young George Washington* (Philadelphia, 1915), ch. 7, "A Boy No Longer," especially p. 113; and James Boyd, *Drums* (New York 1965), pp. 29, 30, 35, 44, 73, 134, 164, 171, 187, 197, 219, 262, 267, 286, 410, 418. Closely connected are all those novels which emphasize ideological cleavage between father and son, and which use the divided family as a metaphor for the divided empire: e.g., *Ambrose and Eleanor* (1834), *Carleton* (1841), *Wyandotté* (1843), *Ernest Harcourt* (1843), *Hugh Wynne* (1897), and *If Not Victory* (1939).

most successful contemporary novelists, wanted to explain why he had accepted an appointment to the Bicentennial Advisory Committee. Here are a few excerpts from his explanation.

> Birth, puberty, acceptance into the adult group, marriage, childbirth, ordination, attaining seventy years, death — these are moments of significance, and a person cheats himself if he fails to observe them ritually.
> The same rule applies to nations. The great moments of attainment and passage ought to be memorialized, for then history is drawn together and the significance of survival is deepened. The rites of passage become logical times to renew our dedication and to look ahead to challenges no less demanding than those whose passing we celebrate.[38]

It is the persistence of this point of view which explains, I believe, the absolutely phenomenal success of *Johnny Tremain* by Esther Forbes. Since its publication in 1943, that book has sold more than two *million* copies, has been made into a full-length film (by Walt Disney) and adapted for television as well.[39] Its plot, quite simply, is an epitome of the American Revolution as *rite de passage*. I cannot rehearse all the details here; but the book, which won the John Newbery medal as "the most distinguished contribution to American literature for children in the year of its publication," and has had at least equal appeal for adults, encapsulates the dominant view of our Revolution in American popular culture.

Johnny was born in 1759, and is nearly fourteen when the book opens in 1772. We are given constant anticipations of what will happen when Johnny is "man-grown." His transformation really starts when he burns his hand severely with molten silver. Looking into the bedroom where he convalesced, he reflects that "in a way he had died in that room; at least something had happened and the bright little silversmith's apprentice was no more. He stood here again at the threshold, but now he was somebody else."[40]

Johnny's time of troubles and symbolic rebirth coincide exactly with that of the colonies. The winter of 1773-74 is pivotal. As the

---

[38]Michener, "A Slice of Cake in Every Hamlet," The *New York Times,* April 5, 1975.

[39]Letter from Houghton Mifflin Company to Michael Kammen, October 1, 1975.

[40]*Johnny Tremain. A Novel for Old & Young* (New York, 1943), pp. 148-49.

pretty Cilla says to Johnny: "This is the end. The end of one thing — the beginning of something else. . . . there is going to be a war — civil war."[41] Later on, in 1775, a woman asks Johnny his age. When he tells her " 'sixteen,' " she replies, " 'And what's that — a boy or a man?' He laughed. 'A boy in time of peace and a man in time of war.' " At the end Miss Forbes refers more and more to manhood, not merely Johnny's achieving it, but his passing through a crisis of confidence about courage, manliness, and even the acceptance of death in a just cause. The book's last words, "A man can stand up . . ." provide a residual refrain throughout.[42]

The fact that Johnny discovers his parentage and true identity in 1775, at the age of sixteen, is quite obviously symbolic though not nearly so heavy-handed as my flat statement of it might sound. Likewise the fact that his tragic injury forces him to rethink his calling. And likewise the fact that all these personal troubles of 1772-1775 have served to prepare him for Lexington, Concord, Independence, and a brave new world beyond that. He has undergone the psychic experience required to transform a boorish, socially *inferior* adolescent provincial into a militant, morally *superior* young American.

Johnny is only the most successful — and fabulously successful at that — in a long line of young men (and sometimes women) going back to Fenimore Cooper's Cornelius Littlepage. Needless to say, this personification of the American Revolution as an individual and collective *rite de passage* raises a huge host of complicated questions about American culture, our imaginative writers, and the whole tortured issue of American uniqueness. Why has this view been the dominant one? What purpose does it serve in the national ideology and self-image? Is it a conservative or a radical point of view? What relationship does it bear to what the anthropologists and ethnologists have in mind when they talk about *rites de passage?*[43] Was the American Revolution in *reality* a rite of passage? Has there not been any other

---

[41]P. 165.

[42]See pp. 17, 26, 45, 112-13, 137, 165, 173, 180-81, 200-201, 233-34, 237, 249, 253, 256.

[43]See Arnold van Gennep, *The Rites of Passage* (Chicago, 1960); Alfred M. Tozzer, *Social Origins and Social Continuities* (New York, 1925); Max Gluckman, "Les Rites de Passage," in *Essays on the Ritual of Social Relations,* edited by Gluckman (Manchester, 1962), pp. 1-52; Victor W. Turner, *The Ritual Process: Structure and Anti-Structure* (Chicago, 1969), especially chap. 3.

enduring perception of the psychological meaning of the revolutionary experience?

I do have some thoughts on all these matters, as well as about the tricky comparative question: what differentiates this genre I have described from the *bildungsroman* of romantic Germany, or from the vast body of fiction set in the days of revolutionary France? I will attempt to explicate all of them in a subsequent book-length study.

Here I simply wish to conclude with two thoughts. First, I must give an ambiguous response to the question I posed at the outset: did Adams and Jefferson really have just cause for anxiety back in 1815? Yes and No. These novelists are just like the little girl with the little curl right in the middle of her forehead. When they are good, they are very, very good; but when they are bad, they are horrid. Now, "horrid" requires no explanation; but "very, very good" means something special. It means that at their best these authors have stunning insights to offer concerning the American Revolution — especially the impact of war upon communities, families and individuals; and most especially the Revolution as a transforming psychological event. In many respects, moreover, the novelists' penetration into the more profound aspects of human and social experience races ahead of even our best professional historians. Fenimore Cooper, for example, anticipates Bernard Bailyn by 120 years; and Harold Frederic, among others, develops the famous "dual revolution" thesis two decades before Carl Becker published his influential dissertation.[44]

My second, and concluding observation, is this. We would do well to recall de Tocqueville's observation that "Revolutions, like love affairs, change your past." What this means in our context, I believe, is that imaginative writers have been perceiving the Revolution as a

---

[44]It is interesting to read, *par passu,* Cooper's *Satanstoe* (1845) and Bailyn's Introduction to *Pamphlets of the American Revolution, 1750-1776,* 1 vol. to date, (Cambridge, Mass., 1965-), pp. 3-202; or Frederic's *In the Valley* (1890) and Becker's *History of Political Parties in the Province of New York, 1760-1776* (Madison, 1909), esp. p. 22. Compare also, Edward Bellamy, *The Duke of Stockbridge: A Romance of Shays' Rebellion,* Joseph Schiffman, ed. (1879: Cambridge, Mass., 1962), pp. 168, 197, with Kenneth Lockridge, "Land Population and the Evolution of New England Society, 1630-1790," *Past and Present,* 39 (1968): 62-80; and Edmund S. Morgan, "The American Revolution Considered as an Intellectual Movement," in *Paths of American Thought,* Arthur M. Schlesinger, Jr., ed. (Boston, 1963), pp. 11-33; cf. also Roberts, *Oliver Wiswell* (New York, 1940), p. 424, and Mary Beth Norton, *The British-Americans. The Loyalist Exiles in England, 1774-1789* (Boston, 1972), especially chaps. 2-4.

rite of passage for so long now that the tradition, that perception, has become virtually as important as the original Revolutionary realities. This tradition of the Revolution has become deeply ingrained in our cultural experience, and therefore constitutes a central part of our self-knowledge as a nation. The curious ways in which the Rights of Man came to be seen as the rites of passage have much to do, I think, with a profoundly complex pattern of cultural change which has taken place in the United States between 1776 and 1976.

THE LEGACY OF
THE AMERICAN REVOLUTIONARY WAR

John W. Shy

In January, 1838, a young Illinois lawyer and politician gave a lecture to the Springfield Lyceum, a group like so many others of its time dedicated to self-improvement through the exchange of information and ideas. In his lecture, the speaker pointed to a phenomenon familiar to his audience. In their midst, he said, lived a handful of old men, one or two of whom died every year, all of whom would soon be gone. This handful of old men, some of them sick, others senile, was all that remained in any tangible sense of the American Revolutionary War. These were the veterans, the men who had served in the Continental army and the Revolutionary militia. Even in 1838, memories were dim and distorted, and the events of sixty years ago were as remote for Abraham Lincoln and his audience as the sinking of the *Lusitania* and General John J. Pershing leading the A.E.F. to France are for us — perhaps more remote, because the people of Sangamon County, Illinois, had no photography, no television, no mass media to bombard them with sense impressions of what Lexington and Valley Forge and Yorktown must have been like. Lacking the technology which keeps our own memories vivid if not always clear, Lincoln in his lecture used these old men and their memories to speak about our subject, the legacy of the American Revolutionary War.[1]

What *was* its legacy? Did, in the long run, the war — except for its obviously crucial outcome — make any real difference? Or did its effects fade quickly after the fighting had stopped in 1783? Historians are better at telling stories accurately than at answering questions, particularly broad and hazy questions like this one. Dozens of historians have told the story of the war without seriously trying to assess

---

[1] *The Collected Works of Abraham Lincoln,* Roy P. Basler et al., ed., 9 vols. (New Brunswick, N.J., 1953), 1: 108-115.

its lasting effects. By doing so, they have suggested two contradictory conclusions: one is that the important effects of the war are too obvious to need discussion; and the other is that the war itself (as contrasted with its outcome) was actually not very important — birth replaced death, damage was soon repaired, and life quickly returned to normal. To observers like ourselves, creatures of the twentieth century, when the hammer blows of war have bent or even broken the lives of almost everyone born during the last hundred years, neither conclusion sounds right. At best, each seems too simple or merely half true; the question, however difficult it may be to answer, deserves better than silence.

Begin by imagining what would have happened had there been no war, or a very short war. General Thomas Gage, commander of British forces in North America, wanted to withdraw his troops from Boston in 1774 and suspend the "Coercive Acts" until Britain was ready for a massive military effort or until the American leaders were ready to negotiate.[2] At the same time, both the British Secretary at War and the Adjutant General, Lord Barrington and General Edward Harvey, argued against trying to fight a land war in North America.[3] None of the three actually opposed a war to enforce Parliamentary sovereignty in the Continental colonies, but their advice might ultimately have meant no war like the one that took place between 1775 and 1783. After the outbreak of fighting in 1775 had led to British failure at Boston and an imminent American declaration of independence, which would foreclose a negotiated reconstruction of the old Empire, others in Britain, like Dr. Richard Price, argued that the best interests of all parties dictated a cessation of hostilities and a recognition of the new political realities. Had Britain done in 1776 what it eventually did in 1783 (as Price argued it should in a pamphlet which sold thousands of copies in a few days), the war would have been brief and left American society relatively unscathed.[4]

---

[2]Gage to Lord Dartmouth, 25 September 1774 (two letters), *The Correspondence of General Thomas Gage,* Clarence E. Carter, ed., 2 vols. (New Haven, 1931-33), 1: 275-77.

[3]Barrington to Lord Dartmouth, 12 November 1774, Barrington Letterbook, Ipswitch Record Office; General Harvey to General John Irwin, 30 June 1775, W.O. 3/5, pp. 36-37, British Public Record Office.

[4]*Observations on Civil Liberty and the Justice and Policy of the War with America* (London, 1776). On Price and the reception given his pamphlet, see the *Dictionary of National Biography,* 46:335.

Stopping the war early, or even before it started, was thus at least imaginable, and by imagining this possibility we can bring what did happen to America during almost eight years of war into sharper focus.

A long war meant that more than 150,000 and perhaps as many as 200,000 American men served actively in the armies of the Revolution.[5] In a population of less than three million, an estimated half million of whom became Loyalists and opposed the Revolution, and another half million of whom were black (almost all enslaved and legally barred from bearing arms), military service approached one in ten of the available population. Colonial governors had usually reckoned that one person in five, allowing for women, children, and old and unfit men, were eligible for enrollment in the militia, which was virtually a universal military obligation. Even allowing for some 5,000 black men who, in spite of legal obstacles, served as soldiers or sailors of the Revolution, and for an indeterminate few thousand men who bore arms for the Revolution only to change their loyalties before 1783, we can say that a very large proportion of the adult white male population of the new United States had served six months or a year or more in the Revolutionary armies.[6] Without a long, hard war, most of these men would never have left their homes, many having seen parts of the Continent they would never have seen otherwise.

A long war killed, in one way or another, perhaps a tenth of the men who served. About 8,000 died in battle, at least as many more died of disease on active service, and an estimated 8,000 died as prisoners of war. The approximate total of 25,000 service-related deaths may not seem a large number for a war that lasted almost eight years.[7] But it is the per capita equivalent of about two million deaths

---

[5]The best estimate I know of the numbers who served actively in the Revolutionary War on the American side is in an unpublished paper by Theodore J. Crackel. Crackel projected backward from the number and age-profile of pensioners in the National Archives, using a modified mortality table. His estimate of 185,000 serving six months or more may be too low, because his working assumptions are uniformly conservative ones.

[6]The best estimate of Loyalist numbers is Paul H. Smith, "The American Loyalists: Notes on their Organization and Numerical Strength," *William and Mary Quarterly,* 3rd ser., 25 (1968): 259-77. For blacks, see *Historical Statistics of the United States, Colonial Times to 1957* (Washington, D.C., 1960), p. 756, and Benjamin Quarles, *The Negro in the American Revolution* (Chapel Hill, 1961), p. ix.

[7]Howard H. Peckham, ed., *The Toll of Independence: Engagements and Battle Casualties of the American Revolution* (Chicago, 1974), p. 130.

in the present United States, and it is about ten times the number of service-related deaths suffered in the 1973 war by Israel, with a population roughly the size of that of the United States in 1780.[8] The effect of the 1973 casualty list on Israel was traumatic; though the tenfold-larger casualty list of the American Revolution was compiled over a much longer period of time, its size in comparison both to modern American equivalents and to recent Israeli experience suggests that 25,000 is a large number.

Death was only the most severe kind of impact felt in the Revolutionary War. The few thousand veterans who are known to have received disability pensions — men who had lost an arm, a leg, or an eye, or whose health was permanently damaged — between the end of the war and the first comprehensive pension act of 1818 can be no more than the visible remnant of a much larger group, most of whom had died before their cases could come up as individual claims or before they could apply under one of the pre-1818 laws, or whose records were lost in the fires of 1800 and 1814 that destroyed War Department files.[9] It is difficult to estimate the total, but evidence from other wars, before the advent of modern medical knowledge, suggests that for each wartime service-related death there is at least one survivor crippled by battle or disease, yielding us a round guess of 50,000 serious American "casualties" — soldiers dead and badly hurt — for the Revolutionary War.[10]

---

[8]The population of Israel was estimated at 3,164,000 by the May 1972 census. The *Annual Register* for 1973, p. 202, lists casualties in the Yom Kippur War as 2,512 dead, 508 missing.

[9]The various pension laws are compiled in Robert Mayo and Ferdinand Moulton, *Army and Navy Pension Laws and Bounty Land Laws* (Washington, D.C., 1852). An account of the number of veterans who were pensioned under these laws is in William H. Glasson, *Federal Military Pensions in the United States* (New York, 1918), pp. 23-96.

[10]On war casualties, the literature is large, but unsatisfactory. The brief discussion in Quincy Wright, *A Study of War* . . . 2 vols., (Chicago, 1942), 1: 224ff, is still a useful guide to the standard works. An even briefer note in Mark M. Boatner, comp., *Encyclopedia of the American Revolution* (New York, 1966), pp. 187, 189, states that three or four were wounded for every man killed; but if we are concerned with *serious* wounds then a ratio of one-to-one seems reasonably conservative. The assertion in the text about death by disease is a guess, but a very conservative one based on study of other pre-twentieth century wars; some historians assert that disease killed many more, but they tend to include non-service deaths. Ernst Kipping, *The Hessian View of America, 1776-1783* (Monmouth Beach, N.J., 1971), p. 39, indicates that 4,626 "Hessians" died in the whole war while 357 were killed but this proportion, if applied to American losses (c. 8,000 known killed) would put total deaths well over 100,000 — an obvious impossibility.

Disrupted lives and communities were also casualties of war. Not even a reasonable guess is possible for the number of civilians killed or hurt by the war but missed in the military recording of casualties. At least 60,000 white persons, loyal to their king or at least not loyal to the Revolution, felt compelled to leave their homes for Nova Scotia, New Brunswick, Canada, the West Indies, or England, most never to return.[11] Slave owners claimed, after the war, that thousands of black people had "disappeared" — seized by British raiding parties, or run away in the midst of wartime weakening of the slave system. Some slaves "disappeared" into freedom, in which case the only sufferers were their owners; but others were simply shipped as slaves to the West Indies, others must have died without leaving a trace for the historian, and still others, who had earned their freedom by joining the British, found life in Canada so unrewarding that they were re-emigrating to West Africa in the 1790s and even returning to a virulently racist United States by the early nineteenth century.[12]

Less ambiguously among the casualties of the Revolution were Indians. The destruction of the great Iroquois Confederation of upstate New York, part of it fleeing to Canada while the remnant came under United States domination, was only the most dramatic case of a general tragedy for the Indian tribes of eastern North America, most of whom when forced to choose sides had supported the Crown, which in the past had offered some protection against the rapacity of white traders, speculators, and frontiersmen. It is not possible to reckon the total number of Indians killed, maimed and displaced by the war, but it is certain that the Revolutionary War shattered beyond repair the power of these Indians to resist white pressure on their lands and their way of life.[13]

Another kind of wartime statistic was created by the army itself,

---

[11]The estimate of "Loyalist" emigrés is lower than that given in Wallace Brown, *The Good Americans: The Loyalists in the American Revolution* (New York, 1969), but Brown recently (November 1974) said at a conference in London on Loyalism that a lower figure of 66,000 was probably correct.

[12]Quarles, *Negro in the American Revolution*, pp. 119, 172-81; Robin W. Winks, *The Blacks in Canada: A History* (New Haven and Montreal, 1971), pp. 29-95, 99, 143, 237. Wallace Brown, at the conference noted above, estimated that 15,000 blacks emigrated.

[13]The best case study of the impact of the Revolutionary War on Indians is Anthony F. C. Wallace, *Death and Rebirth of the Seneca Nation* (New York, 1969); a general account is Jack M. Sosin, *The Revolutionary Frontier, 1763-1783* (New York, 1967).

divided like all armies into the mysterious hierarchy of officers and soldiers. Somewhere between 15,000 and 20,000 Americans became officers in the Revolutionary armies.[14] Before the Revolution, no other institution had made it possible for so many people — approaching one in every hundred of the white population — to achieve a position of equivalent status. Washington and others, including European observers, noted that American officers often were not "gentlemen"; such observations confirm our own hunch that, for many, military service in the Revolution deflected life not only outward but upward. More will be said about this aspect of the war later.

In a society bereft of centralized institutions aside from the remote presence of an imperial government based in London, and an improvised "Congress" comprised of something like ambassadors from the various states, fighting a long war with a centrally directed army imposed an enormous and unprecedented strain. After the first flush of enthusiasm had faded in 1775, and especially after the disastrous campaign of 1776 had made it clear that military service would mean something more dangerous than a day or two of sniping at British soldiers from behind trees and stone walls, recruiting men for the Continental army became a critical problem. The colonial tradition had been one of recruiting "volunteers" for active service. Even in rare instances when men had been "drafted" from the colonial militia for active service, only those who could not buy their way out were required to serve; personal service by the draftee, taken for granted in the twentieth century, was rarely required in the eighteenth.[15] Volunteering and conscription thus tended to boil down to the same thing: economic inducements that attracted those least able to resist them. But money was always in short supply during the Revolution, and by 1776 Congress as well as the States were exploiting the one resource of which America had a vast supply — land. The promise of land seems to have been an effective appeal to enlist men for the duration of the war, particularly those who by the later eighteenth century could not have expected to acquire land by any other means. In the

---

[14]Francis B. Heitman, in compiling a *Historical Register of Officers of the Continental Army* (Washington: 2nd ed., 1914), found about 14,000 officers, although he made no effort to search systematically for militia officers.

[15]John Shy, "A New Look at Colonial Militia," *William and Mary Quarterly*, 3rd Ser., 20 (1963): 175-85; Charles A. Lofgren, "Compulsory Military Service under the Constitution: The Original Undersanding," ibid., 32 (1976): 61-88.

post-war era almost ten million acres, or roughly fifty acres per soldier, were patented from land warrants issued by the federal government alone for service in the Revolutionary War. Even though large part was patented by speculators, who bought up warrants from soldiers at a fraction of their true value, the very act of distributing such an enormous segment of the nation's wealth is one significant effect of the war.[16]

Supplying the Continental soldiers recruited by promises of land was an even greater strain on the improvised, decentralized confederation. At first these men were paid and supplied in the traditional colonial way, by the issuance of paper money — governmental promises to pay (eventually) those who received them, and themselves payable (usually) against taxes. Wars in the past had been financed in this manner, with the additional advantage of pumping badly needed circulating currency into colonial economies chronically short of money. Inflation and governmental recklessness, as in the case of Rhode Island, had sometimes been a problem, but in general the colonial assemblies had kept their wartime issues of paper money under reasonable control. But the American Revolution, in its duration and in the size of its demands, was breaking down the old system by the third year of the war. Once the economy had absorbed about 25 million dollars of paper currency, additional issues began to drive prices up at an accelerating rate. Plans for taxation were administratively difficult under wartime conditions, politically even more difficult in a loose confederation whose members inevitably suffered unequally from the burden of war, and wherever they were tried could never catch up with the heavy and unremitting demands of military operations. By 1778 chaos and bankruptcy loomed; by 1780 they had arrived; a Continental dollar at the end of 1780 was worth one cent in the hard money.[17]

The American States were populous and rich enough to sustain war indefinitely; ideally, no one should have had to serve for long in order to field an army larger than anything the British could muster, nor should that army ever had been in need of food or clothing.

---

[16]Jerry A. O'Callaghan, "The War Veteran and the Public Lands," *Agricultural History,* 28 (1954) : 163-68.

[17]E. James Ferguson, *The Power of the Purse: A History of American Public Finance, 1776-1790* (Chapel Hill, 1961), pp. 3-47.

Bankruptcy, in theory, looks easily avoidable. The actual problem, however, was a predictable product of two factors: weak central direction, both politically and administratively, of a highly centralized military strategy; and the economic and technological difficulties of an unprecedented redistribution of plentiful resources.

Every historian has dwelt on the weakness of central authority during the war, but badly neglected is the story of procuring and transporting supplies.[18] Not until we see the delays, frustrations, and misunderstandings endemic in the task of getting, on some regular basis, cattle from eastern Connecticut and flour from western Pennsylvania and northern Virginia to 15,000 men in New Jersey and New York, where they had eaten the land bare, with the British navy denying use of the cheap and fast water routes and the British army menacing the more direct and better kept roads, can we begin to appreciate why the Revolutionary War brought runaway inflation and, finally, bankruptcy. Simply to find wagons, teams, and drivers on the required scale and frequency was extremely difficult, sometimes impossible; the pre-war market economy had developed in conditions of internal peace and free use of waterways, and was not geared to distribute its products overland at such distance. Competition between government agents and contractors for a hopelessly inadequate supply of transportation drove these costs to fantastic levels, dragging all other prices up with them, widening the gap between public revenue and expenditure, and sowing the seeds of civil war as some people profited and others faced ruin. Even the need to keep experienced, long-service soldiers in the field rather than distribute the burden of military service more equitably, exacerbated the situation. State and local governments were less interested in taking care of long-service soldiers recruited by them at great expense from among the socially expendable segment of the population — in other words, the typical Continental soldier by 1777 — than in supplying their own militia — that is, voters and taxpayers who would soon come home after a few months in the field. By 1779 the Continental forces were often taking what they needed, when they could find it, even plundering supply trains destined

---

[18]Louis C. Hatch, *The Administration of the American Revolutionary Army* (New York, 1904); Victor L. Johnson, *The Administration of the American Commissariat During the Revolutionary War* (Philadelphia, 1941). The most thorough account is in a forthcoming book by Erna Risch to be published by the Center of Military History, U.S. Department of the Army.

for other parts of the Continental army.[19] Under the circumstances, central control, rational planning, good temper, and the spirit of cooperation virtually disappeared. More specifically, two effects of this deteriorating situation, caused solely by the need to support a Continental army, were particularly marked and exceptionally important. One was the loss of authority and prestige by the Continental Congress as it failed to cope with the impossible problem of wartime finance and supply, and the consequent slide of power, from 1778 onwards, down to the state governments.[20] The other was the widespread loss of faith — perhaps a naive faith but nonetheless held by almost everyone committed to the Revolution — in the special ability of Americans, with their absence of poverty and their security and equality arising from widespread ownership of land, to meet the challenge of war without behaving badly. American Revolutionaries had pinned both their hopes on what they called the "virtue" of the people, and that "virtue" most decidedly and spectacularly broke down on the anvil of war. In the words of David Ramsay, who lived through the war as an unswerving Whig and wrote his history of it soon after the peace treaty: "The iniquity of the laws [which vainly tried to regulate the wartime economy] estranged the mind of many of the citizens from the habits and love of justice."[21] More will be said later about the widely ramifying effects of congressional decline and the loss of "virtue" under the impact of war.

Looking far beyond the end of the war, we can specify its impact in yet one more way. As Revolutionary veterans turned gray and arthritic, and their numbers dwindled, the Federal government attempted to solve an embarrassing problem of surplus revenue by doing something for their old age. In 1818 Congress passed a law giving a modest pension to anyone who had served nine months in Continental pay and who stood in need of public assistance. Expecting at most a few thousand applicants, in hardly more than a year Congress found

[19]For example, Washington's General Orders of 29 December 1779, at Morristown, in which he said that American soldiers were behaving more like "a band of robbers than disciplined troops called forth in a defence of the rights of the Community." *The Writings of George Washington,* John C. Fitzpatrick, ed., 39 vols. (Washington D.C., 1931-44), 17: 331.

[20]The best account is still in Allan Nevins, *The American States During and After the Revolution, 1775-1789* (New York, 1924).

[21]David Ramsey, *The History of the American Revolution,* 2 vols. (London, 1793 edition), 2: 136.

almost 20,000 veterans drawing pensions for Revolutionary War services, spurred no doubt by the economic "Panic" of 1819. A new act in 1820 tightened the loose language of the 1818 law, requiring a certified inventory of property; even so, after thousands of names were struck from the pension rolls, about 12,000 remained. Again, in the 1830s when a politically disturbing Treasury surplus and economic depression coincided, new pension laws extended Federal largesse to those who had served six months in the active militia, and eventually to widows and orphans of veterans. Successively broadened through the 1850s, Federal pension files for the Revolutionary War today contain data, much of it rich and fascinating, on about 70,000 veterans and their families.[22] These people, already old when the promise of a pension impelled them to tell their stories, were beneficiaries of the first, little-known Federal program of massive public welfare. The Census of 1840 made a special project of counting these people, and found about 20,000 of them still alive. When Lincoln spoke to the Lyceum at Springfield in 1838, certainly he knew and probably was thinking of Phillip Crowder, Joel Maxcy, and John Lockridge, Revolutionary war veterans in their 70s, living and collecting their pensions in Sangamon County.[23]

Facts and figures do not interpret themselves. Perhaps 200,000 veterans, maybe 50,000 casualties, as many as 100,000 emigrés (counting Loyalists, slaves and Indians), almost 20,000 officers, ten million acres of Federal land, about 70,000 pensioners, hundredfold inflation, and ultimate bankruptcy — these facts acquire meaning only when we explore and even, where evidence fails, speculate on their consequences. One possible consequence may be disposed of quickly: the demographic effects of the war were slight. Historically, war is much less efficient than disease and starvation in altering the structure of a population, and with its rapid rate of growth the population of Revolutionary America easily absorbed its losses. The deaths of 25,000

---

[22]Glasson, *Federal Military Pensions,* and the unpublished work by Crackel mentioned in note 5.

[23]*A Census of Pensioners for Revolutionary or Military Services* (Washington, D.C., 1841). The total listed in the Sixth Census (1840), p. 475, is 20,797, but some of those were veterans of the War of 1812, and the listed age of a few indicate that they were children of veterans. The name of John Lockridge, and the surnames of Maxcy and Crowder, appear in Lincoln's early correspondence, though no connection has been positively established. Sangamon County had a population of about 14,000 in 1838.

young men, plus the loss of other lives through emigration and the delay of births because of military service, hardly dented the long-term upward trend. At most, the abrupt removal of these people, mainly younger males, from the society may have eased some of the pressure against land and opportunity in the more settled areas, which in a relative sense were becoming noticeably "crowded" by the mid-eighteenth century.[24]

But other speculative thoughts on the impact of the war seem more persuasive and of greater lasting importance. Robert R. Palmer has compared the per capita incidence of emigration for Revolutionary America and Revolutionary France, and found it significantly higher for the American Revolution; considering the fact that many French emigrés returned in the early nineteenth century to constitute an intransigent Right wing in French politics thereafter, Palmer suggests that the apparently "mild" character of the American Revolution, and the stability of its post war institutions, were a result of permanently expelling those very people who otherwise might have been the missing party in the politics of the New Republic — the counterrevolutionary conservatives and reactionaries.[25]

A more tenuous, but equally intriguing, thought has been put forth concerning slavery. Where slavery was a minor aspect of society, and where large numbers of blacks served in the Revolutionary armies, the principles of the Declaration of Independence were applied strictly, and slavery was abolished soon after the war. But where slavery was an important social and economic institution, from Maryland south-ward, where the British had recruited numbers of blacks to fight for the king and induced thousands of slaves to run away from their owners, and where plans to recruit black soliders for the Revolution met bitter resistance, the Revolution and its protracted war seems to have made slavery a tighter, more rigorous system than it had been in the last decades of the old Empire. By 1783, Southern slave owners, previously content to run a system more flexible and less harsh in

---

[24]See Kenneth Lockridge, "Land, Population, and the Evolution of New England Society 1630-1790," *Past and Present*, 39 (1968): 62-80; Jackson Turner Main, *The Social Structure of Revolutionary America* (Princeton, 1965); and James A. Henretta, *The Evolution of American Society, 1700-1815* (Lexington, Mass., 1973).

[25]*The Age of the Democratic Revolution: A Political History of Europe and America, 1760-1800,* 2 vols., (Princeton, 1959-65), 1:188-90.

practice than it appeared in the statute books, realized as never before how fragile and vulnerable the system actually was, and how little they could depend on the cowardice, ignorance, and gratitude of their slaves. Troubled by the agitation, even within themselves, created against slavery by the rhetorical justification of the Revolution, slave-owners set about giving legal and institutional expression to a new level of anxiety about the system. New rules governing slavery and a new articulation of racist attitudes may have been one of the most important, enduring, and paradoxical legacies of the Revolutionary War.[26]

The question for the society as a whole may be put in terms of movement, or, as sociologists might prefer, mobility: how much displacement of life was there that would not have happened without a long war? No answer that ignores the variety and particularity of individual human lives can be satisfying; but using our basic facts about the war, fragments of research done so far on the question, and some imagination, we can briefly sketch an answer. First, people began to move across the face of the land — more numerously, more frequently, and for greater distances than ever before. Geographical mobility soon after the war may have approached twice its rate today, when the United States seems to be a society in perpetual motion.[27] The so-called Indian barrier was now breached and crumbling, and the prewar migratory trends simply accelerated. Land grants, land speculation, postwar depression with its uncertainties and frustrations for returning veterans, all drew these men and their families into Vermont, upper New York, and the great Ohio Valley. Uprooted once by the war, veterans were ready to move again when conditions at home disappointed them.

---

[26]This view of the effect of the Revolution on slavery is suggested by Gerald W. Mullin, *Flight and Rebellion: Slave Resistance in Eighteenth-Century Virginia* (New York, 1972), p. 124ff. Winthrop Jordan, *White Over Black: American Attitudes Toward the Negro, 1550-1812* (Chapel Hill, 1968), might disagree (cf. pp. 367-68), but I find much in his book to support the idea advanced herein. In conversation, Duncan J. MacLeod, author of *Slavery, Race and the American Revolution* (Cambridge, 1974), has strongly challenged this causal conjecture, mainly on the ground that "tightening" is not evident until the 1790s when factors other than the Revolution are clearly operative.

[27]This is the conclusion reached by Theodore J. Crackel in his unpublished study of Revolutionary War veterans from New Jersey. John Sellers, in an unpublished study of Virginia pensioners, reached similar conclusions about mobility.

Not only did they begin to pour into the vast territorial openness of transAppalachian North America, but the war had created other kinds of "space" into which veterans could move. The flight of emigrés, many of them holders of property and position, created one kind of space, and mobilization had created another. Without a long, bitter war, Loyalists would not have been forced to flee by the thousands. Without a long, bitter war, a myriad of public offices, major and minor, civilian and military, would not have been needed to represent, to persuade, to guide, to coerce, and to keep watch on three million unruly, scattered, and relatively ungoverned people. We know about the thousands of new military officers, many of whom reappeared later in political roles; and we also know about the wartime creation of a new tier of government at the national level, and about the wartime doubling or tripling in size of State legislatures, both of which often made the reappearance of Continental officers possible. But we are just beginning to learn about the veritable wartime explosion of local government, when a handful of surnames who had run a town or a county were quickly joined and sometimes even displaced by dozens of new names filling up the spaces on those local committees needed to run the war and watch the Tories.[28] Parkinson's law tells us how emergency expansion never wholly contracts once the emergency is passed, and local government in the postwar Republic followed the law; it remained permanently larger than before the war, and so men who chose not to move out could the more easily move up.

But people hit by the war also moved down. There had been a perceptible prewar trend toward a widening gap between rich and poor, rich getting richer and poor getting relatively poorer and more numerous; this trend must have been affected by wartime inflation, bankruptcy, and general economic dislocation.[29] It is possible to recite case after case, at least one for every case of a man moving upward, of men and their families ruined economically by the war. But in our

---

[28]Jackson T. Main, "Government by the People: The American Revolution and the Democratization of the Legislatures," *William and Mary Quarterly,* 3rd ser., 23 (1966): 391-474; Henry J. Young, "The Spirit of 1775," *John and Mary's Journal,* 1 (1975): 53-55.

[29]Charles S. Grant, *Democracy in the Connecticut Frontier Town of Kent* (New York, 1961), pp. 96-103; James A. Henretta, "Economic Development and Social Structure in Colonial Boston," *William and Mary Quarterly,* 3rd ser., 22 (1965): 75-92; James T. Lemon, *The Best Poor Man's Country: A Geographical Study of Early Southeastrn Pennsylvania* (Baltimore, 1972), pp. 11, 69, 88.

present state of knowledge it is impossible to say with any confidence whether we are seeing a further social splitting caused by the war of the fortunate few at the top from the unlucky group near the bottom, or its opposite — a general socio-economic scrambling whose net result may have been to make American society more equal than it had been before the Revolution. Statistical research done so far is inconclusive, but tends to support the former view, that the overall economic impact of the war was to make America less, not more, democratic.[30] Without a solid basis for judgement, however, we can turn again to the informed opinion of the contemporary historian David Ramsay. Ramsay saw inflation, coupled with laws to fix prices and to force the acceptance of paper money, as having ruined widows, orphans, old and retired persons, those with savings and inheritances or who were owed money. "On the other hand," Ramsay continued, paper money was the occasion

> of good to many; it was at all times the poor man's friend; while it was current, all kinds of labor very readily found their reward. In the first years of the war, none were idle from want of employment, and none were employed without having it in their power to obtain ready payment for their services. To that class of people, whose daily labour was their support, the depreciation was no disadvantage; expending money as fast as they received it, they always got its full value. The reverse was the case with the rich, or those who were disposed to hoarding. No agrarian law ever had a more extensive operation, than continental money. That for which the Gracchi lost their lives in Rome, was peaceably effected by the United States, by the legal tender of these depreciating bills. The poor became rich, and the rich became poor.[31]

Whether Ramsay was right in his socio-economic arithmetic must remain an open question, but his concluding sentences drive home a less arguable point — that the wartime economic troubles had made a powerful impression on the lives, including the minds and memories, of those who survived it. He believed that "The experience of this time inculcated on youth two salutary lessons; the impolicy of depend-

---

[30]Allan Kulikoff, "The Progress of Inequality in Revolutionary Boston," *William and Mary Quarterly,* 3rd ser., 28 (1971): 375-412, clearly thinks the Revolution made the distribution of wealth *less* democratic, but Main, *Social Structure,* the only general study so far, is uncertain about the net effect.

[31]*History of the American Revolution* (1793 ed.), 2: 136-37.

ing on paternal acquisitions, and the necessity of their own exertions." But if the wartime economy had stimulated American youth to new heights of initiative and self-reliance in the postwar world, Ramsay, as mentioned earlier, also thought it had been a deeply corrosive experience:

> Truth, honour and justice were swept away by the overflowing deluge of legal iniquity, nor have they yet assumed their ancient and accustomed seats. Time and industry have already, in a great degree, repaired the losses of property, which the citizens sustained during the war, but both have hitherto failed in effacing the taint which was then communicated to their principles, nor can its total ablution be expected till a new generation arises, unpracticed in the iniquities of their fathers.[32]

Ramsay's speculations lead us to a final question about the legacy of the Revolutionary War, concerning its psychological effects, especially insofar as those effects can be seen in the political institutions and character of the postwar nation. Historians generally agree that a marked feature of pre-Revolutionary America was "deferential" political behavior. Although a large proportion of adult white males had the right to vote, they regularly chose their political leaders from a few families of high social and economic position; that is, the mass of voters seemed to "defer" instinctively to a "natural" elite or aristocracy, and the pattern was as plain in New England as it was in Virginia and South Carolina.[33] Though not destroyed by the war, the deferential pattern of political behavior was definitely undermined by it. Nearly every observer, American and foreign, had noted that the weakest point in the Revolutionary army was its officer corps — lieutenants and captains who claimed all the pay and perquisites of military leadership without either displaying the competence or commanding the respect that would have justified their elevated positions. Washington had complained about the problem from his first glimpse of the Yankee regiments at Boston in 1775, and until the end of the

---

[32]Ibid.

[33]Leonard W. Labaree, *Conservatism in Early American History* (New York, 1948), and James K. Martin, *Men in Rebellion: Higher Governmental Leaders and the Coming of the American Revolution* (New Brunswick, N.J., 1973), describe the colonial elite, while J. R. Pole sets forth the concept of a "deferential" society in "Historians and the Problem of Early American Democracy," *American Historical Review*, 67 (1962): 626-46.

war one encounters similar observations.[34] These officers, to a surprising degree for a revolution ostensibly democratic in its premises and goals, came from the same families that had supplied magistrates, selectmen, and representatives to colonial government. More important, perhaps, was the prevailing image of the military officer as "a gentleman" — an extension of the natural political, economic, and social aristocracy. Whether an officer in fact came from the natural aristocracy or not, his commission gave him some claim to be so regarded, and his performance was judged accordingly. The military performance of the typical American officer in the Revolutionary War was not good; after all, very few had been schooled to lead men into eighteenth-century battle, or even to keep them clean, clothed, fed, sheltered, and sober under field conditions. Discipline was poor, and the junior officers were obviously to blame. So after eight years in which about 200,000 of the masses watched perhaps 20,000 of the so-called elite perform more or less incompetently, the post war voter had lost much of his habitual deference to men allegedly "better" than he was. The rhetoric of the Revolution articulated these new social theories and political attitudes, but the experience of war gave a compelling concreteness to what otherwise might have been merely words.[35]

While the unprecedented experience of a long war weakened the position of the aristocracy, it also created a new basis for social prestige and political power. American Revolutionaries let their fears of militarism and standing armies carry them to extremes that now seem almost ludicrous, but at the same time they were deeply impressed by the martial virtues. Before 1775, only Benjamin Franklin had enjoyed the kind of American "fame" that the war, chiefly through military service, would make possible for dozens of men, heroes of the

---

[34]To Richard Henry Lee in 1775 (29 August), Washington wrote of "an unaccountable kind of stupidity" which "prevails but too generally" among the Massachusetts officers, who made it "one of the principal objects of their attention . . . to curry favour with the men." (*Writings,* 3: 450-51). To Brigadier General Charles Scott in 1778 (8 October) he wrote of "the unpardonable inattention of Officers, and their scandalous sacrifice of every other consideration to the indulgences of good Quarters." (*Writings,* 13: 47). Examples could easily be multiplied.

[35]This idea, that more or less incompetent military service during the Revolutionary War weakened the position of the early American elite, emerged from discussion in a seminar for college teachers during the summer of 1975 at Ann Arbor, and I hereby acknowledge my debt to that lively group.

Revolution. Washington's God-like reputation gave a lustre to his whole corps of general officers, and at the local level colonels, majors and even common soldiers, back from the war, often commanded a measure of respect that heretofore only a few clergymen and other local worthies had enjoyed. There is no contradiction between this point and the one preceding: the old colonial elite was tested by the war and found wanting, but the war rewarded all those who had met its test. Revolutionary Army officers, as a group, may not have been highly regarded by their men, but individual officers, as well as soldiers, often emerged from the war as "famous" persons in the eyes of their fellow citizens. America is not a militaristic society, so runs one cliché about its history, but historians have often remarked on how readily, ever since the Revolution military "fame" has found its natural expression in postwar politics.[36]

Lincoln, in preparing his Lyceum lecture, surely was thinking of those old men, drawing their pensions and telling their stories, too ancient to wield power or stand for office, but, with all the others who had been dying off through the years, a constant reminder of the Revolutionary past. Lincoln's message, specifically, was a plea for law and order and for an end to runaway violence. By linking the American propensity for violence with the struggle against Britain and with the Revolutionary generation, he tactfully suggested that violence was once an acceptable, even admirable, form of behavior, but in the new generation, his own, violence was obsolete, even dangerous, and that only respect for law and the rights of others would keep American society intact. Lincoln went further than we dare go, suggesting that part of the legacy of the Revolutionary War was to encourage the violent side of the American character. But it is an intriguing thought, as are some other conjectural connections between the Revolutionary War and the later course of American history. How far, for example, did the long military struggle implant an ineradicable national pride that hardly existed before 1775? Or did that sickening slide of power under wartime pressure, out of the hands of Congress, down to the States, who were then unable to bring it to

---

[36]"Fame" as an influential factor in American Revolutionary behavior is best set forth by the late Douglass Adair, *Fame and the Founding Fathers: Essays by Douglass Adair,* Trevor Colbourn, ed. (Williamsburg and New York, 1974), *pp.* 3-26.

bear on the key problems of Revolutionary strategy, induce the strange ambivalence built into the federal system? Or did massive participation in the war convince Americans, once it had been won, that sheer numbers and raw courage, not professional diplomacy or professional armies, gave the nation guaranteed security from any foreign threat, and so permitted Americans to grow up without thinking much about the rest of the world? Like our original question, these are more easily asked than answered. But, however difficult to define precisely and to prove beyond doubt, the legacy of the American Revolutionary War was real, and it shaped American life unto Lincoln's day and beyond.

FREEDOM AND PROSPERITY IN THE AMERICAN REVOLUTION

BY RICHARD L. BUSHMAN

Reflection on the meaning of the American Revolution began even before independence was declared and has never ceased. John Adams was speculating on the implications with Mercy Warren in January of 1776, and at the end of his life was still raising the question, "What do we mean by the American Revolution."[1] The Bicentennial more than simply celebrating the event has become an occasion for reopening the inquiry. We still ask John Adams' question. We want to know what really changed with independence, and what fundamental principles underlay the Revolutionary movement.

The revolutionaries' own reflections almost always began with one basic point: the change from monarchy to republic. That was the transformation which one nineteenth-century orator said was "the most important event, humanely speaking" in world history.[2] After independence a writ from the king was no longer necessary to call an election, his representative, the royal governor, was not required to complete the legislature and enact a law, and the king was not present symbolically in the courts. There had been two potent components in the government under monarchy, king and people, each represented in all significant decisions. Now there was but one, the people, and the great network of officials who had derived their commissions from the king and governed according to his instructions, received their authority from the people and ultimately were accountable to them. All that had gone on in the king's name now transpired under the authority of a government based on popular consent.

As significant as all that was and is, does that exhaust the meaning of the Revolution? The transition from monarchy to republic occurred

---

[1]*Works of John Adams,* Charles Francis Adams, ed., 10 vols. (Boston: 1850-56), 10: 282.

[2]Edward Everett, *An Oration, Delivered at Cambridge* . . . (Boston, 1826), p. 14.

at the level of government. What about ordinary people? Did the substitution of an elected president for an hereditary king affect them in ways that could be felt? What changes occurred in the aspirations, the prospects, the self-image, and the personal relations of individual men and women?

For sixty years historians have been pursuing these questions in a particular form. They have asked if one class of men, defined by their economic or social position, was displaced from power at the Revolution and another substituted. Or to refine the issue, was the authority or advantageous position of one class weakened and the position of another improved? Although the researchers have been assiduous, competent, and numerous, the answer seems to be "no." New men rose to high positions in government and the economy, institutions such as the church establishments in certain colonies were dismantled, and the American population was set in motion as never before, but there is slight evidence that wealth and power were systematically shorn from one class of men and bestowed on another, or even that there was any substantial effort to do so. Although individual faces changed, the same kind of men governed after independence as before.[3]

Republicanism was not without consequences for everyday life, but the changes were not in material relationships. The significant alterations, it is now becoming increasingly apparent, occurred in the realm of values.[4] The values generated and confirmed in the Revolu-

---

[3]Summaries and analysis of the literature on economic and social struggles can be found in two articles by Bernard Bailyn: "Political Experience and Enlightenment Ideas in Eighteenth-Century America," *American Historical Review,* 68 (1962): 339-351, and "Lines of Force in Recent Writings on the American Revolution," (forthcoming publication in the *Proceedings* of the XIV International Congress of Historical Sciences). For a judgment on the absence of focused or pervasive class conflict, Edmund S. Morgan, "Conflict and Consensus in the American Revolution," in Stephen G. Kurtz and James H. Hutson, eds., *Essays on the American Revolution* (Chapel Hill, 1973), pp. 291-293. Among the historians who hold to a notion of class struggle in some form are Gary B. Nash, David C. Skaggs, Jesse Lemisch, Dirk Hoerder, Staughton Lynd, and Kenneth A. Lockridge.

[4]Various aspects of the interplay of values and politics are analyzed in Pauline Maier, *From Resistance to Revolution: Colonial Radicals and the Development of American Opposition to Britain, 1765-1776* (New York, 1972); Bernard Bailyn, *The Ideological Origins of the American Revolution* (Cambridge, Mass., 1967); Gordon S. Wood, *The Creation of the American Republic, 1776-1787* (Chapel Hill, 1969); Gerald Stourzh, *Alexander Hamilton and the Idea of Republican Government* (Stanford, 1970); John R. Howe, Jr., *The Changing Political Thought of John Adams* (Princeton, 1966); Winthrop D. Jordan, *White over*

tion entered deeply into personal aspirations and judgments of the self and ultimately touched virtually all social relationships. The idea of equality, which has had immense influence in the United States, was not the only idea of consequence. Of even greater importance in the years immediately following the Revolution were a series of values associated with republicanism. Those values affected private lives then, and still shape American ambitions and apprehensions. This is the direction we must look to perceive the full significance of the Revolution.

Republican values emanated from a great variety of cultural artifacts of the Revolutionary period: pictures and events, as well as words, and are easily picked out when contrasted with the values embodied in comparable items from Britain's monarchical culture. Take for example the portraits of the two Georges, our first president and our last king. The coronation portrait of George III and Gilbert Stuart's famous head of President Washington strongly suggest the differing ideals of monarchy and republic. The two models of the best and highest in their respective societies establish what was honored and sought after. Important differences are apparent at first glance. George III is magnificent in his intricate attire, colorful, sparkling, rich. George Washington's clothes are simple and plain, almost dull. As a result, in one the emphasis is on the setting; in the other, on the person. George III is amiable, stately, and strong despite his somewhat babyish round face; but his head is lost amidst the ermine robes, the gold brocade fabric, the jewelled necklace, the draperies, the column, and the rug. The setting overwhelms the king's private person. In George Washington's portrait, we see nothing but face. Particularly are we aware of the jaw, the firm line of the lips, and the serene eyes. All the stories of a mouthful of ill-fitting dentures cannot remove the effect of oak-like integrity and will. Character is everything.[5]

Black (Chapel Hill, 1968); Alan Heimert, *Religion and the American Mind, from the Great Awakening to the Revolution* (Cambridge, Mass., 1966).

[5]The portrait of Washington by Gilbert Stuart, called the Atheneum head because it came eventually into the possesison of the Boston Atheneum, was the result of Washington's third sitting for Stuart. The President endured it only because Martha Washington wanted a Stuart portrait of her husband. Stuart prefered it to the other portraits because he was able to bring a little life into Washington's stolid countenance. The President's face lit up when Stuart steered the conversation to horses and farming. The results were so pleasing that Stuart refused to part with the picture; he knew he could make a fortune turning

Courtesy of Colonial Williamsburg Foundation
GEORGE III
Alan Ramsay

Courtesy Museum of Fine Arts Boston
GEORGE WASHINGTON
Gilbert Stuart

The two portraits suggest how rulers were to command respect in monarchy and republic: by the over-awing magnificence and might of office in one, and by the simple grandeur of character in the other. With that lesson, we also learn to what personal qualities men and women were properly to aspire in each society. In a monarchy, life at its best was embellished with a splendor, though scaled down from the king's magnificence, that was stripped from the republican. Personal qualities alone distinguished George Washington and presumably those who took their cues from his example.

As the eighteenth century presented its ideal ruler and person in the portrait, society as a whole was pictured in the procession. Unlike our parades, eighteenth-century processions were carefully crafted depictions of the social structure. Their purpose was to instruct the populace and inculcate respect. The great procession of state in the monarchy exemplified the social ranks descending from the king. Careful attention was given to the exact placement of each individual to avoid any slight to honor or degradation from what was after all one's place in life. Once established, the order of the procession was published throughout the empire for the edification of those who could not join the multitudes lining the route.

The order of George III's coronation procession appeared in the *Boston Gazette* on November 16, 1761. Twenty-eight years later, on October 19, 1789, Boston welcomed George Washington as president with a procession of citizens whose designated places were equally revealing of the social structure of the new republic. What were the differences? The coronation procession was a forthright statement of the structure of honor under monarchy. At the head, the king's herb woman with her six maids strewed sweet herbs in the path, followed by a fife and four drums in livery coats of "scarlet richly faced," a drum major, "eight Trumpeters, four a breast, in rich Liveries of

---

out copies. Put off again and again with the excuse that the portrait was still unfinished, the Washingtons grew increasingly impatient, but to no avail. Mrs. Washington never got her Stuart portrait. It is impossible to know precisely how many copies Stuart made because at least a dozen painters also copied it, and age, later restorations, and skillful counterfeiting make fine discriminations impossible. In any event, the Atheneum head was a golden goose. John Hill Morgan and Mantle Fielding list over seventy Stuart replicas. (*The Life Portraits of Washington and Their Replicas* [Philadelphia, 1931].) Stuart's daughter said that by the end of his life, he could crank out a copy in two hours. For an amusing account of Stuart's various encounters with Washington, see James Thomas Flexner, *Gilbert Stuart: A Great Life in Brief* (New York, 1955), pp. 122-148.

crimson Velvet," kettle drums with crimson banners, and eight more trumpeters. Thence the procession rose gradually — there were eighty-seven entries in all — from six clerks in chancery, chaplains, sheriffs of the City of London, aldermen, the king's solicitor, gentlemen of the privy chamber, through Baronesses and Barons in the "Robes of Estate," Bishops, Viscountesses and Viscounts, Countesses, Earls, Duchesses and Dukes, to the Lord Chancellor and Archbishop of Canterbury. The penultimate climax was the Queen in her royal robes attended by the Lord Bishops of London and Westminster, covered by a canopy and preceded by the ivory rod with the dove, the scepter with cross, the Queen's crown, and followed by the train-bearer with sixty-seven ladies of the bedchamber. At the peak of the procession was the king, also preceded by regalia — St. Edward's staff, the golden spurs, the scepter with cross, the sword of state, St. Edward's crown, the orb with the cross, the chalice, and paten — and followed by supporters of the train, master of the robes, gentlemen of the king's bedchamber, standardbearers, captains, yeomen of the guard and others. The king in his royal robes proceeded under a canopy supported by the Barons of the Cinque Ports and accompanied by the Bishops of Durham and Bath and Wells.[6]

Besides the ascent of titles which all could recognize as boys and girls today know the relative standing of lieutenant and captain, there was in the actual procession a steady crescendo of magnificence in costumes and trappings. The king's climactic position with full regalia signified his leadership in all the dimensions of power — state, church, military, society, wealth. The common people stood to the side, admiring and cheering as the splendor of the realm swept by.

There is verticality in Washington's procession, too, but of a much different shape.[7] At the head are town and military officers, selectmen, treasurer, clerks, magistrates, followed by the educated professions, clergy, physicians, and lawyers, and the economic elite of merchants and ship captains. Then followed forty-six divisions of tradesmen and

---

[6]For a modern explication of coronation processions with reflections on previous coronations, Randolph S. Churchill, *The Story of the Coronation* (London, 1953).

[7]The broadside announcing the procession is reproduced in James Henry Stark, *Stark's Antique Views of ye Towne of Boston* (Boston, 1901), p. 284. Washington's procession is related to others of the era in an unpublished paper by Claudia Bushman, "Federalist Boston in Procession."

artisans, "alphabetically disposed," as the broadside noted, "in order to give general satisfaction." At the tail of this dachshund-shaped society were seamen, out of alphabetical order to signify their marginality. Each group had a yard-square white flag emblazoned with an emblem of its craft. Besides the egalitarian flatness of the body of the procession, the very presence of the citizens in the procession instead of on the sidelines in an undifferentiated mass signified that republican equality implied participation. The ordinary man was a working member of the body politic.

From the vantage point of the cordwainers and rope-makers in Washington's procession, society looked much different than it did to the anonymous London workers observing the coronation procession. Society and government did not tower above the citizens of Boston to such stupefying heights. Washington, the selectmen, the ship-captains certainly took precedence, but none of the trappings of state enveloped them: no drums and trumpeters, no robes, no regalia, no heralds, no canopies, no choirs or musicians. Washington rode into the city on horseback, bare-headed, wearing his old army uniform. Not only were the heights thus reduced, but the lower orders were raised. They were given a position, a name, and an identity in the procession of state. Whereas under monarchy there was height, magnificence, and exclusiveness, republican society was more level, simple, and comprehensive.

The simplicity of the procession's idealized republicanism was not unfamiliar in Boston, nor entirely out of keeping in eighteenth-century Philadelphia. Republican morality grew out of and elaborated Puritan values.[8] The colonies had always been more egalitarian than the mother country, out of sheer necessity if nothing else. Few peers had ever touched foot on the American shore. None of the colonial aristocracy lived with the magnificence of England's greatest nobles. Colonial assemblies met in modest structures; governors conducted the affairs of state from their parlors. The simplicity of Washington's dress was in the Quaker spirit as well as the republican.

The tendency of colonial society before independence, however, was away from, not toward simplicity. As prosperity permitted colon-

---

[8]Edmund S. Morgan had related what I have called republican to another source of similar values in "The Puritan Ethnic and the American Revolution," *William and Mary Quarterly*, 24 (1967): 3-43.

Procession.

BOSTON, OCT. 19, 1789.

AS this town is shortly to be honoured with a visit from THE PRESIDENT of the United States: In order that we may pay our respects to him, in a manner whereby every inhabitant may see so illustrious and amiable a character, and to prevent the disorder and danger which must ensue from a great assembly of people without order, a Committee appointed by a respectable number of inhabitants, met for the purpose, recommend to their Fellow-Citizens to arrange themselves in the following order, in a

PROCESSION.

IT is also recommended, that the person who shall be chosen as head of each order of Artizans, Tradesmen, Manufacturers, &c. shall be known by displaying a WHITE FLAG, with some device thereon expressive of their several callings, and to be numbered as in the arrangement that follows, which is alphabetically disposed, in order to give general satisfaction.--The Artizans, &c. to display such insignia of their craft, as they can conveniently carry in their hands. That uniformity may not be wanting, it is desired that the several Flag-staffs be SEVEN feet long, and the Flags a YARD SQUARE.

ORDER OF PROCESSION

MUSICK.

The Selectmen,
Overseers of the Poor.
Town Treasurer,
Town Clerk,
Magistrates,
Consuls of France and Holland,
The Officers of his Most Christian Majesty's Squadron,
The Rev. Clergy,
Physicians,
Lawyers,
Merchants and Traders,
Marine Society,
Masters of Vessels,
Revenue Officers,
Strangers, who may wish to attend.

Bakers,	No. 1.
Blacksmiths, &c.	No. 2.
Block-makers,	No. 3.
Boat-builders,	No. 4.
Cabinet and Chair-makers,	No. 5.
Card-makers,	No. 6.
Carvers,	No. 7.
Chaise and Coach-makers,	No. 8.
Clock and Watch-makers,	No. 9.
Coopers,	No. 10.
Coppersmiths, Braziers and Founders,	No. 11.
Cordwainers, &c.	No. 12.
Distillers,	No. 13.
Dock Manufacturers,	No. 14.
Engravers,	No. 15.
Glaziers and Plumbers,	No. 16.
Goldsmiths and Jewellers,	No. 17.
Hair-Dressers,	No. 18.
Hatters and Furriers,	No. 19.
House Carpenters,	No. 20.
Leather Dressers, and Leather Breeches Makers,	No. 21.
Limners and Portrait Painters,	No. 22.
Masons,	No. 23.
Mast-makers,	No. 24.
Mathematical Instrument-makers,	No. 25.
Millers,	No. 26.
Painters,	No. 27.
Paper Stainers,	No. 28.
Pewterers,	No. 29.
Printers, Book-binders and Stationers,	No. 30.
Riggers,	No. 31.
Rope-makers,	No. 32.
Saddlers,	No. 33.
Sail-makers,	No. 34.
Shipwrights, to include Caulkers, Ship-joiners, Head-builders and Sawyers,	No. 35.
Sugar-boilers,	No. 36.
Tallow-Chandlers, &c.	No. 37.
Tanners.	No. 38.
Taylors,	No. 39.
Tin-plate Workers,	No. 40.
Tobacconists,	No. 41.
Truckmen,	No. 42.
Turners,	No. 43.
Upholsterers,	No. 44.
Wharfingers,	No. 45.
Wheelwrights,	No. 46.
Seamen,	

N. B.—In the above arrangement, some trades are omitted—from the idea, that they would incorporate themselves with the branches mentioned, to which they are generally attached. For instance—it is supposed, that under the head of *Blacksmiths*, the Armourers, Cutlers, Whitesmiths and other workers in iron, would be included; and the same with respect to other trades.

Each division of the above arrangement is requested to meet on such parade as it may agree on, and march into the Mall—No. 1 of the Artizans, &c. forming at the South-end thereof. The Marshalls will then direct in what manner the Procession will move to meet the President on his arrival in town. When the front of the Procession arrives at the extremity of the town, it will halt, and the whole will then be directed to open the column—one half of each rank moving to the right, and the other half to the left—and then face inwards, so as to form an avenue through which the President is to pass, to the galleries to be erected at the State-House.

It is requested that the several School-masters conduct their Scholars to the neighbourhood of the State-House, and form them in such order as the Marshalls shall direct.

THE Marine Society is desired to appoint some person to arrange and accompany the seamen.

ials to erect great houses and adorn themselves in fine clothes, they happily did so. The southern gentry had been the first to build mansions and mimic the manners of English aristocrats. Philadelphia and Boston merchants never quite attained the same level of dignity in manners, attire, or residence — at the Continental Congress, the Adams cousins deplored the courtly style of the southerners — but New England had seen the erection of scores of mansions in its own port towns. No one was more susceptible to the allure of fine living than John Hancock. To the dismay of the Adamses, Hancock succumbed to "the glare of Southern manners and the parade of courtly living" at the Second Congress. After his election to the congressional presidency, Hancock hired four liveried servants mounted on caparisoned horses to accompany his carriage. Twenty-five horsemen rode before and twenty-five after, holding drawn sabers. Thus his entourage clattered about Philadelphia. The assimilation of republicanism after independence forbade that form of ostentation in a public official. Even one so lacking in sensibility as Hancock would have sensed the rightness of Washington's horseback entry into Boston in his old army uniform. Republicanism reversed the trend toward splendor in colonial society, at least for public officials.[9]

The diminution of grandeur was one quality of republican society. Judging from the portraits of the heads of state, the preeminence of character was another. Republican partisans made much of that contrast. On the eve of independence, John Adams asked one of his favorite correspondents, Mercy Otis Warren, which form of government she preferred. "Pray Madam, are you for an American Monarchy or Republic?" As the sister of James Otis and wife of the patriot James Warren, Mercy Warren's actual preferences were well known to Adams. He adopted the pose of a questioner to make a point:

> Monarchy is the genteelest and most fashionable Government, and I don't know why the Ladies ought not to consult Elegance and the Fashion as well in Government as Gowns, Bureaus or Chariots.
> For my own part I am so tasteless as to prefer a Republic, if We must erect an independent Government in America, which

[9]John C. Miller, *Sam Adams: Pioneer in Propaganda* (Stanford, 1936), pp. 335-336.

you know is utterly against my Inclination. But a Republic, altho it will infallibly beggar me and my Children, will produce Strength, Hardiness Activity, Courage, Fortitude and Enterprise; the manly noble and Sublime Qualities in human Nature, in Abundance. A Monarchy would probably, somehow or other make me rich, but it would produce so much Taste and Politeness so much Elegance in Dress, Furniture, Equipage, so much Musick and Dancing, so much Fencing and Skaiting, so much Cards and Backgammon; so much Horse Racing and Cockfighting, so many Balls and Assemblies, so many Plays and Concerts that the very Imagination of them makes me feel vain, light, frivolous and insignificant.[10]

Adams' chain of images was meant to characterize the pursuits of a courtier under monarchy and the meaning of royal magnificence in the lives of those who lived under a king. In sum they evoked the moral tone of monarchy. "vain, light, frivolous, and insignificant." There was no equivalent set of images for republicanism, but the contrasting morality is sharply defined: "Strength, Hardiness Activity, Courage, Fortitude and Enterprise; the manly noble and Sublime Qualities in human Nature." Subjects of a king were soft, weak, flimsy. Citizens of a republic were strong, enduring, vigorous.

Adams makes explicit what is implicit in the portraits and the processions. Besides being a form of government, republicanism was a distinctive blueprint for social and personal morality. The magnificence which the king rightly claimed for himself under monarchy set the tone for an elegant and self-indulgent courtly style. Such grandeur was inappropriate in a republic where men were more on an equal plane and all participated in government. More important, self-government developed and required virtue in the citizens of a republic. Simplicity and a manly character were the foundations of the state. The courtier could be trivial, weak, soft; the simple republican had to be energetic, determined, hardy. The plain dress and the stern integrity in Washington's face were the grand pattern for every republican.[11]

In 1776, however, they were still a pattern, not a reality. After

[10]January 8, 1776, *Warren-Adams Letters, Being Chiefly a Correspondence among John Adams, Samuel Adams, and James Warren*, Massachusetts Historical Society, *Collections*, 72 (Boston, 1917): 201.

[11]The fullest description of republican morality is in Wood, *Creation of the American Republic*, chaps. 2-3.

expanding upon the sublime qualities of a republican to Mercy Warren, Adams confessed to one difficulty:

> Virtue and Simplicity of Manners are indispensably necessary in a Republic among all orders and Degrees of Men. But there is so much Rascallity, so much Venality and Corruption, so much Avarice and Ambition such a Rage for Profit and Commerce among all Ranks and Degrees of Men even in America, that I sometimes doubt whether there is public Virtue enough to Support a Republic. There are two Vices most detestably predominant in every part of America that I have yet seen which are incompatible with the Spirit of a Commonwealth, as Light is with Darkness; I mean Servility and Flattery. A genuine Republican can no more fawn and cringe than he can domineer. Shew me the American who cannot do all.[12]

So serious was the problem that Adams wondered if Americans were adequate to the task of manning a republic. So possessed were they by avarice and ambition, that men of all ranks pursued gain at the expense of the public interest. Provisioners at Cambridge charged the Continental army the highest possible prices. Soldiers who enlisted for two or three months walked off with the guns issued them. Moreover, instead of displaying the manly independence that was the hallmark of the true republican, Americans cringed before the great. That was the way of monarchy, to kneel before the king, kiss his hand, yield one's will to his, and thus with all who bore his commission or claimed the title of gentlemen. A republican stood alone, defended his rights, resisted domination. The contrary tendency made Americans vulnerable to the poison of corruption and incapable of defending their rights.

The structure of republican values made the Revolutionary leaders acutely sensitive to the indicators of public virtue. The fate of the nation depended on the patriotism, the independence, and the energy of its citizens. The leaders were particularly alert for tell-tale signs of decay, luxury and dissipation.[13] It was the pursuit of courtly

---

[12]January 8, 1776, *Warren-Adams Letters,* p. 202.

[13]Wood, *Creation of the American Republic,* pp. 107-124; Jack P. Greene, "Search for Identity: An Interpretation of the Meaning of Selected Patterns of Social Response in Eighteenth-Century America," *Journal of Social History,* 3 (1970): 189-220. Greene shows how apprehensions about luxury and self-indulgence were lamented well before the Revolution. Republicanism, confirmed, strengthened, and redirected older values.

grandeur that weakened Europe and kept it in chains, and America could easily follow. In the midst of the war, Adams received a doleful report from Mercy Warren's husband, General James Warren, that "all manner of extravagance prevails here in dress, furniture, equipage and living, amidst the distress of the public and multitudes of individuals. How long the manners of this people will be uncorrupted and fit to enjoy that liberty that you have long contended for, I know not." Observing the same symptom a few years later, John Adams deplored "that spirit of dissipation, vanity and knavery, which infects so many Americans and threatens to ruin our manners and liberties, in imitation of the old world."[14]

Through the 1780s the Old Republicans, as they called themselves, found many causes for despair, some great, operating on a national scale, others tiny but symptomatic of inner rot. In 1784-85 Bostonians organized a tea assembly which assumed the title of the San Souci Club. Each male subscriber received one ticket for himself and two for ladies which entitled them to an evening of card-playing and dancing and a choice of free tea, coffee, or chocolate, or wine, negus, punch or lemonade on payment. The assembly circumspectly closed at midnight, but this respect for propriety was insufficient to placate an "Observer" (probably Sam Adams) who launched a series of attacks in the *Massachusetts Centinel* in the winter of 1785.

> If there ever was a period wherein reason was bewildered, and stupified by dissipation and extravagance, it is surely the present. Did ever effiminacy with her languid train, receive a greater welcome in society than at this day. New amusements are invented — new dissipations are introduced, to lull and enervate those minds already too much softened, poisoned and contaminated, by idle pleasures, and foolish gratifications. We are exchanging prudence, virtue and economy, for those glaring spectres of luxury, prodigality and profligacy. We are prostituting all our glory as a people; for new modes of pleasure, ruinous in their expences, injurious to virtue, and totally detrimental to the well being of society.

---

[14]Quoted in Charles Warren, "Samuel Adams and the Sans Souci Club in 1785," Massachusetts Historical Society, *Proceedings,* 3rd Ser., 60 (1926-27): 319-320.

Like so many of his countrymen, "Observer" saw dissipation and extravagance as a cause of the fall of empires. It was that failure at the center that brought great nations to ignominy.

> Did we consult the history of Athens and Rome, we should find that so long as they continued their frugality and simplicity of manners, they shone with superlative glory; but no sooner were effeminate refinements introduced amongst them, than they visibly fell from whatever was elevated and magnanimous, and became feeble and timid, dependent, slavish and false.

"Observer" had many words for the process of degeneration — dull, enervate, languid, softened, poisoned, contaminated, feeble, timid, dependent, slavish, false. Such was the mind robbed of strength and energy, and therefore defenseless against oppression.[15] The Boston Tea Assembly closed, but through the decade corruption manifest itself on every side: paper money assemblies, conventions and riots, Shays's Rebellion, refusals to pay taxes and debts. In 1786 Washington sorrowfully admitted to John Jay: "We have errors to correct. We have probably had too good an opinion of human nature."[16] What was to be done? John Adams had observed to Mercy Warren in 1776 that "it is the Part of a great Politician to make the Character of his People, to extinguish among them the Follies and Vices that he sees, and to create in them the Virtues and Abilities which he sees wanting."[17] Washington and Jay had reached the conclusion that alterations in the fundamental constitution were required to enable the government to perform that role. "The virtue like the other resources of a country, can only be drawn to a point and exerted by strong circumstances ably managed, or a strong government ably administered," Jay wrote in 1786.[18] The "strong circumstances," by which he meant the Revolutionary War, were now behind the nation, and only strong government was equal to the task.

---

[15]The description of the club is found in ibid., p. 322; the quotation is from *Massachusetts Centinel,* January 15, 1785.

[16]*The Writings of George Washington,* Worthington C. Ford, ed., 14 vols. (New York, 1889-93), 11:53-54.

[17]Braintree, January 8, 1776, *Warren Adams Letters,* p. 202.

[18]Jay to Washington, Philadelphia, June 27, 1786, in Henry P. Johnston, ed., *The Correspondence and Public Papers of John Jay,* 4 vols. (New York, 1890-93), 3:204-205.

Washington concurred: "I do not conceive we can exist long as a nation without having lodged some where a power, which will pervade the whole Union in as eneregtic a manner as the authority of the State governments extends over the several States."[19] With that in mind the constitutional convention met in Philadelphia the following June to compensate as best it could for the shortcomings of American virtue.[20]

Adams's and Washington's misgivings were empirical. They and many others were disappointed in the blatant avarice and weakness they observed. Only later, after the war, did Americans come to recognize that beyond mere weakness there was a fundamental contradiction in the heart of republicanism. Republicanism was always thought of as a fragile government because it made such heavy demands on public virtue. In time its weakness came to appear to be theoretical as well as practical. It seemed to carry within itself the seeds of its own destruction.

The source of the contradiction lay at the very heart of the Revolutionary movement and flowered from there into the post war republicanism. It began with the most resonant protest in the Revolutionary years: the objection to taxation imposed without the colonists' consent. The amount of the taxes was not in question, nor was simple devotion to a traditional principle of English governance the crucial point. The objection was to the use of the tax moneys once they flowed unchecked into the treasury. Americans believed they knew what avaricious officials would do with a brimming treasury which could be refilled at pleasure. They would naturally and inevitably use public funds for personal gain and self-indulgence, clothe themselves in finery, build mansions and palaces, ride about in elaborate carriages.

Besides living in ease and luxury, greedy rulers surrounded themselves with underlings who ate at the great ones' tables. Offices, pensions, favors supported a small army of dependents. "Are not pensioners, stipendiaries, and salary men (unknown before), hourly multiplying on us, to riot in the spoils of miserable America?" Josiah Quincy asked, as he contemplated the expansion of the customs service. "Does not every eastern gale waft us some new insect, even

---

[19]Ford, ed., *Writings of Washington,* 11: 53-54.
[20]The moral background of the Constitutional convention is analyzed in Wood, *Creation of the American Republic,* chaps. 10, 12.

of that devouring kind, which eats up every green thing? Is not the bread taken out of the children's mouths and given unto the dogs?"[21] Worse still, Americans themselves were drawn into the ministry's orbit of influence. The ambitious and greedy among the colonists lusted for offices at the government's disposal and fawned and cringed before superiors to obtain them. "Every day strengthens our oppressors and weakens us," Sam Adams wrote. Thus the ministry cruelly used the colonists' taxes to pay for the placemen, pensioners, corrupt legislators, and servants who were the foundation of the ministers' tyrannical power.[22]

The demands of this monstrous system were insatiable. It would consume the wealth of the people until they were totally impoverished. Taxation without representation gave the ministry license to plunder without hindrance.

> If they have right to lay on us one tax, they have another, if they have right to take one shilling from us without our consent, they have as good right to take *all*, and strip us naked of every thing.[23]

In time the nation would divide between those who labored and those who robbed, as the ministry wrested from the colonists the fruits of their labor to pay for the balls and assemblies, horse races and cockfights, and the other indulgences of ministerial lackeys. Tyranny would impoverish the industrious while the lazy and selfish grew rich in positions of honor and power. That was the misery awaiting the colonies should the Parliament lay taxes without the consent of the American people. The Revolution was fought to prevent this conspiracy from reaching its ultimate conclusion in a kind of semi-feudal slavery.

Slavery, the forcible deprivation of the fruits of one's labors, was the negative pole of Revolution. What lay at the positive pole? What was the Revolution fought for? Liberty was to be free of official leeches and bloodsuckers and to enjoy the fruits for oneself. Free and

---

[21]Eliza Susan Quincy, ed., *Memoir of the Life of Josiah Quincy, Junior, of Massachusetts Bay: 1774-1775* (3rd ed., Boston, 1875), p. 17.

[22]To Elbridge Gerry, Boston, October 29, 1772, in Harry Alonzo Cushing, ed., *The Writings of Samuel Adams*, 4 vols. (New York, 1904-08) 2: 341.

[23]Oliver Noble, *Some Strictures upon the . . . Book of Esther . . .* (Newburyport, 1775), p. 26.

equal government, a New Englander said looking back on the halcyon days before Parliamentary taxation, "secured us from oppression and plunder."[24] This was the simple test of governmental rectitude. "Every Ploughman knows a good Government from a bad one, from the Effects of it: he knows whether the Fruits of his Labour be his own, and whether he enjoys them in Peace and Security."[25]

What was left then when tyranny had been subdued but to labor and enjoy the fruits? One could of course write poetry and worship God, but the radical rhetoric implicitly pointed the mass of citizens in a single direction. Designing rules were notable for plundering the people of property. It followed that securing, pursuing, and enjoying property was the most valuable privilege of the free man. "The object of public virtue, is to secure the liberties of the community," a Boston orator said at the end of the war summing up the sequence of historical causes and effects, "a security of liberty admits of every man's pursuing, without molestation, the measures most likely to increase his ease."[26]

This was the beginning of the contradiction, for the conditions of freedom in turn affected the character of the free. The results of liberty had been axiomatic for centuries. Charles II had identified two traits of free men in his Answer to the Nineteen Propositions in 1642: "the good of democracy is liberty, and the courage and industry which liberty begets."[27] John Adams' list of republican virtues had on it "Activity, Courage, Fortitude and Enterprise."[28] The reasons for heightened industry were manifest. Evil governors were "Enemies to private Property. . . . to drain, worry, and debauch their Subjects, are the steady Maxims of their Politicks. . . . In this wretched Situation the people, to be safe, must be poor and lewd: There will be but

---

[24]Samuel Williams, *A Discourse on the Love of our Country* . . . (Salem, 1775), p. 18.

[25]*Boston Gazette,* May 12, 1755.

[26]John Warren, *An Oration, Delivered July 4, 1783* . . . *in Celebration of The Anniversary of American Independence* (Boston, 1783), p. 10. Daniel Boorstin discussed the Jeffersonian preoccupation with the employment of property from a different point of view in *The Lost World of Thomas Jefferson* (New York, 1948), pp. 107-108, 185, 198-199, 227-228.

[27]J. P. Kenyon, ed., *The Stuart Constitution, 1603-1688: Documents and Commentary* (Cambridge, 1966), p. 21.

[28]John Adams to Mercy Warren, Braintree, January 8, 1776, *Warren-Adams Letters,* p. 201.

little Industry where Property is precarious."[29] By contrast, the assurance of securely possessing one's property and the fruits of one's labor infused people with "the efficacious motives of universal industry." "This will take place," said Ezra Stiles in his famous treatise on The Rising Glory of America, "if every one can enjoy the fruits of his labor and activity unmolested." In America the "sweet and attractive charms" of liberty had filled people "with a most amazing spirit" which promised to operate "with great energy." "Never before," Stiles said with some exaggeration, "has the experiment been so effectually tried of every man's reaping the fruits of his labor and feeling his share in the aggregate system of power."[30] The prospects were unlimited because, as Montesquieu had said, "Countries are not cultivated in proportion to their fertility but to their liberty."[31] With no vicious rulers to plunder or oppress and each man lord of his soil, in full command of his own production, the American had every motive to work. The nation was bound to prosper. By 1795 a preacher could congratulate the nation on its achievement:

> To enumerate the marks of private prosperity would lead me beyond the limits of a sermon. It is, besides, unnecessary. They are seen and felt by all the inhabitants of our land. That people in general of nearly every class and occupation enjoy a state of unusual prosperity; that the means of a comfortable

[29]*Boston Gazette*, May 19, 1755. Benjamin Church in his 1773 Boston Massacre oration plaintively asked, *"When will the locusts leave the land?* Then, and not till then, peace and plenty shall smile around us; the husbandman will labour with pleasure; and honest industry reap the reward of it's toil." *An Oration Delivered March Fifth 1773 . . . to Commemorate the Bloody Tragedy of the Fifth of March 1770* (Boston, 1773), p. 18.

[30]Ezra Stiles, *The United States Elevated to Glory and Honor . . .* (New Haven, 1783), in John Wingate Thornton, ed., *The Pulpit of the American Revolution . . .* (Boston, 1876), pp. 431, 439.

[31]John Warren, *Oration*, p. 12. Crevecoeur attributed the industriousness of pre-Revolutionary Americans to the absence of feudal tenancies. "We are all animated with the spirit of an industry which is unfettered and unrestrained, because each person works for himself." "We have no princes, for whom we toil, starve, and bleed." J. Hector St. John Crevecoeur, *Letters from an American Farmer . . .* (London, 1783), pp. 47, 48; cf. pp. 52-53. An English version of Montesquieu's dictum was Charles Davenant's statement "Industry has its first foundation in Liberty." *Political and Commercial Works,* 2 vols. (London, 1771) 2: 35. The king claimed to be the fount of prosperity because he was protector of liberty: "I am fully satisfied that the Trade and Wealth of My People are the happy Effects of the Liberties they enjoy; and that the Grandure of the Crown consists in their Prosperity." King's Speech to Parliament, January 9, 1723/4, *Boston Gazette*, April 6-13, 1724; cf. reply of the Commons, ibid.

> subsistence were never more than now within the reach of all; that industry and enterprize in every line of life are highly encouraged — that they receive a sure and ample reward — is well secured to him who earns it, are facts so obvious, that they can neither be overlooked nor contested.[32]

The paeans of praise in time became almost obligatory, for prosperity was the ultimate endorsement of American government. "Our constitutions of government," it was acknowledged, are "the source of most of our social and domestic felicity."[33] Since prosperity was ever the mark of the free, " we should vouch peace and prosperity; we should call up increase of wealth and population; we should exhibit health, happiness and public and private felicity" to prove the superiority of the American system.[34] Their political advantages virtually obligated Americans to prosper. "Let us have all the means possible of subsistence and elegance among ourselves," Ezra Stiles wrote in 1783, "if we would be a flourishing republic of real independent dignity and glory."[35]

Subsistence, yes, but elegance? As post-Revolutionary Americans pursued the logic of republican freedom, warning signals began to go up. "Let us not flatter ourselves too much," a preacher warned, "with an ideal of the future prosperity and glory of these United States."[36] In 1783, the year of the peace treaty, the Fourth of July

---

[32]Henry Ware, *The Continuance of Peace and Increasing Prosperity a Source of Consolation and Just Cause of Gratitude to the Inhabitants of the United States* (Boston, 1795), p. 20.

[33]Ibid., p. 9.

[34]James Sullivan, *The History of Land Titles in Massachusetts* (Boston, 1801), p. 347.

[35]Stiles, *The United States Elevated,* in Thornton, *Pulpit,* p. 432. For a discussion of the origins of state concern for prosperity, Marc Raeff, "The Well-ordered Police State and the Development of Modernity in Seventeenth- and Eighteenth-Century Europe: An Attempt at a Comparative Approach," *American Historical Review,* 80 (1975): 1221-1243.

The logic of prosperity was used, of course, for partisan purposes. Ware and Sullivan, quoted above (notes 32 and 34) were paying tribute to the federal constitution. During the Revolutionary agitation, the colonists pointed to their initial growth under free government and salutary neglect as reasons for Parliament to cease in its impositions. Thus Samuel Williams in 1775: "Without entering into every particular, 'this government carried prosperity along with it.' We found its happy effects, in rapid increase of our numbers; in a universal spirit of industry; in a gradual increase of wealth; and in a settled peace, quietness, and good order, among ourselves." *Discourse,* p. 18.

[36]Samuel Wales, *The Dangers of Our National Prosperity . . .* (Hartford, 1785), pp. 26-27; cf. pp. 31-33.

orator in Boston, John Warren, Boston's most eminent physician, explicitly laid out the contradictions in republicanism for his audience. The excruciating truth was that the success of a republic brought it to the edge of its own destruction. "So nearly is the most prosperous condition of a people, allied to decay and ruin, that even this flattering appearance conceals the seeds, that finally must produce her destruction." Why was this so? Because the security of liberty permitted every man to pursue his livelihood without molestation and thence "to place him in a state of independent affluence." "Nothing is more conducive to these ends than a free and unlimited commerce, the encouragement of which is undoubtedly the duty of the Commonwealth." While prosperity itself was in the interest of all, the trouble with commerce was that it stratified society. The immediate effect "is usually an augmentation of wealth, but as it is generally impossible for every subject to acquire a great degree of opulence, the riches of the state become accumulated in the coffers of a few." Thus the end of republican egalitarianism. A few were lifted up by wealth and enabled to resume the magnificence and luxury of the court, whence corruption flowed. "The passions of the great almost invariably extend to the body of the people, who to gratify an unbounded thirst for gain, are ready to sacrifice every other blessing to that, which in any degree, furnished them with the means of imitating their superiors." Self-indulgence at the top trickling down, Warren warned, started society on the familiar descent.

> Bribery and venality, the grand engines of slavery, have been called in to the assistance of the aspiring nobles, who, in this case, never fail to make the deluded people pay them the full price of their prostitution.
>
> This accession of power, acquired by the consent of the people themselves, enables their governors to assume the reins of absolute *controul*, to burst all the bonds of social obligation, and finally to extort by violence, what formerly they were obliged to purchase; accustomed to a habit of sloth and idleness, the subjects are rendered too effeminate to apply themselves to labor and fatigue, or if they do it, are soon discouraged by the rapaciousness of their rulers, a spirit of faction and uneasiness becomes generally prevalent; impressed with that awful respect with which the trappings of wealth universally inspire a people that have been accustomed to view it as the measure of human felicity, they are too pusillanimous to relieve

themselves from their burden by an united effort of the whole.

After that come rioting to plunder the rich — a kind of insurrection easily suppressed — discouragement of agriculture, decline of population, impoverishment, " 'til at length they fall an easy prey to the first Despot, whether foreign or domestic, who offers them the yoke; — Such is the fatal operation of luxury, almost invariably the consequence of unbounded wealth." And such the completion of the cycle of history from liberty, security, industry, and prosperity to inequality, luxury, servility, and tyranny. The very success of the republic in achieving prosperity led on directly to its downfall.[37]

Was there an escape from that fateful circle? John Warren himself, the orator of the day, recommended history and more oratory:

> Go search the vaults, where lay enshrined the relicks of your martyred fellow-citizens, and from their dust receive a lesson on the value of your freedom! When virtue fails, when luxury and corruption shall undermine the pillars of the state, and threaten a total loss of liberty and patriotism, then solemnly repair to those sacred repositories of the dead, and if you can, return and sport away your rights.

In objects of patriotic sentiment — "the picture which brings back to your imaginations, in the lively colours of undisguised truth, the wild, distracted feeling of your hearts!" — Americans might find the determination to heed that admonition, "nor barter liberty for gold," and the American star shine on " 'til stars and suns shall shine no more, and all the kingdoms of this globe shall vanish like a scroll."[38]

Mercy Warren, less affected by the rising tides of romantic sentimentalism than John Warren, wondered near the end of her history of the Revolution if reversion to a traditional social order might neutralize the ill effects of overabundant prosperity. Writing after 1800, when the full effects of freedom were becoming visible, she foresaw that "from the rage of acquisition which has spread far and wide, it may be apprehended that the possession of wealth will in a short time be the only distinction in this young country. By this it may be feared that the spirit of avarice will be rendered justifiable in the opinion of some as the single road to superiority." She toyed with the notion of "some mark of elevation" other than "pecuniary compen-

[37]Warren, *Oration* pp. 9-12.
[38]Ibid., pp. 30, 32.

sation" that would inspire Americans to acts of glory in the public service. Recognizing that she skirted perilously close to the return of a titled aristocracy, Warren pondered "how far honorary rewards are consistent with the principles of republicanism." Her scheme rather than being a practical solution to the problem of prosperity was a measure of how desperate one "old republican" had become.[39]

What was the ultimate resolution of the contradictions in freedom and prosperity? Republicanism required simplicity, austerity, rigor, while freedom meant security and industry, and thence prosperity and luxury. At some inevitable juncture the two collided. The elegance and inequality of commerce clashed with the spartan restraint of republicanism. In the twilight of their lives John Adams plaintively asked Thomas Jefferson, "Will you tell me how to prevent riches from becoming the effects of temperance and industry? Will you tell me how to prevent riches from producing luxury? Will you tell me how to prevent luxury from producing effeminacy intoxication extravagance, Vice and folly?"[40] No answer was given.[41]

"A nation's identity," Erik Erikson has said, "is derived from the ways in which history has, as it were, counterpointed certain opposite potentialities."[42] The Revolution endorsed and energized two values, Spartan simplicity and the pursuit of wealth. Both were authentically republican and American; both have survived two hundred years. In the mode of austerity, Americans read Walden and admire Thoreau's twenty-eight dollar house built with his own hands from used lumber. Rebellious American young people in recent years have donned shabby clothes and imitated the poor, knowing full well they strike a chord in adult consciences. The jeremiads of modern ecologists ring true partly because they require us to return to a simpler life.

---

[39]Mercy Warren, *History of the . . . America Revolution*, 3 vols. (Boston, 1805) 3: 415, 416.

[40]December 21, 1819, *The Adams-Jefferson Letters: The Complete Correspondence of Thomas Jefferson and Abigail and John Adams*, Lester J. Cappon, ed., 2 vols, (Chapel Hills, 1959), 2:551.

[41]Discussion of eighteenth century views of the rise and fall of nations may be found in Stow Persons, "The Cyclical Theory of History in Eighteenth Century America," *American Quarterly*, 5 (1954): 147-163; John R. Howe, *The Changing Political Thought of John Adams* (Princeton: 1966), pp. 140-147; and above all in J. G. A. Pocock, *The Machiavellian Moment: Florentine Political Thought and the Atlantic Republican Tradition* (Princeton, 1975).

[42]*Childhood and Society* (New York, 1964), p. 244.

And yet austerity has always been the minor theme. Walden is usually a mere respite preliminary to a more energetic pursuit of wealth. Modern Americans are more likely to purchase a waterbed than to read the *Whole Earth Catalog* or learn to live on five acres of land. Prosperity has become almost a right of citizenship. Today's America would disappoint and disgust Sam Adams: but then so did Boston of the 1780s. He retired from the governorship in 1797 a broken, palsied man and remained, as John Adams observed, "a weeping, helpless object of compassion" until his death in 1803.[43] Like other revolutionaries, he mourned the nation's abuse of its independence.

Americans need not, however, lose confidence because of Sam Adams's lament. He represents only half of the Revolution. Republicanism fostered two impulses, both of them worthy. It is the task of Americans to reconcile the conflicting demands of freedom and prosperity without repudiating either. Rather than locking the Republic in a paralyzing contradiction, history's challenge to America is to find some employment of her great wealth which, instead of softening and enervating character, will, through the self-discipline of compelling purpose, help its citizens rise above selfishness and vanity in the service of the general good.

---

[43]To Thomas Jefferson, July 16, 1814, *Works of John Adams,* 10:100.

THE IDEAL OF THE WRITTEN CONSTITUTION: A POLITICAL LEGACY OF THE REVOLUTION

BY RICHARD D. BROWN

Two hundred years ago the members of the Continental Congress asserted the independence of the United States of America, committing themselves and the people of their states to a war in defense of constitutional liberty. Their Declaration of Independence, our sacred text, was founded on the traditional Anglo-American belief that the powers of government must be restrained. Short of rebellion, a constitution was the only mechanism they believed capable of exerting that vital restraint. For the Revolutionary generation, a written constitution was a crucial necessity.

By committing themselves to the ideal of *written* constitutions, the Revolutionaries chose to uphold an English political tradition that was declining in the mother country. Written charters had been central to English political life since Magna Carta in the thirteenth century. In the recurrent constitutional crises of the seventeenth century, Parliament and the Common Lawyers had used written charters as a bulwark and a battering-ram against Stuart pretensions to divine-right absolutism. Yet though Great Britain emerged from the Glorious Revolution with new constitutional documents, most notably the Bill of Rights, the English commitment to written constitutions, always limited, waned in the eighteenth century. The supremacy of Parliament meant that the gentry and merchants that had once relied on written documents as defenses against government no longer felt threatened. By the time of William Blackstone, the great constitutional-legal theorist who wrote in the 1760s, the doctrine of Parliamentary sovereignty had achieved wide currency. England, which had never possessed a single written constitution, came to relegate written constitutions to a secondary place. If there was no higher law than Parliament, the importance of the old documents was limited.

Of course everyone did not agree. Radical Whigs, also known as Commonwealthmen, voiced vigorous support for written guarantees of a higher law than Parliament. But in England theirs was a minority view. In America, however, the seventeenth-century faith in written constitutions prevailed. Every colony possessed a charter which served as a written constitution, providing the boundaries and forms of their governments. As Parliament challenged the colonial governments in the 1760s, asserting its right in the Declaratory Act of 1766 to legislate for the colonies "in all cases whatsoever," Americans became even more deeply committed to written charters that embodied the concept of a law higher than that of a legislative majority. The conflict with Britain that led to the Declaration of Independence intensified their conviction that written constitutions were essential to the preservation of liberty, and elevated that belief to the level of a universal credo.[1]

Consequently the Continental Congress's recommendation in May 1776 to the states to draw up constitutions aroused no surprise. Two states, New Hampshire and South Carolina, had already enacted constitutions, and two more, Virginia and New Jersey, would create them prior to the Declaration of Independence. Although in a few instances the adoption of a state constitution was delayed for more than a year, by the time the war ended in 1783, every state was operating under a written constitution that prescribed not only the structure of government but also its powers and their limits.[2] By 1790 a similar national constitution had also been ratified.

It is not the purpose of this essay to provide a sustained analysis of the constitutions of the Revolutionary era. Their general outlines — the three-branch government including a bicameral legislature, frequent elections, and a Bill of Rights — are well known. What I shall explore briefly are some of the implicit assumptions that underlay these explicit formulas for govrnment. Such an exploration can reveal some of the fundamental political expectations of the Revolutionary era.

---

[1]Bernard Bailyn, *The Ideological Origins of the American Revolution* (Cambridge, Mass., 1967).

[2]Allan Nevins, *The American States During and After the Revolution, 1775-1789* (New York, 1927), chaps. 4-6.

When commentators celebrate the United States Constitution of 1787, they invariably salute its brevity as part of its excellence. The brief, general character of its provisions, including judicial review and amendment, all agree, has allowed for a flexibility across the genera- tions that has made it the oldest working constitution in the world. The same brevity was characteristic of the state constitutions that were written during the period. One, that of New Jersey, was a mere 2500 words.[3] In such constitutions the framework of government and the rights of citizens were merely outlined, copious elaboration was deemed superfluous.

This approach to constitution-drafting derived in part from the colonial charters which had provided similarly broad, general delega- tions of authority. Like the colonial charters, the constitutions drawn in the Revolutionary era rested on the belief that public officials must enjoy discretionary powers in defining their objectives and in exercis- ing their authority. People assumed that government officials would be an elevated class of men, educated leaders of wisdom and virtue. Such leaders could only rule with justice, moderation, and effectiveness if they were free to use their best judgement within the broad bound- aries established by the written constitution and the narrower ones sanctioned by custom.

One could not, of course, place unquestioning faith in virtuous leaders. The radical Whig tradition and the Revolutionary experience demonstrated the inevitable tendency of power to corrupt officials. But this did not mean that they should be kept on a short rein, without any discretion. Checks and balances within the government would enable leaders to restrain one another, while a virtuous citizenry would be ever vigilant against the abuse of power, always ready to defend its rights. Frequent elections were seen as the key device whereby public scrutiny would keep officials virtuous. Officials who abused their trust would be rapidly replaced by someone of recognized ability and honor. Ultimately the Revolutionary generation believed that the success of constitutional republics, whatever their structural mechanics for self-regulation, relied on the morality of persons, both in and out

---

[3]James Q. Dealey, *Growth of American State Constitutions: From 1776 to the End of the Year 1914* (New York, 1972), p. 39; Julian P. Boyd, ed., *Funda- mental Laws and Constitutions of New Jersey, 1664-1964* (Princeton, 1964), pp. 156-63.

of office. This was an essential reason the written constitutions were brief and general.[4]

The constitutions of Massachusetts (1780) and of the United States (1787) represent culminations of this outlook. Both are considerably longer than New Jersey's brief effort, but both maintain the same general tone.[5] Both are masterful examples of the desire to create self-regulating mechanisms of limited government through functional separation of powers and bicameral legislatures. At the same time they allow wide areas of discretion. The role and powers of the judiciary, ultimately so important, were barely sketched. The leading architects of these constitutions, John Adams and James Madison, both believed that the governments they helped to create would curb the growth of faction and party and so would be staffed by able, honest, and prudent men like themselves, men whose judgement and self-control could normally be trusted because their system harnessed the ambition of one official to counteract ambition in another.

When one comes to the end of the nineteenth century, an examination of written constitutions reveals striking changes. Indeed the divergence between the United States Constitution and the constitutions of the states which were once so similar is dramatic. For the United States Constitution had remained substantially intact, having undergone only two periods of substantial amendment, one at the outset, between 1791 and 1804, when constitutional oversights were addressed, and the other between 1865 and 1870, when the consequences of the Civil War were written into the Constitution. Generally, Americans had not tampered with the written constitution at the national level. Insofar as change and growth demanded it, judicial review provided the means for constitutional flexibility and development.

The life of the state constitutions had been different. At first brief and general, they grew to become lengthy, elaborate documents. Where a mere 600 words had been sufficient to provide New Hampshire with a government in 1776, Missouri required over 26,000 words

---

[4]Gordon S. Wood, *The Creation of the American Republic, 1776-1787* (Chapel Hill, 1969), chap. 2, part 4; chap. 3, part 5; chap. 12.

[5]The Massachusetts constitution was about 12,000 words; that of the United States about 6,000 words.

[6]James Bryce, *The American Commonwealth*, 3rd ed. rev., 2 vols., (New York, 1897), 1: 454.

a century later.[6] Ordinarily the sheer length of the constitutions grew on the order of 300 to 500 percent.

This growth encompassed two types of addition. One was the insertion of new subject matter, such as constitutional provisions dealing with contemporary issues like banking, education, and transportation. The other was the effort to close loopholes through specific provisions that often treated questions in minute detail. As a result, state constitutions moved away from the plane of general principles toward the level of particular regulation. Though in many ways they were different, more and more, they came to resemble statutory codes.

Substantively there were also major alterations. By the end of the nineteenth century state governors, once little more than appendages of the legislature, had been granted enough power so that, as a minimum, they possessed the veto. Likewise the role of the people in government, and the definition of who "the people" included was broadened. While the American public had maintained the original character of the written constitution at the national level, Americans had transformed their written constitutions in the states.

Why had this happened? Why was it that the Revolutionary ideal of the written constitution was so transformed in the one case while being preserved in the other? Should the divergent histories of the national and state constitutions be regarded as evidence of a split political personality, with one set of constitutional ideas for the states and another for the nation? To answer these questions one must begin by examining the process whereby the state constitutions were altered, a process that reveals some of the fundamental dynamics of nineteenth-century public life.

As of 1900 the 45 states had witnessed some 147 constitutional conventions, averaging three per state. In addition hundreds of constitutional amendments had been presented to voters, and hundreds approved. Two states, Georgia and Louisiana, had adopted as many as seven constitutions over the span of a century; three more states had created five constitutions.[7] Lord Bryce, writing in 1892, estimated that the life of a state constitution had been no more than thirty years.[8] These simple statistics suggest the beginnings of an answer to the ques-

---

[7]Compiled from state records. The figures include one pre-statehood convention for each state.

[8]Bryce, *American Commonwealth,* 1: 456-458.

tion of why state constitutions were so transformed. From the numbers it is apparent that altering, or even replacing, constitutions was a relatively easy, and by the second half of the century, an almost commonplace, affair.

The reason it was easy at the state level was part of the reason it was difficult at the national level, the *accessibility* of the constitutions. Compared to the nation as a whole the states were uniform and compact, and within them powerful interest groups and decided majorities readily formed, able to take over a state government and set about revising its constitution. By contrast the United States Constitution was inaccessible. Not only was a two-thirds majority of Congress required, but in addition the approval of the legislatures (or conventions) of three-quarters of the states. As its authors had intended, altering the Constitution of 1787 was possible only in extraordinary cases. The process of changing the Constitution was so cumbersome and required such broad, sustained agreement, that it was substantially inaccessible.

The core of the problem was the structure of politics. Madison had predicted in *Federalist* Number 10 that:

> The smaller the society, the fewer probably will be the distinct parties and interests composing it; the fewer the distinct parties and interests, the more frequently will a majority be found of the same party; and the smaller the number of individuals composing a majority, and the smaller the compass within which they are placed, the more easily will they concert and exercise their plans. . . . Extend the sphere, and you take in a greater variety of parties and interests; and you make it less probable that a majority of the whole will have a common motive . . . ; or if such a common motive exists, it will be more difficult for all who feel it to discover their own strength, and to act in unison with each other.[9]

His analysis proved remarkably accurate for politics in nineteenth-century America. The decentralization of national politics was extreme.

In response, a party structure developed that used electoral competition as the foundation for integrating local, state, and national politics. Yet the ability of parties to overcome the decentralized patterns of settlement and political organization, and the competing

---

[9]Alexander Hamilton, John Jay, James Madison, *The Federalist,* intro. by Edward Mead Earle (New York, n.d. [1937]), pp. 60-61.

economic interests in the United States, was severely limited. For the most part sectional coalitions were more cohesive than the national parties when it came to actual policy decision. It was only at the state and county level that parties achieved substantial coherence and continuity, and even there party systems differed widely according to local circumstances. Some states had one-party systems, others two parties, and a few had multi-party competitions.[10] Such a structure was far more capable of achieving majorities sufficient to alter state constitutions than to muster the necessary two-thirds and three-quarters demanded by the national amendment process. A majority broad enough to support a new national constitutional convention was unthinkable. It is significant that the one major period of nineteenth-century amendments (the Thirteenth, Fourteenth, and Fifteenth), came in the wake of the Civil War, when a national majority had been mobilized for defending the Union and when a condition of readmission for the southern states was acceptance of the amendments. Had southern whites been entirely free to choose, then even these amendments could not have secured the necessary approval of three-quarters of the states.

Yet as important as this phenomenon of structure and accessibility is, it does not provide a sufficient explanation for the differing histories of written constitutions on the state and national level. For the fact that the public *could* alter and replace the state constitutions did not mean they must do so. If majorities had wished to preserve their constitutions intact, as was substantially true in a state such as Massachusetts, they could. What we must examine now is why in so many places people wanted to alter their constitutions so frequently.

On the surface the explanation is fairly simple: many Americans, some attached to particular interests, were unsatisfied with the performance of their elected officials. Between 1800 and 1830 the public had witnessed and participated in the creation of political parties which, as time went on, became a permanent feature of American

---

[10]See David Hackett Fisher, *The Revolution of American Conservatism* (New York, 1965); Ronald P. Formisano, "Deferential-Participant Politics: The Early Republic's Political Culture, 1789-1840," *American Political Science Review*, 68 (1974): 473-487; Richard Hofstadter, *The Idea of a Party System* (Berkeley, 1972); Richard P. McCormick, *The Second American Party System: Party Formation in the Jacksonian Era* (Chapel Hill, 1966); Roy F. Nichols, *The Invention of the American Political Parties* (New York, 1967); James Sterling Young, *The Washington Community, 1800-1828* (New York, 1966).

government. This institutionalization of partisanship, once castigated as factionalism, was only accepted with ambivalence. Public officials, who had been perceived as stewards of the general good, were now seen as self-interested, office-seeking "party politicians." Simultaneously, the public witnessed legislative majorities falling under the discipline of party affiliation. As a result the legitimacy of legislation as the primary expression of the public interest was sapped. Although party politics gave structure to elections, appointments, and the co-ordination of government among the branches, it had not been anticipated when the state constitutions were drafted. Party politics was alien to the Revolutionary ideal of the written constitution, and it made Americans skeptical of the motives and the actions of their officials.[11]

In some instances, moreover, parties effectively subverted the restraints of the system of separation of powers that had been built into the constitutions. Party majorities could control all three branches of state government with relative ease, and so could abuse their discretionary powers. Regional favoritism in transportation and education policy, and special advantages for friends engaged in banking and other corporate activities, became hallmarks of party government. As they had been initially written, state constitutions were not restraining office holders adequately.

Public reliance on the discretion of officials was also undermined by the rapid and dramatic changes that were occurring in the economic and social life of America. The growth of a national market economy, the development of industry and increasing specialization in occupations, the expansion of cities, the rise of "reform" politics, and the emergence of revivalism as a regular feature of Protestantism, were only some of the most conspicuous changes. Earlier reliance on discretion had been partly based on the belief that officials could operate largely within the framework of custom. Now, in a dynamic society, custom provided less and less in the way of guidance. The exercise of discretion now involved fresh policy-making in more and more areas. These discretionary policies lacked any firm base in custom, and so they were far more likely to prove controversial than ever before.

---

[11]Hofstadter, *Idea of a Party System;* Formisano, "Deferential-Participant Politics."

Official discretion, once safely non-partisan and ruled by custom, now became suspect.

Rewriting state constitutions was one of the key public responses to these dissatisfactions with their governments. The ideal of the written constitution, after all, embodied the idea of subjecting government and governors to the higher, natural law as expressed by the sovereign people. If existing restraints were not sufficient, then rewriting them to make them more explicit and iron-clad, was appropriate. Perhaps the climax of public mistrust of officials came in the last third of the nineteenth century when constitutions came to require that officials swear that they had been honestly elected and, in one case, that they had read their state constitution. The revolutionaries' expectation that rulers would be "most wise, sensible, and discreet" was dead.[12]

Beyond closing the loop holes and hemming their rulers in, the remedy was to shift power to the people through state conventions, plebiscites, and the office of the governor. Specially elected state conventions could more faithfully reflect the popular will than legislatures because they were not integrated into the regular party apparatus, possessed only a transitory existence, and were required to submit their proposals to the direct will of the people in plebiscites. In some respects conventions became super-legislatures and their work, when it was popularly ratified, super-statutes.

Strengthening the governor was also an expression of popular power because it was believed that the high degree of gubernatorial visibility led to the greatest public accountability among state officials. Other office holders fell prey to special interests, but the governor possessed the broadest constituency and so could more nearly represent the general interest. On election day voters could pass judgement on him far more readily than a congeries of local party politicians. By mid-century it had become clear that if a governor lacked the veto power, he was no more than a creature of the majority party leaders in the legislature, a group that was not broadly accountable. Paradoxically, strengthening the governor by constitutional revision was seen as reducing the power of rulers. It was a means of establishing popular control.

---

[12]Dealey, *Growth of American State Constitutions*, pp. 239-240, 268; the quotation is from the Maryland constitution.

Yet a similar drive for written restraints on rulers never developed at the national level. Why? Was it because voters were ignorant of the influence of party politics in the national government and continued to view their national leaders as men of wisdom, virtue, and discretion? No. The reason is that the abuses that were perceived at the state level were partially blocked at the national level. In addition judgements as to what constituted serious abuses of national power varied substantially according to region, preventing broad agreement on the need for remedies.

One key reason why the partisan abuses of party were reduced at the national level was the general inability of a single party to gain thorough-going control of all branches of government. During the period of Jeffersonian hegemony, the Supreme Court led by John Marshall was independent of the dominant party. Partly because of his antipathy to the Democratic-Republican party, Marshall cultivated the doctrine of judicial review, providing the foundation for an effective check on party majorities that outlasted his own thirty-five-year tenure as chief justice.

Party influence at the national level was also restricted by the organization and character of the national parties themselves. Their existence as national organizations was shadowy except in the years of presidential elections, and even then they were largely loose coalitions of state organizations. Party coherence and discipline were far more substantial at the state level.[13] National party leaders could not routinely control majorities, so the effects of party government were further limited.

The arena of national politics was, moreover, so large and diverse as to bear out Madison's predictions. Just as it was difficult to mobilize sufficient majorities for constitutional amendments, so it was difficult to secure legislative and presidential agreement except on policies that enjoyed commanding majorities. Sectional interest groups and rivalries provided an unofficial check that had been anticipated by the drafters of the Constitution. Lobbyists who were successful manipulators of parties, and adroit at securing special-interest legislation in the states, did not thrive at the national level until the last third of the nineteenth

---

[13]McCormick, *Second Party System;* Formisano, "Deferential-Participant Politics."

century. For these reasons it was somewhat more difficult for legislators to abuse their discretionary powers in Congress than in the states.

Yet however difficult it may have been, there were still many critics who did perceive grave abuses in the conduct of politicians who held office. They did not turn to constitutional amendments, however, for several reasons. First, of course, there was the problem of inacessibility, a problem compounded by the fact that the perception of abuses was sectional: witness New England's complaints against Jeffersonian foreign policy around the War of 1812; South Carolina's hostility to Andrew Jackson's enforcement of the tariff in 1833; and northeastern opposition to the Mexican War. In addition there was a question of appropriate constitutional remedies. The approaches that were employed in the states were not directly applicable at the national level since the President already had the veto power and national conventions and plebiscites appeared unwieldy and unproductive. Moreover, the scope of national legislation, largely limited to foreign policy, interstate commerce, and public lands, did not touch the social and economic interests of the broad majority of the public with anything like the same frequency as state legislation. As a result the perceived "remoteness" of the national government blunted desires to modify or manipulate the written constitution that controlled it. Judicial review gave the document some flexibility. Proposals for a new constitutional convention, or even amendments, aroused little attention.

These divergent paths of written constitutions in the states and in the nation as a whole were strongly influenced by long-range, "historical" trends in American public life that were tested and strengthened by the Civil War. Chief among these was the gradual ascendancy of the national government over the states. Looking at the nineteenth century as a whole, there is no single turning-point where the states were reduced from quasi-sovereign status to the role of subordinate political and administrative jurisdictions, yet that was the path they traversed during the century. This trend. based on economic, technological, and demographic factors, among others, led to a relative downgrading of states and state constitutions. The state constitution was, after all, no longer the key written document that limited the operations of government. Its function as the citizen's bulwark against tyranny diminished. From 1865 onward it became apparent that the national constitution of 1787 was the primary written constitution for the people of America.

This perception was interwoven with a larger pattern of constitution-worship that applied to the national constitution rather than state constitutions. The Civil War, after all, had pitted state constitutions against the national one, and it was the latter that had triumphed. The blood of Union soldiers rendered the Constitution sacred. Historians like John Fiske, whose *Critical Period of American History* extolled the Constitution, boasted it was "the finest specimen of constructive statesmanship the world has ever seen."[14] An English Prime Minister, William Gladstone, even claimed "the American Constitution is the most wonderful work ever struck off at a given time by the brain and purpose of man."[15] Today, however much we may admire the Constitution, such unqualified enthusiasm sounds like hyperbole. But in the last third of the nineteenth century the Founding Fathers were demi-gods, and educators, clergymen, and politicians clamored to celebrate their masterpiece.

No similar claims were made for the state constitutions. Accessible, oft-amended and revised, they lacked the dignity of age, and in place of grand generalities they had become cluttered with prosaic details. Their authors were usually clay-footed men who were still living and still engaged in politics. Far from sharing in the romanticization and elevation of the national constitution, the state constitutions suffered by comparison. Now when people thought of the written constitution as an ideal principle, it was chiefly the Constitution of 1787 that they had in mind.

Yet by the end of the nineteenth century constitution-worship became tarnished. Political conservatives, eager to block the efforts of Populists and other economic and social reformers, employed the Constitution, with its provision for judicial review, as their bulwark against what they saw as irrational, levelling, democratic excesses. They turned the partisan use of constitution-worship that had begun as part of the effort to legitimate the Union cause to narrower capitalist objectives. Consequently by the early twentieth century the ideal of the written constitution was being critically scrutinized as never before. Progressive scholars, Orin G. Libby, Algie Simons, and

---

[14]*The Critical Period of American History, 1783-1789,* (Boston, 1888), p. *vii.*
[15]Quoted in Fiske, *Critical Period,* p. 223.

Charles Beard, challenged the Constitution's foundations by arguing that it was rooted in mundane, interest-group politics, not altruistic wisdom.[16] Progressives, frustrated by a Supreme Court that interpreted the Constitution to sustain conservative interests, became critical of the document itself. The Constitution had not been so sharply criticized since the days of the Abolitionists. A dramatic turnabout was under way, and the vast distance that had opened up between the once sacrosanct Constitution of 1787 and the state constitutions began to narrow for the first time. Ultimately the way was opened for amendment of the national constitution.

The movement to amend the Constitution was rooted in the conflict between the state constitutions (which tolerated reforms of transportation, labor conditions, taxes) and the national constitution as interpreted by the Supreme Court. It was the Court that used the Constitution to stymie Progressives, who then turned to the amendment route, however difficult. Ironically the first post-Reconstruction amendment, the Income Tax Amendment, was necessary only because of Court politics. There was nothing in the Constitution of 1787 that would have required the amendment, indeed the United States had operated an income tax during the Civil War. But now, because of the Court, a special enabling provision was required for a revenue act. Here was a shift from the general to the particular, as had been common in the states.

The Constitution was accessible now, relatively, because the economic and political organization of the United States had become substantially centralized, and national interest groups and organizations were surmounting the sectionalism that had dominated nineteenth-century politics. Between 1913 and 1920 no less than four substantive amendments were ratified, each having precedents in the state constitutional revisions of the previous century. The direct election of senators was an old democratization of the states, where party control of the upper houses had long been abused. The prohibition of "intoxicating liquors" also possessed a long history in state constitutions.

---

[16]See Libby, *Geographical Distribution of the Vote of the Thirteen States on the Ratification of the Federal Constitution, 1787-1788,* University of Wisconsin, *Bulletin,* Economic. Political Science, and History Series, Vol. 1 (Madison, 1894); Simons, *Social Forces in American History* (New York, 1911); and Beard, *An Economic Interpretation of the Constitution of the United States* (New York, 1913).

The enfranchisement of women was less common, but it too had been part of some state constitutions. The Progressive amendments of the years 1913 to 1920 suggested that the Revolutionary ideal of the written constitution, that had been transformed at the state level during the nineteenth cenutry, might follow the same route at the national level in the twentieth. Doubts had been raised about the wisdom of the Founding Fathers, and the discretionary powers of national officials, the judiciary in particular, could no longer be trusted.

The possibility of a comparable transformation of the Constitution of 1787 existed, but it would be misleading to claim that such a change had occurred by 1920. Actually, the two amendments dealing with election of senators and women's suffrage were directly in the Revolutionary tradition. They modified the basic structure of the system, in both instances broadening the power of the people without limiting in any way the powers or discretion of national officials. Neither of these amendments suggested any likelihood of making the Constitution into a set of super-statutes or a code minutely regulating the conduct of government. Both maintained the concept of the written constitution as a general framework for government that lays out the boundaries of political life.

The income tax and prohibition amendments were of a wholly different character. Both dealt with matters of substantive policy appropriate to legislative action. The income tax was written into the Constitution chiefly as a means of circumventing a hostile process of judicial review. Prohibition was attached to the Constitution so as to declare emphatically and beyond question that temperance was national policy. The proliferation of this type of amendment, in which particular policies are elevated to the level of basic law by attaching them to the Constitution, would indeed render the national constitution similar to those of the states. This was the prospect that opened up during the Progressive era.

Let us turn now to the last fifty years to see whether the Revolutionary conception of the written constitution as a fundamental law, embodying higher principles than mere statutes, still survives. Since 1920 there have been seven amendments to the Constitution, two in 1933, one in 1951, three in the 1960s, and one in 1971. The first and the next to last of these (1933, 1967), dealing with the government calendar and succession, are technical and seem to represent the desire to make the succession of government absolutely cut-and-dried. They close loop-holes and spell out the rules precisely. The second repeals the prohibition amendment (1933). The third, coming in response to Franklin Roosevelt's unprecedented four terms, limits presidents to two terms in office. The fourth (1961) provides for presidential electors in the District of Columbia; and fifth (1964), directed at Southern poll taxes, establishes the right to participate in primary elections for national officials. The last (1971) extends the suffrage to eighteen-year-olds.

What do these amendments signify? Three, creating presidential electors for the District of Columbia, and opening up primary elections, and giving the vote to people eighteen and over, stand within the Revolutionary tradition as extensions of the principle of popular government. The others, it seems, represent the tendency of the state constitutions. Obviously the repeal of prohibition is a shift on a political issue and furnishes the most striking illustration of legislation by constitutional amendment — prohibition having lasted less than fifteen years. The calendar and succession amendments, by establishing greater precision than the Constitution originally provided, display an absence of confidence in custom and discretion together with a desire for absolute certitude that is more characteristic of the nineteenth-century state constitutions than those of the Revolutionary era. The limitation on presidential terms of office, which replicates limits that were placed on the office of governor in the nineteenth century is also an essentially political matter. Here the discretion of the people, not government officials, is limited although there is the implication that presidents may use their powers to extend their rule unduly. As in the state constitutions the descent from general principles to particular policy is aimed at reducing discretion. In light of Roosevelt's successful violation of the custom of a two-term limit begun by George Washington, the amendment is a clear response to the weakening of custom and discretion as companions of the written constitution.

Considering this record alone, the Revolutionary conception of the Constitution as a truly higher law today is seriously threatened. The integration of the national political, economic, and social systems has rendered Constitutional amendment much more accessible than it was in the nineteenth cenutry. National lobbies and interest groups that can promote particular amendments simultaneously in Congress and the fifty states are flourishing in American politics. Sectional differences no longer dominate national politics. Moreover, as in the Progressive era, the readiness of the national judiciary to defend controversial policies like school bussing and abortion against vigorous popular opposition has aroused great interest in constitutional amendment as the remedy for an unresponsive judiciary. Under these circumstances one may well question whether the Revolutionary ideal can, or should, survive.

My own view is that it should be preserved for the same reasons that the Revolutionary generation defended it. Adherence to a time-tested set of general principles, immune to the short-term fluctuations of public opinion, provides the surest guarantee of a government of laws, not of men, that can protect minorities from majority will. Like the Founding Fathers, I believe that there are and should be laws, good ones, that are higher than popular or legislative majorities. Under such a constitution, democracy is the best form of government for this nation. So much for a statement of faith.

But can the written Constitution survive as a form of higher law? The evidence of 1973-74, when a president was forced to resign under threat of impeachment for violating his constitutional duties, suggests that the concept of the Constitution as the controlling, fundamental law endures. In that time of crisis, the politicians and the public found in the Constitution an ark of safety against arbitrary government and a prescription for defense against the threat. Simultaneously, the principle of judicial review, here directed at the executive not the legislative branch, was tested and confirmed. The Revolutionary ideal displayed its merits to a grateful public.

Yet as strong as this evidence is of the vitality of the ideal, the threat remains. Presidential powers remain great beyond precedent, indeed the same decision that required President Richard Nixon to turn over the White House tapes broadly recognized the concept of executive privilege for the first time, thereby extending executive authority. One wonders, for example, whether a Congress dominated by members of the same party as the President would have challenged its leader on constitutional grounds, or whether party discipline and patronage would have served to suppress congressional action. Ultimately it appears that a free press, stimulated in part by the sales appeal of scandal and muckraking, played the crucial role in focusing public attention on constitutional violations. It is here, perhaps, that we possess the best mechanism for continued preservation of the Revolutionary ideal.

Consider. The press, or more broadly the communications networks, rely heavily on constitutional guarantees for their survival and so share a powerful interest in preserving them. Moreover, as they have become *national* they have emerged as a major instrument for disciplining public officials. The insulation from public scrutiny that nineteenth-century public officials enjoyed no longer exists, and so it is possible that the need to rely on elaborate constitutional provisions to prevent abuses of discretion may no longer exist. Publicity, and its threat, may enforce a reasonable exercise of discretion.

Moreover, the consensus as to the reasonable scope of legislation has so broadened since the late 1930s that a resort to constitutional change may become rare. It is significant that the pressure for public disclosure of information, whether the income tax returns of politicians or the once confidential files of citizens, has been focused on legislatures resulting in statutes. There has been no need to seek constitutional amendment. A reasonably flexible, adaptable system of politics operating within a constitutional framework reduces pressures to alter it.

In the final analysis, of course, the Revolutionary generation would have warned us against reliance on any mechanism or system to protect our Constitution and the liberties it encompasses. If we would seek to preserve the Revolutionary ideal of the written constitution, they would urge us to be alert, watchful, active citizens, always jealous of the Constitution and ready at a minute's notice to fly to its defense. A self-seeking citizenry, one concerned more with private gain than the public good, sensitive to short-term advantage but careless of long-term consequences, ignorant of constitutional principles and lazy in defending them, the Revolutionaries predicted, would lose them. As Thomas Paine asserted in 1776, ultimately the preservation of the higher law resides not in *"the constitution of the government . . .* [but] *in the constitution of the people."*[17]

---

[17]*Common Sense,* in Merrill Jensen, ed., *Tracts of the American Revolution, 1763-1776* (Indianapolis, 1967), p. 408, Paine's italics, phrases here inverted.

ECONOMIC CHANGE AND THE POLITICAL ECONOMY OF THE AMERICAN REVOLUTION

BY JOSEPH A. ERNST*

The economic history of the American Revolution is not long. At most it covers a dozen years. Yet, because these few brief years constitute a remarkable period in modern history they are the subject of a seemingly endless quest for an understanding of their meaning and significance. In this search, few issues have escaped scrutiny, and some — such as the importance or irrelevance of the economic situation in America in shaping the revolutionary movement — are matters of continuing dispute.[1]

But ways of seeing the Revolution have seriously affected ways of seeing the Revolutionary economy. For example, members of the so-called "imperial school" of British-American history have viewed the colonial economy as but one of several administrative problems to be explained and understood from the perspectives of Whitehall and Westminster. Neo-Whig historians of the Revolution, on the other hand, have treated the economic situation as a relatively minor factor in their theory of growing fears in America of a British plot against freedom. Somewhat better is the record of the Progressive "school." A leading theme of this group was the question of the impact on the revolutionary movement of a postwar depression coupled with new and restrictive British economic legislation after 1763. Thus, men like Arthur Schlesinger, Sr. and Carl L. Becker investigated the economic problems of the merchants and landholders. Even here,

---

*Mr. Ernst wishes to thank his colleague, Marc Egnal, for his helpful suggestions and comments.
[1]See the discussion in Marc Egnal and Joseph A. Ernst, "An Economic Interpretation of the American Revolution," *William and Mary Quarterly,* 3rd Ser., 29 (1972): 3-36.

however, the economic history of the period "went little beyond the depiction of 'hard times.' "[2]

Studies of the Revolution are not the only source of information about the American economy on the eve of independence. Colonial economic history is a subject in its own right, and over the years it has attracted the attention of a surprisingly large group of scholars. A number of works (some of them unpublished) have examined the economic life of the large port cities. More extensive is the literature that has traditionally focused on the various sectors of the colonial economy: on trade, agriculture, manufacturing, money and credit. The broad framework for most of this writing has been, and remains, political. The American economy has also been analyzed colony by colony, largely because of the way the economic data was kept and because of the essential conservatism of established categories of thought.[3] A regional approach has been customary only in connection with the tobacco trade and the homogeneous Chesapeake economy. Not until recently has a more thorough-going, sophisticated and self-consciously regional view emerged.[4]

Finally, a small body of literature concerns the growth and economic development of the colonies. Much of this work centers on the elusive and controversial question of the cost to America of the Navigation Acts and British mercantilist policies in general.[5] The more important topics — the actual pace of American expansion, the long swings and the short-run fluctuations of the colonial economy, and the relationship between colonial development and growth of the British

---

[2]For a more extensive analysis of the contributions of the several schools, see Egnal and Ernst, "An Economic Interpretation of the American Revolution," pp. 3-9, and my discussion in "Ideology and the Political Economy of Revolution," *Canadian Review of American Studies,* 4 (1973): 137-148, and in " 'Ideology' and an Economic Interpretation of the Revolution," in Alfred F. Young, ed., *The American Revolution* (De Kalb, 1976), pp. 163-69.

[3]See my select bibliography in *Money and Politics in America, 1755-1775: A Study in the Currency Act of 1764 and the Political Economy of Revolution* (Chapel Hill, 1973), pp. 384-393, and the footnote references in Marc Egnal, "The Economic Development of the Thirteen Continental Colonies, 1720 to 1775," *William and Mary Quarterly,* 3rd Ser., 32 (1975): 191-222.

[4]For a brief discussion of the regional approach see Egnal and Ernst, "An Economic Interpretation of the American Revolution," p. 12.

[5]See Egnal and Ernst, "An Economic Interpretation of the Revolution," pp. 4-5, and Egnal, "Economic Development of the Thirteen Continental Colonies," p. 192.

economy — have received far less attention, although this situation is now changing.[6]

Embedded in this mound of qualitative and quantitative writings are numerous discussions and analyses of various aspects of the Revolutionary economy. Although these accounts are fragmentary and partial, and lack methodological consistency, a general synthesis of the economic history of the Revolution based on such work seems possible. To begin with, one must emphasize short-run fluctuations. This at least has the merit of following the contemporary approach to economic conditions. Colonial merchants, planters and mechanics alike judged their possibilities of making a profit according to traditional short-run indicators, namely: prices, exchange rates, the state of the market, the availability of credit and currency, and the cost of freight and insurance.[7]

This emphasis on the short-run should not obscure the importance of long swings and structural changes in understanding the Revolutionary economy. Not only do these aspects of economic growth provide the larger context and long-range perspective for viewing short-term movements, but they, too, figured in the calculations of the colonial economic classes. Americans were fully aware of such shifting patterns as the relative decline in the West Indies market and the growth in the Southern European and British trade; the increase of intercolonial trade; the appearance of new products and cutthroat competition in the import trade; the southward spread of "the Wheat Belt"; the rise and growing importance of domestic manufacturing; the economic diversification of the Staple colonies; the uncontrolled and disruptive credit practices of British trading houses; and the other broad structural and secular changes that were prominent features of the Revolutionary economy. Nonetheless, merchant letterbooks suggest that short-run conditions, not long-run prospects, were the usual concern of the business classes. Only when long-run factors helped explain or offered solutions to immediate problems did they appear important.[8]

---

[6]See Egnal, "Economic Development of the Thirteen Continental Colonies," pp. 191-222.

[7]For an excellent discussion of this point see William S. Sachs, "The Business Outlook in the Northern Colonies 1750-1775" (Ph.D. dissertation Columbia University, 1957), chap. 9.

[8]See Sachs, "Business Outlook," chaps. 6 and 8.

In any consideration of short-run fluctuations, two periods of major change emerge, the one lasting from 1763 to 1772, the other from 1772 to 1775. The first period was bracketed by the financial crises of 1763 and 1772. The crisis in 1763 was possibly the worst in colonial history; the one in 1772 was almost as severe. During the intervening years the economy went through a postwar slump, a time of retrenchment and, finally, a brief recovery. The decade after 1763 was also marked by widespread colonial efforts at remedying these conditions through a program of economic "reform" and of revision of British currency and trade policies; these efforts were at the very core of the revolutionary movement. This same decade was distinguished as well by a number of important structural alterations over which the Americans could exercise little or no control. The second period of major change took place after the panic of 1772, and its chief characteristics were a slow and uneven recovery from the panic and the serious disruptions that accompanied the gathering independence movement and the coming of war.

In analyzing these economic rhythms one may usefully deal with the thirteen colonies as two broad functional regions. First are the commercial economies, or those areas dominated by the centralized marketing and credit structures of the great port cities: Boston, New York, Philadelphia, Baltimore, Charleston, and, by the end of the period, Norfolk. Second are the areas of decentralized arrangements that characterized the tobacco economies of much of Virginia and parts of Maryland and North Carolina.[9]

What I wish to argue in this essay is that it is only from the perspectives of the significant short- and long-run, structural and regional changes in the decade after 1763 that we can begin to understand what seem to me to be the important economic legacies of the American Revolution. The first of these legacies was created by the "new forces for economic growth" that made their appearance in the 1760s. These were "the growing demand of Southern Europe for American grain, the strengthening of the home market, the expansion of textile and shoe production, and the acquisition and exploitation of western lands."[10] They continued to have an impact on develop-

---

[9]This is the approach taken in Egnal and Ernst, "An Economic Interpretation of the Revolution," pp. 11-12.

[10]Egnal, "Economic Development of the Thirteen Continental Colonies," pp. 198-222.

ments after 1776 and were worked into the fabric of the economic life of the new nation in ways that have yet to be fully assessed. Second, and more important from the view expressed in this paper, are the economic collapses of 1762 and 1772 and their ensuing depressions which created a general sense of crisis in the economic order and called into being several schemes for economic change and regeneration. The aim of these programs was "reform" within the empire, "reform" designed to enable the dominant economic classes in America to withstand conditions of economic upheaval, achieve a greater measure of control over their own economic destinies and secure for themselves more of the fruits of their labor. The failure of these efforts helped to reveal the extent of British domination of the colonial economy and to encourage a growing feeling that "reform" could not be achieved inside the imperial framework. The fact of Independence simply gave the economic and political leadership in America the chance to renew their experiments in the broadening of existing economic opportunities and the creation of new ones.

I

The rapid development of the American colonies after the middle-eighteenth century and business upswing in the early years of the French and Indian War gradually, but inexorably, gave way to financial panic, a general slowdown in the pace of economic growth, and depression. By the summer of 1760 merchants in Boston, New York and Philadelphia were complaining of conditions in the West Indies, where a slump in the sugar market had weakened demand for food-stuffs. The situation improved in 1761, and 1762 turned out to be a boom year in northern exports to the Caribbean, but by then commodity sales were suffering from the removal of the British troops from America and the curtailment in army contracts after the fall of Canada. This created a serious obstacle to the flow of remittances that helped close the trade gap between the commercial colonies and Britain, and it quickly forced a reduction of European imports into New England and the Middle colonies from a peak of some £1,800,000 in 1760 to a low of £775,000 in 1762. But despite these efforts to cut supply, domestic markets were reportedly "overdone." This, coupled with a retrenchment in 1761 of British mercantile houses caught in an impending financial crisis at home, quickly led to a rush for liquidity. By the end of 1762 hard-pressed northern merchants were expressing mixed feelings about the promised end to the war. Some feared a postwar depression in agricultural prices and in the sale of British goods. Others consoled themselves with talk of the healing effects of peace and the promise of better times to come.[11]

A steady drift from prosperity to depression also marked the progress of the tobacco colonies in the years 1760 to 1762. In 1760 generally favorable conditions prevailed. Tobacco exports and prices reached high levels, and imports into Virginia and Maryland surged upwards to an all-time record of £760,000.[12] This increase in imports was caused as much by heavy infusions of British credit as by anything else. Several factors were at work here. One was the combination of a burgeoning British economy and good tobacco markets after 1745. Another was the structural change in domestic marketing and credit arrangements. By mid-century, the system of Scottish "stores," wherein factors for the great Glasgow tobacco houses bought the "weed," sold goods, and gave credit, had rapidly expanded operations into the Virginia and North Carolina Piedmont and had become serious competitors in the older consignment trade in the Tidewater areas of Maryland and Virginia and in the Albemarle Sound area of North Carolina.[13]

As British manufactures continued to pour into the tobacco economies through these new channels, hopes of large profits quickly gave way to complaints of the "overcrowding" of goods and poor sales. Yet even as merchants tried to recover by cutting imports in 1761 and

---

[11]See especially Ernst, *Money and Politics,* pp. 90-91, 94-95; Sachs, "Business Outlook," chap. 4; Marc Egnal, "The Pennsylvania Economy 1748-1762: An Analysis of Short-Run Fluctuations in the Context of Long-Run Changes in the Atlantic Trading Community" (Ph.D. dissertation University of Wisconsin, 1974), chap. 6. For other useful discussions of conditions during these years see the footnote references in Ernst above. The statistics are drawn from Jacob M. Price, "New Time Series for Scotland's and Britain's Trade with the Thirteen Colonies and States, 1740 to 1791," *William and Mary Quarterly,* 3rd Ser., 32 (1975): 324.

[12]See Ernst, *Money and Politics,* pp. 67-70; Calvin B. Coulter, Jr., "The Virginia Merchant" (Ph.D. dissertation, Princeton University, 1944), pp. 198-209; Ronald Hoffman, *A Spirit of Dissension: Economics, Politics, and the Revolution in Maryland* (Baltimore, 1974), pp. 28-29; Price "New Time Series for Scotland's and Britain's Trade with the Thirteen Colonies and States," p. 324.

[13]See the discussion in Ernst, *Money and Politics,* pp. 46, 65, 67; Coulter, "The Virginia Merchant," chaps. 4, 5, 8; Jacob M. Price, "The Rise of Glasgow in the Chesapeake Tobacco Trade, 1707-1775," *William and Mary Quarterly,* 3rd Ser., 11 (1954): 179-199; James H. Soltow, *The Economic Role of Williamsburg* (Charlottesville, Va., 1965), chap. 2.

again in 1762, tobacco markets in Europe weakened. Fierce competition among rival Scots helped maintain prices for tobacco sold in the
colonies but only for a little while. By 1762 low prices were common
to both the consignment and store trades. A final blow to prosperity
came at the end of 1761 when tobacco houses in England and
Scotland, finding themselves under increasing financial pressures at
home, curtailed American credit. In Virginia sterling exchange rates
that had held at 140 for two years rose to 145 in October, 1761, to
150 in April, 1762, and then, as coin rapidly drained back to Britain
to cover sterling obligations, rates on paper currency reached a peak
of 165, "a very high exchange . . . no trade can afford." These briefs
were the notable swings in the tobacco economy at the end of the war
that prompted the merchants of the upper South, like their northern
compatriots, to look forward to peace and the return of trade to
"its proper channels."[14]

But the Treaty of Paris brought no relief from the melancholy
state of trade and credit. Instead, as one historian has so elegantly
phrased it, "the big bust came in 1763."[15] Collapse of a speculative
boom in wartime securities and commercial credit in Amsterdam and
Hamburg in August, 1763, brought panic to the London Exchange.
As credit became progressively tighter, business failures, which had
already reached a staggering 205 in England in 1762, climbed to 233
the following year. In the ensuing scramble to save themselves, British
merchant-creditors began calling in their American debts with deva-
stating effects. Equally discouraging were the reports from the West
Indies and the European tobacco markets. Nonetheless the stream of
British goods flowing into America in anticipation of a widely predicted
postwar recovery was again reaching flood proportions. From a low
in 1762 imports into the northern colonies, for instance, took a sudden
spurt in the fall of 1763 and had increased a full 90 percent by 1764,
totalling some £1,450,000. Complaints of a scarcity of credit and
cash, a wave of bankruptcy, poor prices and generally straitened conditions were common to all the colonies, and to all classes, by 1763,

---

[14]Cf. 12n., the graph in Ernst, *Money and Politics,* p. 377, and Coulter,
"The Virginia Merchant," pp. 267-268. The quote is from William Allason to
James Dunlop, February 24, 1763, Letterbook of William Allason, 1757-1770,
Virginia State Library, Richmond.

[15]Hoffman, *A Spirit of Dissension,* p. 28.

as the effects of contraction and retrenchment spread throughout the American economy.[16]

By the beginning of 1764, everything seemed to be "tumbling down."[17] Conditions that year, and throughout the first half of 1765, improved not at all. "Never before," according to one economic historian, "had colonial business experienced convulsions of such magnitude nor had these reversals implicated so many people."[18] From Massachusetts to North Carolina credit and cash continued "monstrous scarce." Business failures in America were on the rise; profits, sales, real estate values and payments on the ebb. The universal distress did not end there, however, as the shock wave threatened to recoil back upon the British commercial classes. As John Dickinson dramatically explained it in *The Late Regulations:* "Trade is decaying and all credit is expiring. Money is become so extremely scarce, that reputable freeholders find it impossible to pay debts which are trifling in comparison to their estates. If creditors sue, and take out executions, the lands and personal estate, as the sale must be for ready money, are sold for a small part of what they are worth when the debts were contracted. The debtors are ruined. The creditors get but part of their debts, and that ruins them. Thus the consumers break the shopkeepers; they break the merchants; and the shock must be felt as far as London."[19]

Markets for American commodities in this period were mixed. In the West Indies, trade remained unfavorable. Import prices were low, export prices high, while the anti-commercial practices and taxes imposed by the Revenue Act of 1764 only increased the costs of doing business with the Islands and decreased colonial returns. On the other hand, strengthening markets for rice, indigo and naval stores largely exempted Charleston and its hinterlands from the gathering

---

[16]Ernst, *Money and Politics,* pp. 90-91, 94-95, 154-155; Sachs, "Business Outlook," pp. 113-142; Hoffman, *A Spirit of Dissension,* pp. 28-29; Coulter, "The Virginia Merchant," pp. 226-243; Price, "New Time Series for Scotland's and Britain's Trade with the Thirteen Colonies and States,' p. 324.

[17]To Scott, Pringle, Cheap and Co., February 5, 1764, *Letterbook of John Watts, Merchant and Councillor of New York* . . . Dorothy C. Barck, ed., New-York Historical Society, *Collections,* 61 (New York, 1928), p. 228.

[18]Sachs, "Business Outlook," p. 132. Cf. 16n. above.

[19]*The Late Regulations Respecting The British Colonies On The Continent Of America Considered* . . . (Philadelphia, 1765), Paul Leicester Ford, ed., *The Writings of John Dickinson* (Philadelphia: Historical Society of Pennsylvania, 1895), pp. 227-228.

gloom, although even Charleston's merchants reported distressed sales of British imports.[20]

Of all the problems facing the commercial colonies, the glut of dry goods seemed the most pressing. The cry of "hard times" in the cities usually meant depressed dry-goods markets, about which the colonial mercantile establishment found it could do little. After mid-century, liberal offers of trade credit became a general feature of the export of British goods to America and a concomitant of the growth of the British economy. Lengthening the terms of credit to about a year and enlarging the amount of credit available to the large American merchants, for instance, was one of several devices designed to boost British sales. This policy drew little criticism from its beneficiaries. Efforts to bypass the merchant elite was another question. Here two structural changes were at work that threatened to transform the nature of colonial business altogether. One was the British supplier's use of "agents" to create new trade outlets in America by opening a line of credit and goods with retail merchants and even with some shopkeepers. Another was the increased access to vendue, or auction, sales by British houses which began to wholesale their goods, or to sell by the lot directly to local consumers. Both of these practices not only disrupted existing merchandising arrangements and helped to flood the market, but also vexed the old merchants who held firm to the ancient adage that competition was the death of trade — their trade.[21]

---

[20]For a discussion of conditions in the West Indies trade see Sachs, "Business Outlook," pp. 144-156, and Marc Egnal, "The Changing Structure of Philadelphia's Trade with the British West Indies, 1750-1775," *Pennsylvania Magazine of History and Biography*, 99 (1975): 156-179. However inadequate, the best account of the economic history of South Carolina during the Revolution is Leila Sellers, *Charleston Business on the Eve of the American Revolution* (Chapel Hill, 1934); but see also Richard Walsh, *Charleston's Sons of Liberty: A Study of The Artisans, 1763-1789* (Columbia, 1959). For a general discussion of the Revenue Act of 1764 see Merrill Jensen, *The Founding of a Nation: A History of the American Revolution 1763-1776* (New York, 1968), pp. 177-180, 206-207, 222. Commodity prices in the period are to be found in Ann Bezanson et al., eds., *Prices in Colonial Pennsylvania* (Philadelphia, 1935); Arthur Harrison Cole, *Wholesale Commodity Prices in the United States, 1700-1861* (Cambridge, Mass., 1938); and United States, Department of Commerce, Bureau of the Census, *Historical Statistics of the United States, Colonial Times to 1957* (Washington, D.C., 1960).

[21]For a more extensive discussion of this matter see Egnal and Ernst, "An Economic Interpretation of the American Revolution," pp. 15-16; Sachs, "Business Outlook," pp. 253-254.

By the end of 1765 beleaguered American merchants were anxious to do what they could to ease conditions. The Stamp Act presented these merchants with an opportunity to merge their interests with the general concern over the threat against liberty and the constitution. The consequent call for repeal, backed by a boycott of British goods, offered an ideal means to defeat a tax on business, to retrench and to cut off the damaging flow of imports.[22]

In 1764 and 1765 the tobacco economy also was ailing. Tobacco markets and prices continued at a low ebb, and in 1764 exports of the "weed" declined nearly fifteen percent from the previous year. The effect of these conditions, coupled with the severe financial pinch at the time, was a general distress: the supply of good sterling bills fell sharply; credit grew more stringent; hard cash was drained away to Britain or was withdrawn from circulation; demand for sterling bills reached unprecedented heights; exchange rates remained high; protests became a commonplace; bankruptcies climbed; payments slowed to a halt and sales of British goods slumped badly.

In a word the tobacco economies verged on insolvency, and contemporary observers portrayed a desperate scene. In Virginia, merchant William Allason ordered a pair of pistols for protection against the small planters and farmers who were being "pressed for their old balances" and were retaliating by threatening merchants and law officers, tearing down the debtors' prisons, or simply running off.[23] Less violent but more difficult to deal with were the large planters who simply connived at obstructing the law courts. A similar situation prevailed in Maryland. "Our trade is ruined," lamented the secretary of the province, Benedict Calvert. "We are immensely in debt, and not the least probability of our getting clear. Our gaols are not half large enough to hold the debtors; upon every road you ride you meet people going from different Parts of the Province to get out of the way of their Creditors."[24] In North Carolina Governor William Tryon

<hr>

[22]Sachs, "Business Outlook," pp. 168-169, 255-256.
[23]See Ernst, *Money and Politics,* pp. 144-145, 194-195; Hoffman, *A Spirit of Dissension,* pp. 28-36; Robert Polk Thompson, "The Merchant in Virginia, 1700-1775" (Ph.D. dissertation, University of Wisconsin, 1955), also has information on short-run conditions in this period scattered throughout his work. For additional reference see the citations in Ernst above. The quotes are from Allason to Bogle and Scott, July 29, 1764 in Allason Letterbook.
[24]To Cecil Calvert, June 24, 1765, in "The Calvert Papers, Number Two," Maryland Historical Society, *Fund Publications,* 9 (Baltimore, 1894), pp. 261-262.

likewise reported a general shortage of hard cash and other symptoms of the postwar depression in the tobacco trade. There was a significant difference among these colonies, however. Unlike Virginia where paper currency was in abundant supply, Maryland and North Carolina faced a monetary stringency after the war. By 1765 all paper would be retired, and the fiat money system would be at an end. In North Carolina less than £70,000 served the needs of a population of 200,000. With coin swept away to settle sterling accounts in Britain, and paper rapidly disappearing from circulation, the pressure in both Maryland and North Carolina for an additional issue of paper money became intense and added greatly to the growing anxiety of the planting and mercantile classes.[25]

In brief, like the commercial colonies to the north, the tobacco economies in 1765 suffered from a dearth of hard money and credit as well as a prolonged slump in business, trade and agriculture. Once again the coming of the Stamp Act served to focus the rising discontent and to offer a chance for action. Economic boycott, at least in Maryland, together with the debt moratorium that accompanied the closing of the courts, gave both merchants and planters a chance to strengthen their market position, to retrench, and to straighten out finances.

News of repeal of the Stamp Act, of the revision of the Revenue Act, and of the creation of free ports in the Caribbean reached America by the summer of 1766. Merchants in Boston and New York were not impressed. They wanted further changes in the Revenue and Trade Acts to encourage business with the West Indies. But elsewhere in the commercial colonies Parliament's actions were seen as a step toward economic recovery. Conditions did get better in 1766. One reason was an easing of British money markets and a return to the generous credit practices of former years. Another was the sudden and dramatic rise in the wheat and flour trade with Southern Europe and Britain. Most important, however, non-importation had allowed the merchants to sell off excess goods at reasonable prices and to settle sterling obligations at exchange rates that were favorable for the first time in several years.

The promising signs of recovery did not last long, however, and business prospects dimmed again in 1767 and 1768. For one thing,

---

[25]See Ernst, *Money and Politics,* chaps. 5-6, and pp. 199-200.

markets in the West Indies never did mend after the war. But of all the complaints registered by merchants in the commercial colonies, the most frequent was of the declining sales of European manufactures.[26]

A scarcity of cash and an oversupply of goods were the notable symptoms of this new crisis. By 1767 merchants were once more reporting a shortage of money, dull sales and cutthroat competition among sellers as British "firms stood ready to elbow their way through their competitors with liberal credit policies."[27] The following year exports to America were higher than they had been for a number of years, and they precipitated a renewed demand for debt collections, cries of slow payments, and a spreading wave of bankruptcy on both sides of the Atlantic. In fact, the only bright spot in the picture was the continuing rush to ship wheat and flour to Southern Europe and Britain. Orders and prices remained firm. Yet even here difficulties arose. The increased purchase of grain in the colonies placed heavy cash demands on the shrinking wartime currency supplies. It also aggravated the declining condition of the urban poor and unemployed. "Is money grown more plenty?" asked a New Yorker in 1767. "Have our tradesmen full employment? Is grain cheaper?" By the summer of 1767 the continuing rush for liquidity coupled with the increased demand for cash payments had created a monetary shortage so chronic that merchants throughout the commercial colonies decried the lack of "enough money circulating to do business."[28] Even Charleston was affected. Large rice shipments to grain-short markets in 1767 and 1768 gave the local planters a chance to insist on being paid in money,

---

[26]*Ibid.,* pp. 102-103, 250-253; Sachs, "Business Outlook," pp. 193-208; Virginia D. Harrington, *The New York Merchant on the Eve of the Revolution* (New York, 1935), chap. 8. For a discussion of the origins and impact of the new grain and flour trade to Southern Europe and Britain see William S. Sachs, "Agricultural Conditions in the Northern Colonies before the Revolution," *Journal of Economic History,* 13 (1953): 274-290, and "Business Outlook," pp. 140-143, 187, 274-275; Hoffman, *A Spirit of Dissension,* pp. 41-43; Gaspare J. Saladino, "The Maryland and Virginia Wheat Trade from Its Beginnings to the American Revolution" (Master's thesis, University of Wisconsin, 1960); and Max Schumacher, "The Northern Farmer and His Markets during the Late Colonial Period," (Ph.D. dissertation, University of California, Berkeley, 1948).

[27]Sachs, "Business Outlook," p. 206.

[28]The quote is from William S. Sachs, "Business Depression in the Northern Colonies, 1763-1770" (Master's thesis, University of Wisconsin, 1950), pp. 206-7; see also Price, "New Time Series for Scotland's and Britain's Trade with the Thirteen Colonies and States," p. 321, and 26n. above.

not the usual sterling bills or credit. In addition, a prohibiting tax on slave imports in these same years had left the planters with large amounts of cash on hand which ordinarily would have gone to purchase black labor. The result was that the demand for a medium of exchange peaked at a time when supply appears to have dropped off sharply.[29]

Repeal of the Stamp Act also raised expectations in the tobacco colonies of better conditions in trade and agriculture. Profitable markets and prices for tobacco did return in 1766. Exports, however, fell slightly from the relatively high figures of the previous period. The following year exports remained at about the same levels, while prices declined somewhat, but in 1768 both exports and prices were up. The business outlook also improved as a result of the end of the British credit stringency, and imports multiplied again in 1767 and 1768. On the other hand, exchange rates fell, and merchants now found it easier to pay sterling debts. The only serious difficulties, as in the case of the commercial colonies, were the overcompetition among traders and the tightening cash situation brought on by a combination of factors — the contraction of the wartime currency supply, the shortage of coin, the heavy burden of taxes to redeem former paper money issues, the growth of population, and the increasing demand for money as opposed to credit purchases of tobacco and other commodities, especially wheat. In Virginia there was the additional complication of the Robinson Scandal and the shaky condition of the public credit. Nonetheless, merchants who only a short while before had bitterly opposed any new currency issue were increasingly coming to feel that the money supply had fallen considerably short of the "Occasions of Trade," and that something had to be done about it.[30]

By contrast to the merchants' situation, conditions among the Tidewater planters appeared less promising. In the words of one historian, the records of these planters reveal "a steady decline in prosperity, and a steady increment in indebtedness." Their heavy reliance on English consignment merchants for goods and credit, and the depression in the tobacco trade earlier in the decade, had left many of them deeply in arrears. Despite relatively favorable markets and

---

[29]Ernst, *Money and Politics,* pp. 217-218.
[30]Ibid., chap. 6 and pp. 230-231.

prices after 1766, they had failed to extricate themselves, possibly because tobacco yields in the Tidewater reportedly fell as much as two-thirds in the period and because merchant-creditors continued to dun for payment of old debts. Under these circumstances, planters who had failed to diversify or to extend their holdings outside the Tidewater turned to monetary solutions and the promise of a bank and access to public credit in an attempt both to meet current obligations and to expand their output.[31]

During these years of depression and of slow and partial recovery, one can discern a broad attempt at colonial "reform" of the mercantile system. Its principal aim was the repeal or revision of the anti-commercial legislation of the years 1764 and 1765, namely, the Revenue and Trade Acts of 1764 and 1766, the Stamp Act of 1765, and the Currency Act of 1764. Underlying this first "reform" movement was a conviction that metropolitan control of money, trade and manufacturing should be exercised wisely, that is, with an eye to the needs of all classes operating within Britain's trading community. However, while the various American interests offered conflicting explanations of and solutions to the accumulating problems of the period 1762 to 1767, the economic leadership generally felt that the cut in the molasses tax and the Parliamentary retreat from the Stamp Act would not go very far in promoting recovery. Consequently, when "hard times" returned after 1767, merchants as well as planters took another and a closer look at their place in Britain's commercial empire. A few, like Charleston merchant, Christopher Gadsden, began to talk of a complete break with the "formal system of Empire," with the Navigation Laws and the other mercantilist legislation, and the creation of "a free and open trade with all the powers of Europe, instead of the present, limited and restricted one both inwardly and outwardly with the discontented, monopolizing selfish Great Britain."[32] The majority, however, pushed for greater local control over what may be termed the "informal system of Empire," or the British commercial intrusions into the colonial economy. By this time the colonists' faith in the ability and willingness of parliament, and imperial authorities generally, to do something about the economic situation in America was

---

[31]The quote is from Thompson, "The Merchant in Virginia," p. 285; see also ibid., pp. 316-317 and Ernst, *Money and Politics* pp. 234-236.

[32]Robert M. Weir, ed., "Two Letters by Christopher Gadsden, Feb. 1766," *South Carolina Magazine of History,* 75 (1974): 175.

greatly weakened. The goal, therefore, was a larger measure of economic sovereignty.

This renewed effort after 1768 at economic relief and regeneration may be said to have formed the second broad attempt at "reform" of the British mercantile system in the years between the financial crises of 1763 and 1772. It focused on two related problems, the shortage of money and the balance of trade. The money question embraced short-run as well as secular considerations and was both a cause and a symptom of the current economic downturn. Merchants were already complaining that the scarcity of cash in 1767 had disrupted the marketing of goods, but in 1768 the cry reached a crescendo. Throughout America, in the tobacco no less than the commercial colonies, merchants, farmers and mechanics bemoaned the lack of sufficient currency to cover short-run contingencies such as an increasing volume of goods, an expanding demand for the payment of domestic debts and the declining values of property and land. Nor was this solely a matter of the paper currency supply, which was unquestionably contracting; similar complaints issued from New England where currency was on a limited metallic basis. The fact was that an insufficiency of money to meet transaction and liquidity demands preserved a problem common to all colonies and to all classes. Certain major secular changes were equally as important as short swings in creating these heavy cash requirements. The most significant were: the rapid growth of the colonial population, averaging almost 3.5 percent per annum in the decade after 1760; the increased production of grains and flour for the Southern European market after 1766, and the southward spread of the "Wheat Belt"; the "gathering strength of inter-colonial trade"; and the appearance of new, and the expansion of older and established, industries after 1760 such as iron, potash, whale products, hats, shoes, textiles, iron and furniture.[33]

But the urgent call for more and more money after 1768, for repeal of the Currency Act of 1764 and an end to British intervention in this area of the colonial economy, also involved another question: the contemporary belief that moderate injections of bills of credit by colonial land banks could provide a temporary relief for business slumps. The idea was that by providing a ready source of public credit at low interest local governments could stimulate short-run changes in

---

[33]Egnal, "Economic Development of the Colonies," pp. 217-222.

the pattern of spending, an idea especially appealing to hard-pressed merchants in the Middle colonies where domestic markets collapsed under the combined pressures of a glut of British imports and the stringency of money.[34]

New infusions of "fiat" money and public credit seemed to many to be "the soverign remedy" for the several ailments plaguing the colonial economy after 1767. And it undoubtedly received more public attention than any other of the economic "reforms" at the time. Still, paper money was only one of a number of specifics aimed at bolstering the weakened economy, expanding the area of local economic control, and serving the major colonial interests. The established merchants in the commercial colonies still faced "overcrowding" of British goods, and their efforts to curb vendue sales and convince British suppliers to cut off the flow of credit to shopkeepers and small traders were continuous, if unsuccessful. More promising were the programs, sponsored by many of the same merchants and by the local artisans, for domestic manufacturing and the production of goods for export to Britain. In a period of declining dry goods markets, this was good business. Over the long run it was also an acknowledged way to achieve a favorable trade balance, and thus stabilize and lower exchange rates, cut the swelling volume of sterling debts, reduce the pressure on money, and, generally, return the economy to a sounder position and to the control of the established elite.[35]

A short-run solution that embraced several of these propositions, and thereby appealed to a number of different interests, was non-importation, associated this time with the effort to repeal the Townshend Acts. The timing of, and reasons for, non-importation varied from place to place. The movement commenced in Boston and spread to New York, then Philadelphia. In all three cities the distressed dry goods merchants joined ranks with the artisans and mechanics whose own economic grievances now brought them into the main-

---

[34]Ernst, *Money and Politics,* p. 354.
[35]For an extensive discussion of this point see Ernst, " 'Ideology' and an Economic Interpretation of the Revolution," pp. 166-180.

stream of revolutionary activity. The broad objective of this new alliance was to inaugurate a program of "Oeconomy," industry, and frugality, a program designed to give both groups the chance to retrench as well as to boost local industry and employment. Next in line was Baltimore, a new and rapidly growing city that was enjoying a boom in wheat sales to Southern Europe. Adoption of non-importation in Baltimore seems to have been largely a matter of following the example of the Philadelphia merchants, with whom there were close commercial ties, and of meeting local artisan demands for manufacturing. Last among the great port cities to enter non-importation was Charleston, where the artisans also played a leading role. The latter maneuvered the old economic leadership of planters and merchants into granting them equality of representation on the committee to enforce the pact, a stratagem that provoked the first public discussion in America of the theory and practice of interest-group politics.

Finally, there was Norfolk. Norfolk, a comparatively small port just emerging as the local emporium for Virginia's growing trade with the West Indies, only agreed to non-importation in the summer of 1770. The action reflected less of an immediate concern with economic problems than a desire to establish Norfolk's leadership in the creation of a colony-wide mercantile organization for the advancement and protection of commercial interests. The objective was to build Norfolk into a great and independent metropolitan hub before the Dominion's new wheat trade fell prey to Philadelphia merchants (who already were buying up vast quantities of local grain), in the same way that the tobacco trade had earlier fallen prey to the merchants of London, Glasgow and Liverpool. A short-run goal was to reduce trade long enough for local merchants to collect their debts and to clear overstocked inventories. Whatever the precise reasons for non-importation in the several cities, by the beginning of 1770 merchants in the northern colonies had already sold off much excess stock. With rising prices, falling exchange rates and shortages of British goods reported in various lines, the merchants now swiftly and successfully moved to end non-importation despite opposition from the artisans, whose interests were not as easily served by reopening trade. Unwilling to grant any competitive advantage to their northern neighbors, merchants to the south also quickly abandoned their agreements and their artisan allies.[36]

From 1770 to mid-1771 the economic outlook in the commercial colonies noticeably brightened. Dry goods sales rode on the crest of an upsurge that lasted a full year before a combination of easy credit and booming British exports again toppled domestic markets. Conditions in the Southern European trade remained favorable for almost as long, while for the first time since the end of the French and Indian War West Indian markets encouraged large shipments of high-priced foodstuffs. There was even a rush of exports to the mother country.[37]

In the tobacco colonies the call for more money also continued undiminished throughout the late sixties. But refusals by imperial authorities to countenance additional issues of treasury notes or public loans momentarily directed attention away from currency to other problems, especially the balance of trade and long-term needs for improving the economy. In Virginia the solutions favored in the public press included: exploiting new markets through the diversification of agriculture; producing new and selected raw materials; encouraging secondary production of such items as flour and breadstuffs; prohibiting slave imports; reducing the purchase of foreign manufactures; manufacturing cheap cloth to replace imported dry goods; developing local cooperative stores to drive down the price of British goods; making the large plantations autarkic through the increasing use of black craftsmen; and accelerating the shift out of tobacco and into foodstuffs through the encouragement of urban marketplaces, such as Norfolk. These last few plans formed part of a larger scheme to lessen dependence on British exporters and, in general, to extend local control over the economy.[38]

Most of these policies for broadening the area of economic

---

[36]A general discussion of non-importation that presented a different point of view is Jensen, *Founding of a Nation,* chap. X. For non-importation in Baltimore see Arthur Schlesinger, Sr., *The Colonial Merchant and the American Revolution, 1763-1776* (New York, 1918), p. 138 and Thomas W. Griffith, *Annals of Baltimore* (Baltimore, 1824); in Charleston, Sellers, *Charleston Business,* pp. 203-220; in Norfolk, Ernst, *Money and Politics,* p. 236, and Thompson, "Merchant in Virginia," pp. 327-330.

[37]Sachs, "Business Outlook," pp. 214-218, and Hoffman, *Seeds of Dissension,* p. 97.

[38]Ernst, *Money and Politics,* pp. 236-239, Carville Earle and Ronald Hoffman, "Staple Crops and Urban Development in the Eighteenth-Century South," *Perspectives in American History* 10 (1976): 7-78.

sovereignty arose out of agricultural needs and reflected the interests of the ailing planters. Merchants were left to fend for themselves. They did so by establishing a number of short-lived trade organizations designed to cut down on growing competition, especially in the purchase of tobacco and sterling bills and in the sale of goods, and to facilitate payments among themselves. A measure of the difficulty with regulating competition in an area of decentralized marketing and credit structures is that fact that the volume of imported goods during non-importation actually increased. Other and similar far-ranging plans for encouraging growth also came up for discussion in neighboring North Carolina and Maryland.[39]

In 1769 and again in 1770 tobacco exports increased markedly over previous years. Prices held at relatively high levels. In 1771 exports reached an all-time high. Prices continued to be good, and sterling exchange rates remained steady and slightly below par. The future of the market seemed assured. In the wheat trade, which was becoming an increasingly important factor in the Virginia, Maryland and North Carolina economies, conditions appeared equally favorable, at least through 1769 and the first half of 1770. Prices and markets slumped somewhat thereafter, but had already begun to recover by the beginning of 1772. Under the circumstances, merchants as well as planters could look forward to profitable returns. In fact, the only weak spot in the economy remained the continuing scarcity of money and the failure of the currency supply to meet accelerating demands for cash. In Maryland this requirement was met in part by a loan office issue of £300,000 in the fall of 1769; in Virginia by a treasury emission of £30,000 in 1771 to cover flood-damaged tobacco; in North Carolina, by a debenture issue of £60,000 in 1771 to defray the costs of the War of the Regulation.[40]

II

In 1772 the British economy collapsed for the second time in ten years. The crash produced an international financial panic greater

[39]Ernst, *Money and Politics,* pp. 153-154, 204-205 and Thompson, "Merchant in Virginia," pp. 295-330.

[40]Ernst, *Money and Politics,* pp. 166-167, 237-239, 293-303; Hoffman, *Seeds of Dissension,* p. 96-97, and Price, "New Time Series for Scotland's and Britain's Trade with the Thirteen Colonies and States," p. 324.

than in 1763 and ushered in the second of the two worst colonial depressions. For many Americans this latest calamity accentuated the pressure for economic reform. For others it shattered any hopes of finding an easy solution to their problems within the existing system of mercantile empire. Indeed, the periodic and progressively more destructive credit and commercial upheavals seemed to be an endemic problem that signalled a serious crisis in the whole imperial order. After 1772, therefore, the debate over the economy increasingly centered not on the long-term advantages of empire as opposed to immediate needs for practical change and for greater local control in the sensitive areas of land, labor, marketing and money, but on the possibility of having to restructure the imperial framework or even to break the imperial connection altogether to protect American interests. Moreover, the practical plans and programs for economic reform that shaped the decade of Revolution following the end of the French and Indian War swiftly gave way before the rising independence movement and the disruptions of politics and war.

A commercial and speculative boom in Britain, the end of non-importation, and the "dumping" tactics of British houses again led to an "overcrowding" of American markets. Exports to the colonies in 1771 topped all previous marks, and the results were predictable. Merchants throughout the commercial colonies were already reporting markets "glutted and overdone" late in 1771. Nevertheless, shipments in 1772 declined only slightly as exporters chalked up their second best year in American sales, confident that conditions in the colonies represented a temporary disorder that would soon end. What nearly ended was the boom. On June 10, 1772, the London banking house of Neal, James, Fordyce and Down stopped payment, and it quickly became apparent "what an immense chain of circulation was carried on, and a great part of it without any solid foundation." London was in "an uproar; the whole city was in tears." Bankruptcies and stoppages became a common occurrence, and suicides, too. The failure in London of the Scottish firm of Bogle and Company led Robert Bogle to jump from a window and thereby setting the fashion for stockbrokers during the Great Crash of 1929. The wave of panic rapidly spread out across Britain, Europe and the Atlantic, and sent the American economy reeling. In all the colonial cities merchants voiced the same complaints: "A general scramble for liquidity had caused forced sales, falling prices, hoarding of cash and heavy inventory losses."[41]

The pall of gloom continued well into 1773, and while confidence showed some signs of returning early the next year, reports of dead stocks, slow payments, shortages of money and a contraction of credit generally persisted through 1774. By then, however, agitation over the Tea Act and the Intolerable Acts had greatly disrupted the normal market mechanisms. Conditions in the export trade were only marginally better. Foreign demand for commodities floundered in the last half of 1772, but strengthening markets in Southern Europe and the Caribbean raised prices in 1773 to former levels, where they generally held until upset by the threatened embargo in 1775. The same period also registered a marked decline in freight earnings in the British and West Indies trade.[42]

The crisis of 1772 struck the tobacco economies with even greater force as the spreading collapse overturned European tobacco markets. It was 1763 all over again. Tobacco prices plunged, British credit dried up, demand for payment swiftly mounted and the pressure on money intensified. Hard cash once more disappeared from circulation and drained back to Britain. Good sterling bills became scarce. Those available were high-priced and highly suspect. All classes suffered as the tobacco colonies struggled to pay for the massive imports of previous years, to retrench, to remain solvent, and, in a word, to survive. The depression wore on through 1773, and tobacco markets weakened further. But declining tobacco prices were not accompanied by falling prices of imported goods. Merchants opted instead to restrict credit and collect their outstanding debts, and acts of violence again became a familiar means of venting popular frustration. Conditions improved marginally in 1774 when pressures began to work themselves out, and the tobacco trade started slowly to recover. It was too late, however. By year's end, markets everywhere in America came

---

[41]The quotes are all from Ernst, *Money and Politics,* p. 309. The standard discussion of the collapse in 1772 is Richard B. Sheridan, "The British Credit Crisis of 1772 and the American Colonies," *Journal of Economic History,* 20 (1960): 161-186. See also Sachs, "Business Outlook," pp. 218-222; Hoffman, *Seeds of Dissension,* pp. 100-103; Thompson, "Merchant in Virginia," pp. 327-330; and Robert W. Coakley, "Virginia Commerce during the American Revolution" (Ph.D. dissertation, University of Virginia, 1949), chap. 8.

[42]Idem.

more and more under the influence of the gathering independence movement and the schemes for commercial retaliation against British "tyranny."[43]

The economic legacies of the Revolution were few. They were not great or enduring. They did not reverberate down through the ages. The plain fact is that fundamental business skills and knowledge in agriculture and manufacturing easily survived the upheavals of Revolution without any change at all. Economic events and issues of the period were not charged with transforming qualities. They did not give rise to any system of economic thought, to any approach to economics and economic problems that was radical — in the original sense of the word, that went to the roots — or even especially novel. After the Revolution, as before, Americans assessed their situation and their interests almost entirely in conventional short-run terms. Times were good when prices, markets and exchange rates were good, when currency and credit were adequate. If times were bad, the colonists' "solutions" to the problem were also customary: to adjust, retrench, turn to new products and explore new markets, end destructive over-competition, and enlist government in removing any barrier to trade and in easing the demand for money and creating a source of public credit. Whatever the limitations of these remedies, they at least gave contemporaries the feeling that the economy functioned in ways they understood and according to patterns that offered some possibility of practical control. And there was nothing that happened during the scant dozen years after 1763 to change their views of the matter. But if the economic history of the Revolution does not represent any serious break in the economic theory and practice of the age, the event did not pass without any economic consequences.

What I have suggested in this paper is that the most important economic legacy of the Revolution was the creation of an economic "reform" movement in the decade after 1763 that continued on past Independence. Scholars of the so-called "Critical Period" have generally failed to make this point, and to tie their discussion of economic

---

[43]Hoffman, *Seeds of Dissension,* pp. 101-102; Thompson, "Merchant in Virginia," pp. 344-348, and Coakley, "Virginia Commerce," chap. 8.

events and issues following 1781 to the Revolutionary experience for two reasons. First, there has been no broad synthesis of the economic history of the Revolution available for them to draw upon. Second, it has been a commonplace that the drive for economic change and the restructuring of government was a product of the conditions of sovereignty that came with Independence, of the wartime disruptions of money and trade, and of a new economic panic and depression after 1783. But this idea that the movement for the Constitution may be said to have originated in self-conscious efforts at economic "reform" at the time of the Revolution is a starting point for another and a different story.

THE DIPLOMATIC LEGACY OF AMERICA'S REVOLUTIONARY GENERATION

by Jerald A. Combs

For the past thirteen years I have walked into the first meeting of my course on the American Revolution and asked the students to pick the single word that best describes the United States. My purpose has been to show the students how the words they selected were related to the sense of national identity we have inherited from the American Revolution. Until the past few years, this was an easy task. My students selected words like "liberty" "democracy," "equality," or "opportunity." But in recent years I have been getting words like "imperialism," "aggression," "racism," and even "atrocity." In the 1960s the war in Vietnam and racial problems at home have destroyed the image of America as the exemplar and defender of freedom for many students.

Earlier students had seen America's foreign policy as worthy of the traditions of liberty handed down to us by the Revolutionary generation. They were particularly proud of America's role in the struggle against Adolph Hitler and Joseph Stalin. Recent students, on the other hand, have argued that we have betrayed the legacy of the American Revolution, or worse, that we have been living up to a darker side of that legacy, ravishing the Vietnamese just as the Founding Fathers ravished the Indians, British, French, or Spanish who got in their way.

Our present time of guilt and confusion is not a happy one in which to celebrate the nation's 200th birthday. It makes the self-congratulatory slogans dominating the Bicentennial seem inflated and fatuous. Yet I think a deep look at our Revolutionary legacy will show that the alternate vision, that of America the bestial, is equally fatuous. Our legacy comes neither from gods nor beasts, but from a remarkable generation of human beings like George Washington, Alexander Hamilton, Thomas Jefferson, John Adams, James Madison, and

James Monroe. These men led the United States not only through the Revolution, but also through the first critical half-century of the new nation's existence, culminating in the Monroe Doctrine of 1823. The diplomatic legacy of this Revolutionary generation still has an impact today, and a study of it should help us understand how we have come to the present confused state of our foreign policy.

Was the diplomatic legacy of the Revolutionary generation an idealistic one, a commitment to liberty, democracy, equality, and peace, as many of our nationalist historians would say? Or was it an aggressive, sometimes rapacious, struggle for economic and territorial expansion, as more radical historians would maintain? The remarkable thing about the diplomatic legacy of the Revolutionary generation is that it was both. The Founding Fathers' contribution to the diplomacy of their own time and to ours has been a series of policies and maxims that combined lofty ideals with quite selfish interests. They convinced themselves and their progeny not only that the advancement of American power and prosperity would benefit liberty and democracy, a rather simple rationalization of interests and ideals, but also that liberty and power, democracy and prosperity, could actually be mutually reinforcing rather than antagonistic goals. They did this in so compelling a way that until the last few years this idea has been an almost unquestioned premise of American foreign policy. Thus the United States holds itself up to the Third World as an example of the fact that new nations do not need to accept political dictatorship or wholesale property confiscation as the price of a descent standard of living. Unlike the Communist nations, America argues that emerging nations can have liberty, power, democracy, and prosperity all at the same time, without the need to sacrifice one to another.

When the American Revolution first began, the Founding Fathers were not at all convinced of this proposition. They believed that power and liberty were antagonists. A large measure of individual liberty would inevitably weaken a nation's domestic and foreign power, while great power would endanger liberty.[1] The Revolutionaries were willing to sacrifice considerable power to ensure their liberty.

This was the price they thought they were paying when they formed a republic instead of a monarchy. Each of the major principles of republicanism seemed likely to weaken the state. Government by

---

[1]See Bernard Bailyn, *The Origins of American Politics* (New York, 1968).

consent of the governed would be cumbersome and indecisive; the protection of individual rights would necessarily involve denying certain powers to the state; a commitment to equality would undermine social stability and unquestioning obedience to the states' rulers. Yet, despite the cost in national power, the Revolutionaries proceeded to establish state governments which relied on written constitutions with bills of rights to protect individuals against overweening state power. They reduced the powers of their states' executives or did away with the office of governor entirely. They shackled the federal government by requiring a two-thirds vote of all the states for the passage of any substantive legislation, and by giving the Congress no power to enforce its votes in any case. They protected private property against state taxing power by ensuring the state legislatures were beholden to property holding and tax-paying citizens. This, in their mind, was the ultimate protection of liberty. Property permitted a citizen to support himself and his family without dependence on government or employer; so long as his property was protected against confiscatory taxation, a property-holder would be free to exercise independent political judgment. This view of liberty, of course, coincided nicely with the Americans' economic interests in avoiding taxes and government regulation of overseas trade, but that fact does not undermine the considerable libertarian idealism which lay behind these concepts.[2]

With such a weak government, it is not surprising that the Revolutionaries euphoric expectations for the spread of liberty throughout the world were accompanied by deep anxieties. They knew from their study of history that republics were fragile, and that no such government had ever maintained itself for more than fifty years. Looking across the sea to a powerful and hostile set of European monarchies, seeing themselves surrounded by the colonies of Great Britain and Spain, they knew there would be no dearth of helping hands to aid the collapse of the infant government.

Yet beneath America's apparent weakness, the Revolutionary generation detected an enormous latent power. The nation's population was doubling every twenty-five years, and its land was as fertile as its people. The United States had an extensive seacoast and good harbors, with many rivers to furnish transportation from inland areas

---

[2]See Gordon S. Wood, *The Creation of the American Republic, 1776-1787* (Chapel Hill, 1969).

to the sea. Its western boundaries, ably negotiated at the end of the Revolution by Benjamin Franklin, John Jay, and John Adams, encompassed territory far beyond the limits of the nation's actual settlements. These boundaries extended to the Mississippi River on the west and to the Great Lakes on the north, giving access to the key transportation routes of North America's interior. Control of these waterways, in the days before the railroad, would mean domination of much of the continent. With the nation's population exploding, while those of the neighboring British and Spanish colonies remained fairly static, America's potential power was enormous.

Spain, hoping to short-circuit the future, closed the Mississippi at its mouth to U.S. navigation immediately after the Revolution. Yet even at this nadir of America's foreign relations, Thomas Jefferson could proclaim, "My fear is that [the Spanish] are too feeble to hold [the border territories] till our population can be sufficiently advanced to gain it from them peice by peice [sic]."[3]

Great Britain, of course, posed a more substantial threat than Spain. Still, England was 3,000 miles away and had already suffered defeat at the hands of the Americans. The United States, geographically remote from the strongest nations of the eighteenth century, in position to dominate the key waterways of North American, surrounded by a vacuum of power, was a potential giant among nations as it began to grow in population and agriculture. Even England recognized this fact. One London newspaper bewailed the results of the Revolution with the lament that now "Yankees shall become High and Mighty Lords!"[4]

The vision of a powerful and prosperous country tempted the Founding Fathers. Yet they were fearful of the effects of power and prosperity on republicanism. So the Revolutionaries embarked on an attempt to weld their ideals and interests together. Through the development of a series of policies, maxims, and rationales, they succeeded in demonstrating both to their own satisfaction and that of future Americans that indeed America could have power and liberty at the same time. This became the essence of the American dream. It is the primary diplomatic legacy of the Revolutionary generation.

---

[3]Thomas Jefferson to Archibald Stuart, January 25, 1786, *The Papers of Thomas Jefferson,* Julian P. Boyd, ed., 21 vols. to date (Princeton, 1950-), 9: 218.
[4]*The Public Advertiser,* January 31, 1783.

One of the first steps in rationalizing power and liberty was the Constitution. It created a strong executive, it lessened the power of the states to block decisive federal action, it gave the federal government power to tax, and it laid no roadblocks in the way of regulating foreign trade or raising an army and navy. Fears that these provisions would expand power at the expense of liberty were somewhat allayed by the checks and balances in the Constitution, by addition of a national Bill of Rights, and by the knowledge that Washington would be the first president.

Not all the people's fears were laid to rest, however. They had learned from the greatest political theorists of the day that a republic could not survive if it attempted to rule a large area, and the United States was a very large country by eighteenth-century standards. Political scientists of the day believed that a large area required strong and decisive rule to keep its dispersed and heterogeneous population from quarreling and splitting. If the government became strong enough to do this, it would no longer be republican; if it did not become strong enough, it would descend into anarchy. But James Madison, in his famous *Federalist* Number 10, effectively countered this view. He claimed that a republic could actually fare better in a large area than in a small one. In a small area the population would probably divide into only two or three interests. The majority interest could well be a permanent one and impose its will on the minority without challenge. A large area would contain many interests. None could expect to be in a permanent majority. Thus every faction, knowing it would sooner or later be among the minority, would see the benefit of protecting minority rights and liberty.[5]

The Federalist defenders of the Constitution made yet another major contribution to the rationalization of power and liberty. They explained that a system of Federalism would divide power between local and national governments. Opponents of national power had claimed that states would struggle continually with the federal government for sovereignty until one or the other was victorious, thereby

---

[5]See William Appleman Williams, *Contours of American History* (Cleveland, 1961). Williams sees Madison's argument as one designed to encourage expansion. Given the context of the *Federalist Papers,* I think Madison was being more defensive than that. He was trying to convince his constituents that a republican form of government could rule a nation as large as the United States already was, not that it could rule an area even larger. Nonetheless, the argument was easily adapted to later expansionist movements.

destroying the system of checks and balances, and liberty with it. But the *Federalist Papers* pointed out that sovereignty lay with neither the national government nor the states, but with the people as a whole. If either the states or the federal government gained too much power, the people could step in to rectify the situation by amending the Constitution. Thus the federal system, which permitted a disparate people to live together by balancing local agencies responsive to local conditions against the federal government concerned with national and international policy, could be preserved from degeneration.[6]

Another important contribution made by the Revolutionary generation to this federal system was the admission of new states as equal entities under the Constitution. It was this policy, along with the division of power between federal and local governments, which permitted the United States to govern relatively efficiently and happily such a large area. The only relevant precedents for governing so large a territory were those of the Roman and British empires. There were many Americans who believed that colonialism was the only means by which America could rule its western territories, fearing that the wild westerners might otherwise someday outnumber and dominate the more civilized East. But Virginia, prodded by Thomas Jefferson and James Monroe, refused to turn over its western territorial claims to the federal government unless the new territories were guaranteed the right to enter the union as equal, self-governing states. Since Virginia's western claims were stronger and more extensive than those of any other state, the nation was forced to accede. So, in a stroke, one of the major barriers to the growth of American power was struck down. The nation's expansion would not necessarily lead to colonial problems like those that had disrupted the British Empire.

This new confidence in the compatibility of republicanism and expansionism laid the basis for the march to the Pacific. It made possible American dominance of such a large and rich area that the United States became the super power in the twentieth century. The Revolutionary generation's confidence that America could have both liberty and power has undergirded our foreign policy from that day to this.

But how did the Founding Fathers translate this commitment to

[6]*Federalist* Number 46; see also Gordon Wood, *Creation of the American Republic,* pp. 543-547.

domestic liberty and power into specific foreign policies? What diplomatic maxims have come down to us as the legacy of the Revolutionary generation? Until recently most Americans would probably have echoed Ernest May, one of our country's leading diplomatic historians, who described these traditions as "pacifist and isolationist."[7] To what extent do the policies of pacifism and isolationism actually constitute the diplomatic legacy of the Revolution?

Obviously they do have some significance in early American foreign policy, especially with regard to Europe. The Revolutionary generation would not have used the word "isolationism," however. "Isolationism" was coined in this century as a term of opprobrium. The Revolutionaries would have called their policy "neutrality" or occasionally "non-entanglement." Although the Revolutionary generation recognized and welcomed America's growing power, it had no wish to become entangled in wars of the major powers of Europe. These men wanted to take advantage of America's geographical remoteness from Europe to isolate their country from such wars. This policy would also permit them to avoid a standing army and the heavy military expenditures which the nations of Europe were compelled to accept but which the vacuum of power surrounding the United States permitted our nation to escape. In 1776 Thomas Paine summarized this policy well in his pamphlet, *Common Sense:* "As Europe is our market for trade, we ought to form no partial connection with any part of it. It is the true interest of America to steer clear of European contentions. . . ."

Notice that although Paine wished to avoid European alliances and wars, he did not want to isolate America from the commerce of Europe. In fact, one of the major reasons for renouncing partial connections was to avoid contentions that would hinder trade. Some Americans realized that if the United States maintained extensive commerce with Europe, we might well be drawn into European wars despite our political neutrality. Jefferson, for one, warned that commerce would mean "frequent wars without a doubt," for Americans' "property will be violated on the sea, and in foreign ports, their persons will be insulted, imprisoned, etc. for pretended debts, contracts, crimes, contraband, etc. These insults must be represented, even if we had

---

[7]Ernest R. May, *The World War and America Isolation, 1914-1917* (Cambridge, Mass., 1959), p. 3.

no feelings." He thought it might be better for the peace and liberty of the United States "to practice neither commerce nor navigation."[8] But Jefferson knew such an idea was hopeless. His countrymen were unwilling to sacrifice the power and prosperity that came with foreign trade.

Instead, Americans combined their commitment to foreign trade with their desires for neutrality and peaceful relations with Europe. Trade, many argued, would actually bring peace.[9] Nations would become dependent on one another for economic necessities and thus be reluctant to fight one another. Trade could even be used as a substitute for war. Commercial retaliation might compel other nations to respect America's rights, relieving the United States of the need to resort to military action. As Americans had rationalized power and liberty, so they rationalized peace and neutrality with extensive foreign commerce. Jefferson, too, would come to accept this rationalization, proclaiming in his First Inaugural Address in 1801 that America sought "Peace, commerce with all nations; entangling alliances with none."

Prior to the twentieth century, the United States was tempted by two types of situations to abandon its commitment to neutrality in European affairs. The first was a threat to the nation's own security. During the Revolution itself, the United States signed a perpetual alliance with France to secure that nation's aid against England, and was ready to sign treaties with Spain and other nations as well. The French Treaty of 1778, which was ended by mutual agreement in 1800, was the only such alliance signed by the United States until 1942. Nevertheless the United States showed itself ready to accept alliances in times of emergency in several later situations. Jefferson professed a willingness to "marry ourselves to the British fleet" if France acquired New Orleans and blocked the Mississippi River. Monroe, Jefferson, and Madison came close to accepting a British alliance while shaping the Monroe Doctrine in 1823. Even Washington's Farewell Address made provisions for such alliances, counseling the United States "to steer clear of permanent alliances with any portion

---

[8]Jefferson to John Jay, August 23, 1785, *Papers of Thomas Jefferson,* Boyd, ed., 8: 426-527; Jefferson to G. K. Hogendorp, October 13, 1785, ibid., 633.

[9]See Felix Gilbert's discussion of the antecedents of this view in *To the Farewell Address: Ideas of Early American Foreign Policy* (Princeton, 1961). In the paperback edition, title and subtitle are reversed.

of the foreign world," but adding that the country should "trust to temporary alliances for extraordinary emergencies."

The second type of situation that tempted the United States to intervention in European affairs was America's ideological sympathy for republican revolutions. The French Revolution of the 1790s, the Latin American revolutions of the Napoleonic era, the Greek Revolution of the 1820s, and the general European revolutions of 1848 excited the sympathy of most Americans. At the same time, these revolutions promised material benefits to the United States. Such revolutions could be expected to weaken the hostile powers of Europe and even to replace some of them with republican regimes that might actually be sympathetic to the United States. In addition, Americans expected republics to be more peaceful than monarchies. Republics would be governed by ordinary people, for whom war meant death and taxes, rather than by kings, for whom war meant glory.

Despite these ideological temptations and occasional security threats, the United States maintained its neutral posture toward Europe through the eighteenth and the nineteenth centuries. But this neutrality was no more pacifist than it was isolationist. A few of the Revolutionary generation advocated a restrained, impartial, and gentle neutrality. For others, however, neutrality meant an aggressive pursuit of neutral rights. This was one of the major disputes between the Founding Fathers, helping to lead to the formation of the first two parties, the Federalists and the Republicans. Alexander Hamilton and the Federalists, often with Washington's support, called for restraint in pursuing neutral rights during the wars between France and Great Britain, fearing that war with England might destroy the infant republic. Thomas Jefferson, James Madison, and the Republicans condemned this neutrality as appeasement, and advocated a more active protection of our neutral rights. After Jefferson swept the Federalists from office, the Republicans pursued their vigorous course first with the Embargo and finally with war itself in 1812. Although many Americans opposed the declaration of war in 1812, within months of the conclusion of the war, they capitulated to a broad national concensus which agreed that it had been a glorious and proper action. From that time on, neutrality was regarded as an active rather than a passive policy. When Charles Francis Adams praised a policy of restraint toward Britain during and after the

Civil War, and cited the neutral policies of the Founding Fathers as support for his position, he was roundly attacked. One historian told him that the Founding Fathers had followed a "spirited and manly" neutrality quite in contrast to Adams' own "weak-kneed" conduct as minister to Great Britain.[10] Neutrality, then, could take forms that were far from pacifist.

Nevertheless, a study of the Revolutionary generation's policies toward Europe could well conclude that it was peaceful and neutral, if not "pacifist and isolationist." While sympathizing with republican revolutions and being willing to form European alliances in an emergency, the United States did avoid serious intervention in European politics. Still the nation insisted on the continuance of its foreign trade, even at the risk of war. Meanwhile the United States avoided large expenditures for standing armies or navies, and prided itself on its enlightened, republican, peaceful, non-interventionist policies.

But America's foreign policy toward Europe was only part of the diplomatic legacy of the Revolutionary generation. What about its policies toward other parts of the world?

In Asia, the Mediterranean, and the distant countries of South America, the Revolutionary generation did not have many significant interests. Consequently, neither these men nor their immediate descendents saw much distinction between their policy in Europe and their policies in these areas. That policy was non-intervention. Thus Martin Van Buren wrote to several of our ministers in Latin America in 1829 that "It was the ancient and well-settled policy of this government not to interfere with the internal concerns of any foreign country," a policy which he said was "regarded by its constituents with a degree of reverence and submission but little, if anything, short of that which is entertained for the Constitution itself."[11] Surely Van Buren was correct about the sentiments of most Americans. But those sentiments were severely qualified. Americans made a distinction between political intervention, of which they disapproved, and non-political intervention for the protection of the lives and property of American citizens abroad, which they and all European nations of the time

---

[10]A review by Henry Dawson in *The Historical Magazine,* 2d Series, 9 (1871): 129-150.

[11]Martin Van Buren to the Minister to Colombia, June 9, 1829, quoted in John Bassett Moore, ed., *International Law Digest,* 8 vols., (Washington, D.C., 1906), 6: 14; Van Buren to the minister to Mexico, October 16, 1829, ibid., 14-15.

regarded as perfectly proper. Such interventions could range from forced debt collections to bombardment of towns imprisoning American sailors. There were over one hundred so-called non-political interventions by the United States prior to 1900. Of course, as the *Mayaguez* incident of May 1975 showed, there is a thin line between political and non-political intervention. But Americans were convinced that there was a difference. They could support non-political interventions, such as the war with the Barbary pirates (1801-5), while still considering their country an anti-interventionist nation. Naturally, most non-political intervention took place in Asia and Latin America, where domestic order was tenuous and where governments were incapable of resisting intervention from abroad.

A second major exception to the policy of non-intervention in distant countries was the Monroe Doctrine of 1823. In a sense this was actually a non-interventionist policy, warning Europe away from attempts to subvert Latin American governments or obtain further colonies in the Western Hemisphere. At the time it was clear that our government could not enforce this policy, let alone use the Doctrine to stake out its own empire in Latin America. Great Britain was the dominant outside power in South America and was expected to remain so. Later, the Monroe Doctrine served as a basis for a more active and interventionist policy, ultimately being used by Theodore Roosevelt and later presidents to justify American intervention in the internal affairs of Latin American nations as a means of preventing European powers like Germany from gaining a foothold in the Western Hemisphere. But wholesale American intervention in Asia and Latin America would wait until the turn of the century; and though certain attitudes and doctrines of the Founding Fathers set the stage for later interventions, we might well regard their diplomatic legacy in these areas to be only slightly more interventionist than their policy toward Europe.

The same cannot be said for the Revolutionary generation's diplomatic legacy in North America and the Caribbean. Here the policy was aggressive, pugnacious, even rapacious. The Revolutionaries fought continuous wars with the Indians; twice they attacked Canada; they purchased Louisiana with a measure of propriety, but they secured Florida by trickery and military pressure. Later their descendents would conquer much of the west by making unjust war on

Mexico. How is it, then, that most American people can still regard early American foreign policy as having been "pacifist and isolationist"?

One way to avoid the obvious implications of United States policy in North America has been to regard this as essentially domestic rather than foreign policy. We have covered it under rubrics like "The March Westward" or "the gallant adventures of the pioneers on the frontier." We have thus avoided charging the aggressiveness exhibited by Americans on this continent to our diplomatic record and continued to call ourselves pacifists and neutralists.

Rationalizing American policy in North America took more than this, however, even for the Revolutionary generation. Many Americans could not help but see some conflict between America's democratic ideology and the westward march of conquest. New Englanders especially, urged some restraint in the handling of the Indians, although this came after they had already "solved" their "Indian problem" by exterminating or removing the natives. The issue of slavery also provided some rein on all-out expansionism, with northerners and southerners alike restraining their enthusiasms for expansion when it seemed likely that a new territory would adopt the opposing social system. These turned out to be flimsy bonds, however, as the riches of the west beckoned, as technology provided ways to communicate with and control far-flung territories, and as time-tried rationales quieted the consciences of the bumptious citizens of the United States.

Primary among those rationales was the federal system established by the Founding Fathers. America's march westward expanded the area of freedom, it was said, since we freed territories from colonial status under monarchical powers like Spain and Britain and brought them in as equal, self-governing states. Often we moved in at the behest of the inhabitants themselves, as in Texas, West Florida, and California, where the residents rebelled against their colonial masters and asked to be annexed to the Union. Thus freedom, republican revolution, and anti-imperialism were all served by the expansion of the United States; liberty and power were still entwined in America's destiny.

This did not quite dispose of the fact that many of the inhabitants of the western territories annexed by the United States came into the nation unwillingly. Other rationales had to be devised. Perhaps most important of these was the fact that there were so few of these people blocking America's westward march. The United States seemed to face an "empty continent." We were not imperialists, like the Europeans, conquering and exploiting foreign civilizations. We were expansionists, developing land that was poorly used by its few motley inhabitants. As the *New York Morning News* put it in 1845,

> . . . our way lies not over trampled nations, but through desert wastes, to be brought by our industry and energy within the domain of art and civilization. We are contiguous to a vast portion of the globe, untrodden save by the savage and the beast. . . . Public sentiment with us repudiates possession without use. . . . It has sent our adventurous pioneers to the plains of Texas, will carry them to the Rio del Norte, and even that boundary, purely nominal and conventional as it is, will not stay them on their march to the Pacific, the limit which nature has provided. . . . Rapacity and spoilation cannot be the features of this magnificent enterprise, not perhaps because we are above and beyond the influence of such views, but because circumstances do not admit of their operation. We take from no man; the reverse rather — we give to man.[12]

The Indians, along with the beasts, were merely the objects that kept the continent from being completely empty. Indian tribes were defined as "domestic dependent nations," to be dealt with by the Secretary of War rather than the Secretary of State. Their title to their lands was tenuous, at best. As barbarians, they were considered to have few rights against the needs of a "superior" civilization.

Citizens of the United States could push aside those they considered savages with few qualms. The other European inhabitants of North America — Spaniards, Mexicans, British, and French — posed a slightly different problem for American consciences. But in most areas of North America, the Europeans were even fewer than the Indians. Their populations were static, their governments backward, and they were regarded by Americans as culturally inferior, lazy, and incompetent. They, too, could be seen as little more than barriers to progress. Nevertheless, where there was a large and hostile European population, the United States steered clear. For instance, after the Mexican War, when American troops had actually conquered Mexico City and could well have claimed all of Mexico, thoughtful

---

[12]*New York Morning News,* October 13, 1845.

Americans quickly abandoned the prospect. Annexing empty areas from which the few angry but incompetent inhabitants would be quickly overwhelmed by Anglo-American immigrants was one thing, ruling a hostile and concentrated population was quite another. It would demand a standing army, large military expenditures, and oppressive government. That would be imperialism rather than expansionism, calling for the sacrifice of too much in the way of liberty for too little in the way of power and prosperity.

What, then, can be said of the diplomatic legacy of the Revolutionary generation? To label it "pacifist and isolationist" is surely foolish. Such a label may indeed have some relevance to the Revolutionaries' policy toward Europe; but, in fact, the Founding Fathers had three foreign policies — one toward Europe; a second toward Asia, the Mediterranean, and the most distant nations of South America; and a third toward North America and the nearer nations of Latin America.

The diplomatic legacy of the Revolutionary generation toward Europe counseled a minimum of political entanglement but demanded extensive trade with that continent even at the risk of political involvement and war. It called for neutrality in European quarrels, although this came to mean an aggressive pursuit of neutral rights rather than a policy of restraint. It permitted temporary alliances with European powers in emergencies. It sympathized with republican revolutions, although it did not expect much to come of these movements where the inhabitants did not have proper Anglo-Saxon genes and experience in self-government.

The diplomatic legacy toward Asia, the Mediterranean, and the more distant parts of South America was somewhat different. Here the United States had only two significant interests, those of trade and later the protection of a few missionaries. The Revolutionary generation sympathized with anti-imperialist revolutions in these areas, such as those in Greece and South America. The Founding Fathers knew that these revolutions would open markets formerly monopolized by the mother countries of Europe, and hoped that the establishment of republics would encourage a world-wide movement toward peaceful, free trading, self-governing nations. Nevertheless, they refused active intervention on behalf of the revolutionaries, confining their interventions to what they considered non-political actions for the protection of American lives and property abroad.

The diplomatic legacy toward North America and the Latin American nations in close proximity to the borders of the United States diverged still further from that toward Europe. Here American policy was expansive, aggressive, and far from pacifist and non-interventionist. The United States did not arm itself as the European powers did. With the vacuum of power existing in the western hemisphere, America had no need to do so. While pioneer settlers served as the cutting edge of the frontier, the United States swept aside Indians, French, Spanish, Mexicans, and British in the march to the Pacific, meanwhile casting covetous eyes on Cuba and the Caribbean. Still the Revolutionary generation considered its policy peaceful, anti-imperialist, and non-interventionist. The Founding Fathers deemed the continent to be relatively empty, they considered the west's few inhabitants to be savages or inferiors, and they condemned the nations competing with the United States for the continent as monarchical and colonialist. Rescuing the west from European imperialists and native savages, guiding it toward independence as a fellow republic, or bringing it into the union as a group of equal, self-governing states, was seen not as imperialism, but as simple expansion. Thus the United States reconciled its ideals with its interests, and the Revolutionary generation convinced the country that it could have power and liberty at the same time.

What has become of the Revolutionary generation's diplomatic legacy in our own time? Some historians would argue that the legacy is still with us. The Founding Fathers' aggressive policy toward North America, now backed by immense economic and military power, has spilled out of our own continent into the entire world. We have dominated and exploited all the nations we could until recent revolutions began to roll us back. These historians would argue that the capitalist system bequeathed us by the Revolutionaries made such imperialism inevitable. It bred selfish competitiveness into the American character. It forced America to expand, providing ever new economic frontiers to divert the poor from the revolutionary idea of socializing and equalizing economic holdings in the United States. Thus any idea that the diplomatic legacy of the Revolution included real commitment to liberty, peace, or isolationism they would deem mere propaganda.[13]

Certainly they are right to point out a measure of continuity between America's expansive policy in North America during the Revolutionary era and America's policy in this century. Certainly they are correct when they deny that America's sole concern, then or now, was with liberty, peace, and isolationism. But they, like those who claimed that the diplomatic legacy of the Revolution was indeed pacifist and isolationist, are looking at only one part of that legacy. They are also dead wrong in failing to see that a concern for power and liberty had at least as much influence on American foreign policy as economic interest. The significant thing for us to understand is that the Revolutionary generation succeeded in rationalizing all of these goals, and convincing Americans that they could achieve them all without sacrificing any one of them. Thus we have seen that many Americans really believed trade was beneficial to all parties involved because it encouraged world interdependence and peace as well as prosperity. "The Open Door" did not constitute simply a means of dominating other countries through control of their economies. The Founding Fathers believed that private property and a free economy were security against tyrannical government. We may now see some of the shortcomings of that view; but one should not doubt the sincerity with which the view was held in the previous centuries. The fact is that the world has changed, and the ideas and rationales willed us by the Revolutionary generation do not work the same way for us as they did for them.

In fact, many would argue that modern conditions have brought the United States to reject much of the diplomatic legacy of the Revolutionary generation. As we became an industrial power, we abandoned free trade for a protective economic policy, and in turn abandoned that for a selective policy designed to protect our domestic market while expanding into foreign ones. We have abandoned isolationism for the role of global policeman, signing numerous entangling alliances. We have abandoned an anti-military policy for a huge military establishment. We have abandoned our support for revolution

---

[13]See William Appleman Williams, *Contours of American History;* Lloyd C. Gardner, Walter F. LaFeber, and Thomas J. McCormick, *The Creation of the American Empire* (Chicago, N.Y.; 1973); Gabriel Kolbo, *The Roots of American Foreign Policy: An Analysis of Power and Purpose* (Boston, 1969).

as those revolutions turned from republican to socialist ideologies; and we have abandoned anti-imperialism for support of European colonialism, even to the point of replacing European nations as colonial masters when they were forced to give up their empires.

Despite these changes, Americans have not been terribly conscious of having lost the Revolution's diplomatic legacy until very recently, following the Vietnam debacle. How did Americans of the pre-Vietnam era rationalize these tremendous deviations from the policies of the Revolutionary generation with their continued abstract devotion to the diplomatic legacy of the Founding Fathers?

First, in a most significant way, modern foreign policy did not violate the Revolution's diplomatic legacy in the eyes of most Americans. The Founding Fathers sought the twin goals of liberty and power, and twentieth-century America seemer to have achieved them, using its global power to protect the "free world."

Second, the achievement of enormous power made interventions (which would have been major incidents in the nineteenth century) seem minor annoyances in the twentieth. Most Americans failed to see the full extent of American interventions because American power allowed them to be carried on so quickly and silently. As long as these interventions were quiet, cheap, and did not involve the threat of a major war, the American public tolerated them. This allowed vested interests to dictate policy in areas which existed only on the fringes of the American public's attention. Corporations, missionaries, and diplomats stationed in Asia, the Mediterranean, or South America could call for military help in response to their own narrow interests, justifying this by good Revolutionary precedents such as the protection of American lives and property, the enforcement of the Monroe Doctrine against European imperialism, or even the defense of liberty against domestic or foreign tyranny. Because so many of these interventions were indeed cheap and quick, the American public had little time or cause to worry about them as violations of their Revolution's heritage.

When lengthier and more serious interventions occurred, the American people demanded much more thorough justification. They rallied fully behind the Spanish American War because it did oppose Spanish imperialism, while defending the Monroe Doctrine and significant U.S. strategic and economic interests in Cuba. Having destroyed the Spanish empire, and not knowing quite what to do with the Philippines, the public briefly supported taking them as American colonies. But the guerrilla war that errupted in the islands, along with the difficulties that occupation of the Philippines created with Japan, forcibly reminded many Americans of their Revolutionary generation's diplomatic legacy. Soon, even foreign policy activists like Theodore Roosevelt regretted the decision to keep the islands. Americans could consider imperialism in the Philippines a great aberration, one compensated for by our voluntary abandonment of a large territory we were unwilling to grant statehood.

American intervention into World War I posed a different problem. Justified at first on the good Revolutionary grounds that we were defending our neutral rights against submarine warfare and at the same time making the world safe for democracy, our intervention, like that in the Philippines, came to be seen as a mistake and an aberration, brought about by British propaganda, Wall Street bankers, and munitions makers. So, by the 1930s, the United States readopted a neutrality policy, combining it with a "good neighbor" policy in Latin America. Once again the United States seemed in harmony with its diplomatic heritage.

World War II changed all of that. A whole generation, traumatized by the war, adopted the lesson of Munich. Appeasement of Communist aggressors like Stalin would bring World War III, just as appeasement of Hitler had brought World War II. America had to abandon neutrality, become a global policeman, and stop Communist aggression wherever it reared its head.

This required huge standing military forces, the creation of numerous entangling alliances, opposition to revolutions that might be subject to Communist influence, in short the abandonment of almost every maxim of the Revolutionary generation's diplomatic legacy. It had been difficult enough to rationalize the foreign policies of the Founding Fathers with such deviations as the conquest of the Philippines, World War I, and the Big Stick in Latin America, but bringing traditional policies into line with the Cold War role of global policeman would be even harder.

In the short run, squaring the Cold War with the Founding Fathers was not terribly important. The threats of Hitler and Stalin were so obvious in the 1940s that most Americans could be rallied to interventionism by calls to defend the libertarian ideals of the revolution throughout the world against aggression or else face another Munich. But if the United States was to contain the Soviet Union over the long term, a fuller and more sophisticated rationale would be needed. Otherwise Americans would revert to their old maxims as soon as the obvious threat to their security diminished. Opinion leaders of the country would have to be won to a new vision of foreign policy, a new set of maxims which would explain in a sophisticated and credible way the need for America to remain politically and militarily, as well as commercially, involved in the outside world.

This was done by the conglomeration of historians, politicians, philosophers, and columnists we have come to call the Realists, men like Reinhold Niebuhr, George Kennan, Walter Lippman, Hans Morgenthau, and a bright young Harvard professor named Henry Kissinger. They hoped to convince the American people that United States foreign policy had been based too long on a self-righteous and parochial sense of ideological superiority. This had led either to isolationism to protect the United States against the evils of the outside world, or to crusading, all-out wars to purge the world of evil and make it "safe for democracy." Americans should adopt a more moderate and realistic policy based firmly on national interest and dedicated to the maintenance of a worldwide balance of power, they claimed. Limited goals wedded firmly to adequate power would be the best hope for peace in a fallible world. Thus America's policy should be containment of Russia and Communism, not their eradication. The Realists hoped to achieve a steady, long-term policy which neither provoked nuclear war by pursuit of utopian goals nor collapsed before Communist pressure in another Munich.

To achieve such steadiness in a democracy, where volatile public opinion was far more influential than in a dictatorship, the American people had to be educated to a sophisticated overview of diplomacy. Hans Morgenthau's book, *In Defense of the National Interest,* was a major landmark in this effort. In it, Morgenthau was able to convince many that the Realist outlook was in line with the diplomatic legacy of the Revolutionary generation.[14] He called the early national period, "the golden age of American diplomacy." The Founding Fathers, he said, had supported liberty in the world, but never to the

[14]Hans Morgenthau, *In Defense of the National Interest: A Critical Examination of American Foreign Policy* (New York, 1951).

point that it endangered the national interest or the balance of power. They had realized that so long as there was a balance of power in Europe, European nations would be too afraid of one another to devote extensive resources to a war in North America. Thus, even during the Revolution, America's leaders had not tried to cripple England permanently, but to leave her powerful enough to check their own ally, France. They had tried to remain neutral in the wars of the French Revolution; and despite the high ideals of the Monroe Doctrine, they had not risked serious intervention in South America.

So long as the balance of power existed in Europe, the Founding Fathers counseled neutrality, non-entanglement, and the devotion of resources to production rather than to the building of military power. But for the Revolutionary generation, according to Morgenthau, these were policies, not dogmas. These men were ready to accept temporary alliances in an emergency, and to intervene in world politics if America's power allowed it and national security required it.

Morgenthau and the Realists argued that this century had witnessed the destruction of the European balance of power, thus endangering America's interests and security. In both World Wars, the United States had intervened to stop the unification of Europe under an aggressive and militaristic country, but in neither case had the American public fully understood its country's role. Americans had seen their participation in both world wars as altruistic sacrifices for the protection of the liberties of others, rather than realistic interventions for the protection of their own interests and the restoration of the balance of power. Thus, after World War I, when it was clear the world had not been made safe for democracy, they retreated, leaving Europe to plunge into war once again when Germany threatened the balance.

Now, after World War II, the power of Europe had been permanently diminished. Germany, France, and England were shattered, leaving Russia supreme on the continent, with only the United States capable of checking its expansion. A return to non-entanglement and disarmament in such a situation would not be a return to the diplomatic legacy of the Revolutionary generation, but a betrayal of their flexible and realistic policies which later generations had erected into dogmas.

Until the fiasco in Southeast Asia, the Realist rationale for the

Cold War received wide-spread acceptance. In fact, with its emphasis on restraint and its de-emphasis of inflated ideology, the Realist outlook was often the refuge of liberals and moderates against more aggressive Cold Warriors. People like Morgenthau, Kennan, and Lippmann were among the earliest and most articulate opponents of the Vietnam War. They argued that the war was not vital to America's interests, that lack of public support in Southeast Asia made it unwinnable, and that it repelled rather than attracted the major powers of the area we needed to help contain China — nations like India, Japan, and Indonesia.

Despite these counsels of restraint from leading Realists, the Vietnam War has gone far to discredit the Realist outlook and with it much of the more sophisticated rationale for the Cold War. Vietnam was seen at its outset by the Realists as an attempt by the Communists to circumvent containment with wars of national liberation, wars that America's alliances and conventional forces could do little about. The war in Vietnam became a test case for America's ability to maintain the balance of power against this kind of threat. But Vietnam turned out to be more a civil war than aggression exported from Moscow or Peking. In addition, it soon became clear that American ideas of liberty and humanity were no better served by the South Vietnamese government than by the Viet Cong. Since America was moving toward detente with the Soviet Union, and since no great material interests were involved in Vietnam, it became increasingly less clear to Americans why they were fighting there. Atrocities, accepted in World War II or Korea as tragic but inevitable concomitants of modern warfare, seemed intolerable in Vietnam, where the threat to the United States was so much less imminent. In the process, the policy of containment and the Realist arguments which had supported it came under severe attack.

Henry Kissinger, like most of the Realists, understood this situation. He desperately wanted the United States out of Vietnam. But he wanted even more strongly to maintain the balance of power. He feared that a precipitate retreat from Indo-China would weaken the United States too much in the eyes of China and the Soviet Union, tempting them to aggression and destroying the detente. To prevent this, he and President Nixon took severe actions at enormous risk, mining and bombing North Vietnam and invading Cambodia.

Fortunately for Nixon and Kissinger, peace was made. But disillusionment with the Cold War had already set in. The Munich analogy had been replaced by the Vietnam analogy. Appeasement would no longer need nearly as much justification as intervention. Kissinger obviously believes that this movement has gone too far. The use of the Central Intelligence Agency to topple the government of Salvador Allende in 1973 in Chile shows a willingness to intervene to support even infamous regimes in order to prevent the erosion of the alliances balancing China and Russia.

Kissinger is probably right in thinking that Americans will accept interventions on the cheap, such as Chile or the *Mayaguez* incident. But the support is very thin. The disillusionment with the Cold War and with past American administrations is very deep. It is time for a complete reassessment of our foreign policy to redefine the occasions and areas in which American intervention would be justified. In that process, Americans should reconsider and reevaluate the diplomatic legacy of the Revolutionary generation and of the interpretation placed on it by the Realists.

About certain basic things, I think the Realists have been correct. Certainly we should understand, as the Founding Fathers did, that in the absence of some secure world government, a balance of power is probably the best that fallible man can do to preserve peace. Still, I think the Realists have been too cynical in their actions to maintain that balance. This has led them not only to policies which were morally unpalatable to those who take seriously the idealistic side of our Revolutionary legacy, but also to policies which were not realistic even in their own terms. The American people turned away from support of their own government, undermining America's strength. The people had accepted the tragic necessities of immoral actions in support of a greater morality so long as there was a clear and over-whelming threat to the United States. Now that the threat has diminished, those actions seem more heinous.

Kissinger's interventions in Chile, along with our continued support of men like Park Chung Hee in South Korea or Anastasio Somoza Debayle in Nicaragua may shore up a balance of power in the short run but will lead to long-run disaster. Revolutions inevitably are going to come in areas ruled as cruelly as these are. We, as supporters of the old regime, will be cast as enemies of the new governments, and may well find the revolutionaries throwing their military and economic weight to our competitor's side of the balance of power.

I do not think, however, that we should actively encourage revolutions abroad. Our own sense of values, and even our own revolutionary heritage, will not condone what will probably take place in those revolutions that are to come.

The American Revolution was a conservative one which did little more than alter the political structure of the nation. The coming revolutions of the Third World will be far more drastic and terrible than that. They will be radical social revolutions combined with attempts to industrialize under-developed economies at the same time. They will probably not be much concerned with individual liberty as we perceive it, and almost certainly not with the preservation of private property. Under the circumstances, perhaps our best hope is to return to the neutrality policy of the Founding Fathers, but this time toward the Third World rather than toward Europe.

Meanwhile, it would be wise to maintain, as best we can, a reasonable balance of power among the developed nations. This can be done with far less tinkering in the fringe areas of our concern than we have had in the past few years. Surely the nuclear balance of terror, even if greatly reduced by recent Strategic Arms Limitation (SALT) agreements, is adequate to prevent outright invasion of Western Europe and Japan, the heart of America's security area. Our major concern should be with regaining our own sense of worth by a re-dedication to liberty, civility, and economic justice at home. This is going to be difficult, because inevitably America's economic and military strength is going to decline relative to that of other nations. For years, the United States, with about seven percent of the world's population, has consumed thirty-five percent of the world's goods. The energy crisis has given us graphic warning that this will not continue. How will we respond to the erosion of our standard of living?

Jefferson had flickeringly hoped that the United States would accept a modest standard of living if necessary to ensure a humane and libertarian society. This hope was overriden as the Revolutionary generation decided it could have great power and prosperity without diminishing liberty. Now, perhaps, it is time to reconsider not only the Realists' vision of the world, but that of the Founding Fathers as well.

We can see now that power and prosperity are finite, and that they can indeed have deleterious effects on liberty and the spiritual values of the nation. Obviously we should not reject the American dream of combining liberty, prosperity, and power, but perhaps it is time to see that there are limits to their compatibility. We should seek a new balance between the elements of this diplomatic legacy. Perhaps then we might see words like "liberty," "democracy," and "equality" begin to appear again in student assessments of America's national identity.

IGNOBLE SAVAGISM AND THE
AMERICAN REVOLUTION

BY BERNARD W. SHEEHAN

(The author wishes to acknowledge a fellowship from the Henry E. Huntington Library, San Marino, California, that facilitated the preparation of this essay.)

The success of the American Revolution marked a significant defeat for the American Indians. Not because the tribes had been beaten in war. They had not. Or, at least, the Iroquois and the northeastern tribes had come through the conflict without a crippling defeat. The Cherokees lost badly to the Virginia and Carolina militia in 1776, but in the later years of the struggle they took to the warpath once again. Yet, despite the survival of native military power, the peace signaled a collapse of Indian opposition east of the Mississippi. True enough, the northwestern warriors maintained an intermittent belligerency until 1794, but the southern tribes surrendered substantial segments of territory and the Iroquois League disintegrated. After the Revolution the eastern tribes gradually receded under the pressure of American power.

One need not be surprised at the irony of this situation. From the beginning of relations between white and Indian, the tribes always lost, even when they seemed to win. The Iroquois League may have seemed startlingly successful in maintaining its independence during the seventeenth and eighteenth centuries, but the appearance masked a far more important development. While the league played off the English against the French, acculturation and the growth of factions in the tribes dissolved the independence of separate peoples. By the time of the Revolution the dependence of the Iroquois made it inevitable that they would join the white man's fight. The same story could be told of the southern tribes. The Indians may have engaged in war with the appearance of autonomy, but they emerged from the conflict with their independence decisively impaired. The reason can be discovered in part in an examination of the intricate skein of relationships that by the time of the Revolution had come to constitute a peculiar sort of bond between white and Indian. Each side depended upon the other, albeit with different results. For the native tribes the white man was at once a threat to survival and a necessity for that survival. For white men of the Revolutionary era, the Indian represented an exemplar for the realization of republican order, but as an ignoble savage he also constituted an obstacle to the creation of that order.

Seen as an ignoble savage, the Indian reversed the major attributes of civilization. Civilized men in this interpretation endured in prudential balance with other human beings; savages existed without the benefit of institutions. The savage world lacked the political and domestic accomplishments that made civilized life tolerable. Savages had yet to discover the state, and they had created none of the social attachments that gave richness and texture to civilization. Civilized men confronted limitation, wherever they turned, and this curbed a latent tendency to violence. Even when violence did occur, civilization checked its worst excesses. Violence for the ignoble savage was a way of life. In civilization war and rapine were exceptions, to be regretted and ended as quickly as possible. For the savage, war and brutality nourished the deepest needs of his being. Savages killed without compunction, mutilated and devoured the bodies of their victims, and tortured prisoners. Civilized men engaged in violence defensively or for explicit purposes. Savage violence was an end in itself, undifferentiated and without instrumental object. The idea of savagism stemmed from deep mythic roots in European culture. It was devoid of anthropological validity, and, consequently, it explained nothing about the nature of native society. But because white men believed it, ignoble savagism held profound meaning for the relations between white and Indian.

Very soon after the outbreak of the Revolutionary War both sides settled the question of acquiring Indian allies. Except for the Oneidas and Tuscaroras among the Iroquois and factions among the Cherokees and Creeks, the Indians joined the British. Both the king's government and the rebels professed a reluctance to admit the warriors to the struggle. The Indians themselves announced their neutrality. But the precedents favored their inclusion. In the imperial wars the native tribes had long played an important role. Though many Indians had come to see the disadvantages in fighting the white man's battles, the warrior impulse still held a powerful place in native culture. Even had the whites wished to exclude them, it was probably inevitable that they would join the fighting.[1]

It would be easy to assume that the reluctance of the white men to employ Indian allies was merely a sham. And it may well have been. After all the Iroquois did make it plain that they considered the conflict none of their business and intended to stay out.[2] The Continental Congress began by protesting strongly its opposition to native allies, even while Stockbridge Indians had joined the army around Boston.[3] Washington hoped in the beginning to keep the conflict free of the consequences of savage war, but he soon conceded the advantages of recruiting Indian scouts and "light troops."[4] And surely both side protested too much and too piously in blaming the enemy for first introducing the Indians into the war.[5]

The dispute over native allies hinged on the question of savagism. Whether or not the Indians engaged in a singularly brutal mode of warfare, white men on both sides believed that they did, and this belief colored their attitudes towards native society throughout the Revolutionary period.[6] Thomas Paine set the tone of American

---

[1]Jack M. Sosin, "The Use of Indians in the American Revolution: A Re-Assessment of Responsibility," *Canadian Historical Review,* 46 (1965): 101-102; Don Higginbotham, *The War of American Independence: Military Attitudes, Policies, and Practices, 1763-1789* (New York, 1971), pp. 320-21.

[2]Barbara Graymont, *The Iroquois in the American Revolution* (Syracuse, 1972), p. 98; "Talk of Guyasutha at Fort Pitt, July 6, 1776," *The Olden Time* . . . , Neville B. Craig, ed., 2 vols. (Pittsburgh, 1846-47), 2: 113.

[3]E. B. O'Callaghan, ed., *Documents Relative to the Colonial History of the State of New-York,* 15 vols. (Albany, 1853-87) 8: 605-08, 619; 622; Graymont, *Iroquois in the American Revolution,* p. 80.

[4]Washington to Nathaniel Gist, January 14, 1777, *The Writings of George Washington,* John C. Fitzpatrick, ed., 39 vols. (Washington, D.C., 1931-44), 7:11-12; Washington to President of Congress, February 15, 1777, ibid., 102; Washington to Commissioners of Indian Affairs, March 13, 1778, ibid., 11:76.

[5]Earl of Dartmouth to Guy Johnson, July 24, 1775, *The Sullivan-Clinton Campaign in 1779,* Division of Archives and History, ed. (Albany, 1929), p. 51; James H. O'Donnell III, *Southern Indians in the American Revolution* (Knoxville, 1973), p. 30.

[6]See Bernard W. Sheehan, *Seeds of Extinction: Jeffersonian Philanthropy and the American Indian* (Chapel Hill, 1973), for an effort to strike a balance between the seemingly contradictory consequences of the idea of savagism. For emphasis on the negative consequences, see Richard Slotkin, *Regeneration Through Violence: The Mythology of the American Frontier, 1660-1860* (Middletown, Conn., 1973) and Michael Paul Rogin, *Fathers and Children: Andrew Jackson and the Subjugation of the American Indian* (New York, 1975); for the author's review of the Rogin book, see *Pennsylvania Magazine of History and Biography,* 100 (1976): 129-31.

propaganda on the subject of Indian allies by referring in *Common Sense* to "that barbarous and hellish power" that had stirred up the Indians and the slaves in order to destroy American liberty.[7] Jefferson included a condemnation of the king in the *Declaration of Independence* for unleashing the "merciless Indian savages" on the frontier. The Americans seemed to have the better of the argument because they attracted fewer Indians and because the frontier settlements attacked by the warriors usually favored independence. As a result the British tended to be defensive on the subject. The Earl of Dartmouth and General Gage favored native auxiliaries but were careful to note that the Americans acted first. Governor Tryon of New York frankly recommended sending the tribes against the patriots, though he felt obliged to caution against the killing of women and children. Few Englishmen could approach the issue with the equanimity of Guy Johnson, who contended that the Indians were "much misrepresented in the article of cruelty." "The Tomahawk . . . ," he insisted, "is seldom used but to smook thro', or to cut wood with. . . ." But even so he was defensive. True, the Indians scalped the dead, but they might be easily restrained. And, besides, the Americans had first solicited Indian aid.[8]

When Burgoyne marched into New York in 1777 with a motley army of British regulars, Canadians, Germans, and camp followers, he depended on a native contingent to lead him through the wilderness. Although he threatened the Americans with the direst consequences if they persisted in rebellion, he was terribly sensitive about the behavior of his Indian allies. He instructed them to "strike at the common enemies of Great Britain and America — disturbers of public order, peace, and happiness — destroyers of commerce, parricides of the state." But what he gave with one hand he took back with the other. He asked of the Indians nothing less than the abandonment of their habitual mode of war. The warriors would have to moderate their passions; they would have to be selective rather than indiscriminate in attacking the enemy. Loyal colonists must not be molested. There should be no bloodshed unless the warriors were opposed by

---

[7]Paine, "Common Sense," *The Complete Writings of Thomas Paine,* Philip S. Foner, ed., 2 vols. (New York, 1945), 1:30.

[8]William Tryon to George Germain, December 24, 1778, *Sullivan-Clinton Campaign,* p. 71; Guy Johnson to Germain, March 12, 1778, *Documents Relative to New-York,* O'Callaghan, ed., 8:740.

arms. Old men, women, children, and prisoners must not be harmed. The British would pay compensation for prisoners but not for scalps. Indians were free to scalp enemies killed by their own fire in a fair fight. Of course the tribesmen fought their own kind of war, and Burgoyne could do little about it.[9]

The crisis came when a western Indian named Wyandot Panther arrived in the British camp carrying the scalp of Jane McCrea (silky black or delicately blond, according to the source). The young woman came from a loyalist family, and her fiance was an officer in Burgoyne's command. These facts merely compounded a difficult situation. Burgoyne went to the Indian camp, confronted the culprit, and threatened retaliation. But the general knew the weakness of his position. He could not afford to lose his native scouts, hence he swallowed his principles and let off Wyandot Panther with a reprimand. In the history of border warfare the incident was trivial, but it illustrated the intensity of feeling on the issue of savage war. Horatio Gates recognized an opening and wrote to Burgoyne, twitting him for hiring savages to kill Europeans — and for paying for scalps. In reply Burgoyne's usual bombast failed him. He explained the rules he had imposed on the Indians and described the McCrea incident. But he revealed his weakness when he admitted that Wyandot Panther had not been punished. Gates had the better of the exchange. The countryside rose against Burgoyne in part because American propaganda exploited the murder of Jane McCrea.[10]

Burgoyne's misgivings in associating Indians with the British army were echoed by other Englishmen. Two of his officers, Thomas Anburey and William Digby, recorded their hesitations in fighting alongside the tribesmen. Both admitted that forest warfare required native aid and that the Americans must be opposed with their own weapons. But both also made it clear that native behavior was deeply repugnant to them.[11] In Parliament the opposition seized on

---

[9]James Phinney Baxter, *The British Invasion from the North. The Campaigns of Generals Carleton and Burgoyne . . . with the Journal of Lieut. William Digby* (Albany, 1887), pp. 357-60.

[10]Graymont, *Iroquois in the American Revolution*, pp. 151-52; Baxter, *British Invasion from the North,* pp. 262-65; Arthur Reid, *Reminiscences of the Revolution, Le Loup's Bloody Trail from Salem to Fort Edward* (Utica, N. Y., 1859), pp. 26-28, tells a different tale of the McCrea incident.

[11]Sydney Jackman, *With Burgoyne from Quebec* (Toronto, 1963), pp. 93, 129; Baxter, *British Invasion from the North,* pp. 120-21.

Burgoyne's bravado and his naïvete in believing he could modulate the activities of his native allies. Edmund Burke invented a little tale to make the point. "Suppose," he told the Commons, "there was a riot on Tower Hill. What would the keeper of his Majesty's lions do? Would he not fling open the dens of the wild beasts and then address them thus: 'My gentle lions — my humane bears, my tender hearted hyenas, go forth! But I exhort you, as you are Christians and members of civil society, to take care not to hurt any man, woman, or child.' "[12]

Jefferson took the opportunity later in the war to clarify American attitudes on the subject. In 1776 he had already made his opinions plain on the threat of Indian attack. He told the Iroquois that if they did not exercise greater care in preserving neutrality "we would never cease waging war with them while one was to be found on the face of the earth." When George Rogers Clark captured Henry Hamilton in 1779, Jefferson seemed to lose all perspective. Hamilton represented a perverse alliance between savagery and civilization, and civilization could only be defiled by it. Indians fought without a sense of limit; they obeyed none of the rules of warfare that he believed inhibited the violent propensities of white men. By associating with savages, Hamilton became the "butcher of Men, Women and Children."[13]

The portrayal of Indians as the very incarnation of violence had a long history.[14] Jefferson invented nothing new, nor did the Revolution add anything to the history of border warfare as it had been perceived in the past and would be for many years after. It may be that the special circumstances of the Revolution intensified the tendency of Americans to believe the worst about native society. As the Americans saw it, the British threatened liberty itself, the very hope of humane existence. One can see in this a certain reciprocal contamination; in a sense the British and Indians deserved each other. Both seemed bent on obliterating everything the white Americans held most dear. Is it surprising, then, that John Adams could sit down to dinner with a party of Caughnawaga mixed-bloods and describe them as "carnivorous Animals devouring their Pray"? Or that he could laugh

---

[12]Fitzpatrick, ed., *Writings of George Washington,* 8:387n.
[13]Sheehan, *Seeds of Extinction,* pp. 209-10.
[14]Howard Mumford Jones, *O Strange New World: American Culture in the Formative Years* (New York, 1964), ch. 2.

uproariously to himself when, in an imaginary exchange, Rousseau should assert that "Savages do no ill because of the '*calmness of their passions*' "? What could be more absurd?[15]

Fantasy and reality mingled in the white man's mind. After the uprising of the Virginia Indians in 1622, frontier inhabitants knew how uncomfortable the Indians could make life. During the Revolution the Carolina backcountry retreated before the attacks of Dragging Canoe and his Cherokee warriors. The southern Indians were soon cowed by the white militia, but in the north not even Sullivan's expedition in 1779 could keep the Iroquois from laying waste to some 50,000 square miles of colonial territory. In 1780 Guy Johnson reported 836 warriors engaged in forays against the settlements. The following season 2,945 warriors of various tribes ravaged the frontiers of New York, Pennsylvania, and Ohio. Late in the war John Filson reported of the Shawnees: "They evidently saw the approaching hour when the Long Knife would disposses them of their desirable habitations; and anxiously concerned for futurity, determined utterly to extirpate the whites out of Kentucke." Most Americans found it easier to grasp the reality of the Indians' intentions than the causes of their hostility.[16]

Indiscriminate murder, scalping, torture, the taking of prisoners for adoption, all these native practices struck white men as the very antithesis of civilized behavior and hence not only a threat to life and limb but a menace to the delicate balance of human society. Perhaps the contrasting experience of Europe intensified American feelings on the subject. From the close of the Thirty Year's War, Europeans had been evolving a technique of conflict that pitted armies and diplomats against each other but limited the damage to the society at large. No similar development took place in America. On the contrary the imperial wars, in great measure because of the involvement of the native tribes, revealed the vulnerability of society in the New World. The American demand for total victory over the

---

[15]L. H. Butterfield, ed., *Diary and Autobiography of John Adams,* 4 vols. (Cambridge, Mass. 1961), 2: 226-27; Zoltan Haraszti, *John Adams and the Prophets of Progress* (Cambridge, Mass., 1952), p. 85.

[16]O'Donnell, *Southern Indians in the American Revolution,* pp. 42-43; Guy Johnson to George Germain, July 26, 1780, *Documents Relative to New-York,* O'Callaghan, ed., 8:797; Graymont, *Iroquois in the American Revolution,* p. 245; John Filson, *The Discovery and Settlement of Kentucke* (Ann Arbor, 1966), p. 66-67.

French arose from the conviction that nothing short of that would provide the security needed for the creation of civilization in America. In the Revolution the British and loyalists with their Indian allies seemed to threaten once again the very existence of American society[17]

In her later years Mary Jemison described the education of her Seneca husband in a way that American frontier residents would have found convincing:

> In early life, Hiokaoo showed signs of thirst for blood by attending only to the art of war, in the use of the tomahawk and scalping knife; and in practising cruelties upon every thing that chanced to fall into his hands, which was susceptible of pain. In that way he learned to use his implements of war effectually, and at the same time blunted all those fine feelings and tender sympathies that are naturally excited by hearing or seeing, a fellow being in distress. He could inflict the most excruciating tortures upon his enemies, and prided himself upon his fortitude, in having performed the most barbarous ceremonies and tortures, without the least degree of pity or remorse. Thus qualified, when very young he was initiated into scenes of carnage, by being engaged in the wars that prevailed amongst the Indian tribes.[18]

Perhaps William N. Fenton exaggerates when he claims that "the Iroquois warrior could be a homicidal maniac . . . ," but during the Revolution Americans would have thought the description quite apt.[19]

Two incidents stood out in the American memory: the attacks of Indians and loyalists on Cherry Valley and Wyoming. The facts counted for little. With a party of 110 loyalist rangers and 464 Indians, John Butler led the attack on Wyoming in July 1778. Two forts surrendered without a fight, but the defenders of the third came out to meet the enemy. As happened with uncanny regularity, the Indians and loyalists out-flanked the militia which then panicked and the slaughter began. The Indians and rangers took 227 scalps and five prisoners. The Americans had been defeated in

---

[17]John Shy, "The American Military Experience: History and Learning," *Journal of Interdisciplinary History*, 1 (1971): 212-16.

[18]James Seaver, *A Narrative of the Life of Mary Jemison, The White Woman of the Genesee,* Charles Delamater Vail, ed., 20th ed. (New York, 1918), p. 105.

[19]William N. Fenton, "The Iroquois in History," in *North American Indians in Historical Perspective,* Eleanor Burke Leacock and Nancy Oestreich Lurie, eds. (New York, 1971) p. 142.

battle and suffered the consequences. At Cherry Valley in November 1778 Walter Butler (John's son) with Joseph Brant and Cornplanter attacked with such swiftness that the Americans offered little organized resistance. At Wyoming the warriors had not killed unarmed civilians, but at Cherry Valley they could not be restrained. Sixteen soldiers and thirty-two inhabitants (mostly women and children) were killed. The Indans took more than seventy captives. Forty were sent back, but the Indians tomahawked some on the path.[20]

Without embellishment frontier war was brutal enough, but for the Americans, Wyoming and Cherry Valley came to symbolize British and Indian viciousness. James Thacher, a doctor in the Continental Army, pictured the people of Wyoming enjoying "all the happiness which results from harmony and the purest natural affection," set upon by a band of "tories, Indians and half-blooded Englishmen." The result was "one of the most dreadful instances of perfidious savage cruelty that can perhaps be found on the records of history."[21] The Americans accused Esther Montour, who had been at neither Wyoming nor Cherry Valley, of "Barbarity unparalleled in former ages." The story went about that she had tied some of the prisoners to trees and then "the old infernal Savage brute would go with her knife cut their throats with it and scalp them at the same time repeating 'She should never be tired of killing rebels.' "[22] According to one diarist the British and Indians had "rendered a scene of desolation and horror, almost beyond description, parallel, or credibility." Had it not been for the testimony of the sufferers themselves, "it would be impossible to believe that human nature could be capable of such prodigious enormity."[23] Ultimately, the culprit was the British government and the king. The Oneida missionary, Samuel Kirkland, asked a rhetorical question and answered it: "Are these the fruits and effects of thy clemency, O George, thou tyrant of Britain and scourge of mankind? May He, to whom vengeance

---

[20]Graymont, *Iroquois in the American Revolution,* pp. 167-74, 183-91.

[21]James Thacher, *Military Journal of the American Revolution* (Hartford, 1862), pp. 142-43.

[22]"Journal of Lieut. Samuel M. Shute," August 11, 1779, *Journals of the Military Expedition of Major General John Sullivan Against the Six Nations of Indians in 1779,* Frederick Cook, ed. (Auburn, N. Y., 1887), p. 270n.

[23]"Contemporary Account of Attack on Wyoming," *Sullivan-Clinton Campaign,* p. 66.

belongeth, put forth his righteous indignation in due time."[24]

In time it seemed that hatred of the king, his soldiers, and the loyalists might erase the image of the savage Indian. After the skirmishes at Lexington and Concord, American propagandists made it customary to compare the behavior of the British with the activities of the Indians — sometimes unfavorably. As the Reverend Jonas Clarke described that first confrontation: "They approach with the morning light; and more like *murderers* and *cut-throats* than the troops of a *Christian king,* without provocation, without warning, when no war was proclaimed, they draw the *sword of violence* upon the inhabitants . . . , and with a *cruelty* and *barbarity* which would have made the most hardened savage blush, they *shed* INNOCENT BLOOD!"[25] But the British did more than shed blood. "The savage barbarity exercised upon the bodies of our unfortunate brethren who fell, is almost incredible: not contented with shooting down the unarmed, aged and infirm, they disregarded the Cries of the wounded, killing them without Mercy, and mangling their Bodies in the most shocking Manner."[26] Ethan Allen found it difficult to distinguish the British from the Indians. He accused the British of murdering prisoners after they had surrendered their arms. A militia officer was "hacked to pieces with cutlasses (when alive)" and another officer "thrust through with a bayonet, of which wound he died instantly."[27] Of all the British leaders whom the Americans implicated in a savage assault on liberty, the Butlers, father and son, were the most brutal. In American propaganda they merged into one personality. For Henry Dearborn, Butler was an "inhuman savage." Wyoming, wrote an American

[24]Samuel Kirkland Lothrop, *The Life of Samuel Kirkland* (Boston, 1847), pp. 247-48.

[25]Jonas Clarke, "A Sermon: The Fate of Blood-Thirsty Oppressors and God's Care of his Distressed People," *The Magazine of History,* 41 (1930): 191.

[26]Peter Force, ed., *American Archives,* 9 vols. (Washington D.C., 1837-53), 4th ser., 2: 392.

[27]Ethan Allen, *A Narrative of Colonel Ethan Allen's Captivity* . . . (Philadelphia, 1779) pp. 26-27. Richard Slotkin, *Regeneration Through Violence,* pp. 251-52 traces the savage British theme to Allen. In this, he may be correct. Certainly Allen used the theme. But the incident recounted by Slotkin from the *Narrative* will not make the point so neatly. He quotes a passage in which Allen described an attack made on him by an Indian after his capture. The unquoted portion tells how Allen was saved from the Indian when he gingerly placed a British officer between himself and his assailant. In this incident, at least, there would seem to be an alliance between civilized men against savagism. At best Allen was ambivalent on the issue of British savagery.

officer, had been "attacked by a merciless band of savages, led by a more savage Tory, the Unnatural monster Butler. . . ." Although Joseph Brant endured his share of vilification, in contrast to Butler his reputation shone. One anecdote described the scene in the British camp before the assault on Cherry Valley. When Butler read his orders to the assembled "Tory rabble," Brant wept and asserted that he made war on the Americans from principle, that he "wod never have a hand in massacring the defenceless inhabitants."[28]

The brutality of the native warriors paled before the atrocities committed by Ebenezer Allen, a white savage described by Mary Jemison. Allen was a frontier entrepreneur who became a thief, polygamist, and murderer and capped his career by joining the Iroquois in their attacks on the settlements. He became legendary as a Tory who, because he had forsaken civilization, had fallen lower than the savage Indian.[29] Time after time, the loyalists seemed more relentless in their determination to destroy civilized life. In an attack on Schoharie, the Iroquois warriors burst into a house and killed and scalped a woman and her children. An infant remained alive in its cradle. When an Indian "noted for his barbarity" approached the cradle, the child smiled up at him and he dropped his tomahawk — "the feeling of nature triumphed over the ferocity of the savage." At this moment a loyalist skewered the infant on his bayonet exclaiming "this too is a rebel."[30] An incident told many times by the soldiers on Sullivan's expedition into the Iroquois country drove the point home. A young man named Henry Pensell managed to escape from the slaughter at Wyoming. He hid on an island in the Susquehanna where he was discovered that evening by a party of loyalists headed by his brother. Henry Pensell begged on his knees for mercy. He offered to be his brother's slave if he were spared. All to no purpose. In Dearborn's description, "this unatural & more than savage brother Cain" shot his younger brother, then tomahawked and scalped him. A party of Indians who had viewed the scene "curs'd

[28]"Journal of Lieut.-Col. Henry Dearborn," June 27, 1779, *Journals of the Military Expedition of Major General John Sullivan,* Cook, ed., p. 64; "Journal of Major James Norris," June 23, 1779, ibid., pp. 224-25; Graymont, *Iroquois in the American Revolution,* p. 191.

[29]Seaver, *Narrative of the Life of Mary Jemison,* pp. 91-92.

[30]William W. Campbell, *The Border Warfare of New York, During the Revolution; or the Annals of Tryon County* (New York, 1849), p. 171.

his unnatural behaveyer & threten'd to serve him the same way[.]"[31]

A ruse by Benjamin Franklin gave the American charge of British savagery an urbane but macabre twist. In 1782 he wrote what he called a "Supplement to the Boston *Independent Chronicle*." The bogus newspaper reported that a grisly package had arrived in London containing a collection of American scalps (sorted according to size and quality), accompanied by a message from the Senecas. The Americans, it appeared, had once been like "young Panthers," "but now their Bodies are become big as the Elk, and strong as the Buffalo; they have also got great and sharp Claws." Because of this transformation, the Indians have been driven from their country. The Senecas have sent their gift of scalps as a token of the alliance between the Indians and the king. For Franklin the point was clear: one could not distinguish the cause of the king and his loyalist adherents from the savage customs of the American tribesmen.[32]

Yet a closer look at the revolutionary conflict revealed that it was every bit as difficult to distinguish the tactics of the American patriots from the savage manners attributed to the Indian warriors. The irony seemed patent even at the time. In order to defend civilization against the assault of savagery, frontier fighters inevitably found it necessary to adopt the manners and tactics of the savages they wished to kill.[33] Richard Slotkin sees a progression of wilderness proficiency in the careers of such Indian fighters as John Mason, Benjamin Church, and Robert Rogers. Not only did some white men become more adept in the wilderness, but increasingly they killed Indians with less compunction.[34] Rogers was a professional woodsmen who saw himself engaged in total war with the French and Indians. Although cautioned by General Gage to avoid excessive brutality, he attacked the St. Francis Indians with ruthless finality, intending their total destruction.[35] In the Revolution the Indians and loyalists

[31]"Journal of Lieut.-Col. Henry Dearborn," July 5, 1779, *Journals of the Military Expedition of Major General John Sullivan,* Cook, ed., p. 65.
[32]"Supplement to the Boston *Independent Chronicle,*" *The Writings of Benjamin Franklin,* Albert Henry Smyth, ed., 10 vols. (New York, 1905-1907), 8: 437-47; Franklin to John Adams, April 22, 1782, ibid., p. 433.
[33]Roy Harvey Pearce, "The Metaphysics of Indian-Hating," *Ethnohistory,* 4 (1957): 29.
[34]Slotkin, *Regeneration Through Violence,* pp. 188-89.
[35]Robert Rogers, *Journals of Major Robert Rogers* (Ann Arbor, 1966), pp. 145, 154; Lawrence Henry Gipson, *The Great War for Empire: The Victorious Years, 1758-1760* (New York, 1936-70), pp. 265-66.

faced men every bit as skillful in the wilderness as Rogers and equally determined to sweep the continent of savage opposition.

During the Seven Years' War the British organized detachments of light troops that supplied mobility to the otherwise slow-moving eightenth-century army. Also groups of rangers acted as scouts and contested with the French and Indians on their own ground. Rogers commanded only the most famous of these contingents. By the time of the Revolution light troops had fallen from favor in the British army, although the German mercenary forces contained jaeger contingents which were the continental version of light troops. Both sides employed lightly armed forces throughout the war. Such American leaders as Daniel Morgan, Michael Cresap, John Sevier, and James Smith were matched on the British side by Joseph Brant, the Butlers, and Banastre Tarleton.[36]

The Seven Years' War had stimulated thinking on the subject of light troops and forest warfare. In 1765 William Smith's account of Bouquet's expedition contained a treatise written by Thomas Hutchins, who would later be geographer of the United States. Hutchins proposed three tactical maxims which he hoped would aid the Americans in their contest with the Indians. The settlers should attempt to surround the enemy, "fight scattered," and never hold firm when attacked. Instead they should give way in order to lure the enemy on and then return to the attack. In fact these were the main tenets of Indian war. In so far as the whites employed them, they would be imitating the Indians. For the implementation of these principles, Hutchins recommended that troops sent against the Indians should be lightly armed and clothed; they should never be exposed to the enemy by being drawn up in close order; they should be taught to make battlefield maneuvers with great rapidity.[37]

The second formal examination of Indian warfare did not appear until 1799, but it was drawn from the experience of the Seven Years'

---

[36]Ernest A. Cruikshank, *The Story of Butler's Rangers and the Settlement of Niagra* (Welland, Ont., 1893) ; Don Higginbotham, *Daniel Morgan: Revolutionary Rifleman* (Chapel Hill, 1961) ; "Light Infantry," in Mark Mayo Boatner III, *Encyclopedia of the American Revolution* (New York, 1966), pp. 634-35; "Riflemen," ibid., pp. 934-36.

[37][William Smith], *Historical Account of Bouquet's Expedition Against the Ohio Indians in 1764* (Cincinnati, 1868), pp. 109-10; John K. Mahon, "Anglo-American Methods of Indian Warfare, 1676-1794," *Mississippi Valley Historical Review*, 45 (1958) : 260.

War and the Revolution. The author, James Smith, had been captured by Indians in 1755 and lived with them until 1759. He seems to have enjoyed the love-hate relationship with his native hosts that afflicted many captives. In the 1760s, with the aid of two assistants who had also been Indian captives, he organized the "Black Boys."

> We dressed them uniformly in the Indian manner, with breech-clouts, leggins, mockesons and green shrouds, which we wore in the same manner that the Indians do, and nearly as the Highlanders wear their plaids. In place of hats we wore red handkerchiefs, and painted our faces red and black, like Indian warriors. I taught them the Indian discipline, as I knew of no other at that time, which would answer the purpose much better than British. We succeeded beyond expectation in defending the frontiers, and were extolled by our employers.[38]

During the Revolution Smith commanded a similar frontier contingent. He believed the Indians to be "the best disciplined troops in the known world," and he could counsel no better way to defeat them than by adopting their tactics. Indians could bring together large bodies of men, although in truth their numbers were a good deal smaller than the whites believed. The settlers usually outnumbered them. Indian leaders, he contended, made general plans, but the warriors did the fighting and would respond to commands when required. Corporal punishment was not necessary to insure discipline. The Indians fought unencumbered by clothes. They were well armed and knew how to use their weapons. In a march up the Allegheny in 1778 Smith moved in three columns, well spaced, and with flankers out. He ordered his men to fire from behind trees when attacked. Smith deplored the tendency of frontiersmen to imitate the brutality of Indian warfare, but his own men took scalps.[39] He lived a half-Indian existence and his prescription for success in the wilderness relied on his own experience as a captive.

When Morgan arrived before Boston in July 1775 with ninety-six Virginia riflemen, Washington was pleased with this addition to his

---

[38]James Smith, *An Account of the Remarkable Occurrences in the Life and Travels of Col. James Smith . . .* , Wm. M. Darlington, ed. (Cincinnati, 1870), p. 107.

[39]Ibid., pp. 150-55, 134-37, 159-60.

[40]Higginbotham, *Daniel Morgan*, pp. 24-26.

British had experienced similar inconveniences during the Seven Years' War and had relied on Rogers precisely because he proved able to discipline them.[41] On at least one occasion Washington expressed reluctance to add another frontier contingent to his army. When James Smith appeared at Morristown in 1777 with a recommendation from the Pennsylvania Council of Safety that he be permitted to organize a ranger batallion, Washington turned him down. According to Smith, Washington did not fall in with the scheme of white men turning Indians. Instead he offered Smith a commission as major in the Continental army.[42]

But this action was untypical. Washington favored ranger forces and encouraged their use repeatedly during the war. He told Patrick Henry in 1776 that he believed the frontier militia "peculiarly adapted" to Indian warfare. He was particularly sensitive to the effects that Indians and frontier riflemen might have on loyalists unused to frontier life or on raw levies from Europe.[43] The frontier companies from Virginia, Pennsylvania, and Maryland. that joined Washington in 1775 were armed with rifles, the conventional hunting weapon. Each man carried a tomahawk and scalping knife and dressed in a long hunting shirt, leggins, and moccasins. As one disapproving observer commented, "it was the silly fashion of those times for riflemen to ape the manners of the savages."[44] Later Washington promoted hunting shirts with long breeches made of the same cloth and worn like gaiters for American troops who had not yet been provided with clothing. He hoped that the British would mistake every American infantryman for a marksman, and he did not seem displeased to command an army that resembled the native enemy.[45]

Evidence that civilization broke down on the frontier could be

---

[41]Douglas Southhall Freeman, *George Washington: A Biography*, 7 vols. (New York, 1948-57) 3: 522-24; Gipson, *The Great War for Empire*, 7: 154-55; Higginbotham, *Daniel Morgan*, p. 26.

[42]Smith, *An Account of the Remarkable Occurrences in the Life and Travels of Col. James Smith*, Darlington, ed., pp. 132-34.

[43]Washington to Patrick Henry, October 5, 1776, *Writings of George Washington*, Fitzpatrick, ed., 6: 166; Washington to Joseph Reed, April 19, 1779, ibid., 14: 406; O'Donnell, *Southern Indians in the American Revolution*, p. 71.

[44]Higginbotham, *Daniel Morgan*, p. 23; Lynn Montross, *Rag, Tag and Bobtail: The Story of the Continental Army, 1775-1783* (New York, 1952), p. 50.

[45]"General Orders," July 24, 1776, *Writings of George Washington*, Fitzpatrick, ed., 5:336.

seen in the western habit of dressing like Indians. In 1768 Sir William Johnson reported an attack on a trader near Fort Pitt by thirty white men disguised as Indians. It was apparently a common practice for whites to dress as Indians, loot canoes and packhorses, and blame the crimes on innocent warriors.[46] Tactics in war often required similar behavior. When the Shawnees broke on to the frontier in 1778 in retaliation for the murder of their chief, Cornstalk, and besieged the whites in the fort at Point Pleasant, Grenadier Squaw (Cornstalk's sister) painted and dressed two white men as warriors and sent them through the Indian lines for help.[47] Daniel Brodhead, the American officer in command at Fort Pitt during the Revolution, employed "light parties" that he painted and dressed as Indians and sent to retaliate in kind for the taking of scalps. Apparently his strategem met with some success.[48] Washington himself seemed attracted to the idea. He suggested that Daniel Morgan should "dress a Company or two of true Woods Men in the right Indian Style and let them make the Attack accompanied with screaming and yelling as Indians do. . . ." He thought such tactics would be more successful if the enemy believed they faced real Indians.[49]

Washington instructed Sullivan to deliver his attacks "with as much impetuosity, shouting, and noise, as possible." Formations should be kept loose and the troops should be encouraged to rush upon the enemy with the war whoop and fixed bayonets. In fact Sullivan trained his men in bush fighting, and at the Battle of Newtown in the critical flanking movement the troops rushed upon the loyalists and Indians just as Washington had commanded. Sullivan also managed to avoid ambush though he failed to entice the enemy into a decisive engagement.[50] In the frontier war in the South, leaders

---

[46]Arthur C. Parker, "The Indian Interpretation of the Sullivan-Clinton Campaign," The Rochester Historical Society, *Publication Fund Series*, 8 (1929): 51; Smith, *An Account of the Remarkable Occurrences in the Life and Travels of Col. James Smith,* Darlington, ed., pp. 108-10.

[47]Alexander Scott Withers, *Chronicles of Border Warfare* . . . , Rueben Gold Thwaites, ed. (Cincinnati, 1895), p. 242.

[48]"Journal of Lieut. William Barton," August 26, 1779, *Journals of the Military Expedition of Major General John Sullivan,* Cook, ed., p. 7; Daniel Brodhead to Sullivan, August 6, 1779, ibid., p. 307.

[49]Washington to Daniel Morgan, June 13, 1777, *Writings of George Washington,* Fitzpatrick, ed., 8: 236-37.

[50]Washington to John Sullivan, May 31, 1779, *Sullivan-Clinton Campaign,* p. 91; Mahon, "Anglo-American Methods of Indian Warfare," p. 268.

such as William Christian and John Sevier fought the Indians and loyalists with native tactics. They dressed Indian style, carried tomahawks, fought from ambush, and seldom failed to give the war whoop. At King's Mountain the Americans surrounded the loyalists and kept up a peppering fire. Each time the loyalists charged in order to disperse them, the Americans withdrew as Indian tactics demanded only to push a little closer to the top of the mountain when the loyalists pulled back.[51] The conflict never turned out to be as simple as Ethan Allen described it to the Caughnawagas. "I know how to shute and ambush just like Indian," he bragged, "and want your Warriors to come see me and help me fight Regulars[.] You know they Stand all along close Together Rank and file and my men fight so as Indians Do and I want your Warriors to Join with me and my Warriors like Brothers and Ambush the Regulars. . . ."[52] Much of the western fighting did indeed follow the native pattern.

Occasionally the tendency of the Continental Army to adopt the manners of the Indians went beyond the requirements of discipline. Washington may have been pleased with the addition of Morgan's riflemen to his musket-carrying forces around Boston, but he soon saw the disadvantages. After a few days of sharpshooting the British learned to keep their heads down, but the riflemen kept up the fire. Washington finally had to order them to stop wasting ammunition.[53] On Sullivan's expedition the consequences of indianization revealed deeper strains in the white man's mind. The general was forced to order his soldiers to cease firing their guns and giving the war whoop each time warriors were thought to be in the vicinity.[54] Two men sentenced to run the gauntlet for stealing rum seemed an open enough adaptation to native habits.[55] But the gauntlet was imposed for more than one crime: "One of Colln. Spensers men Run the Ganlet

[51]John P. Brown, *Old Frontiers: The Story of the Cherokee Indians from Earliest Times to the Date of Their Removal to the West, 1838* (Kingsport, Tenn., 1938), pp. 150-52, 160, 189-90, 192-93; J. G. M. Ramsey, *Annals of Tennessee to the End of the Eighteenth Century* . . . (Charleston, S. C., 1853), p. 235.

[52]Graymont, *Iroquois in the American Revolution*, p. 68.

[53]General Orders," August 14, 1775, *Writings of George Washington*, Fitzpatrick, ed., 3: 384-85; Freeman, *George Washington*, 3: 524.

[54]"Journal of Rev. William Rogers, D.D.," August 16, 1777, *Journals of the Military Expedition of Major General John Sullivan*, Cook, ed., p. 262.

[55]Journal of Sergeant Thomas Roberts," August 22, 1779, ibid., p. 243.

Through 3 Regiments and Every man had a whip and one had one hundred Lashes at the post[.] thear Crime was for painting themselves [and] threthnging Two officers Lives as Indians[.]"[56] Imitation of savage ways may have been useful, but it could also be inconvenient. More important it could threaten the very basis of discipline in a civilized army.

To many observers the Indian appeared to be an incorrigible individualist and so did the unruly frontiersman. But this was probably no more true of the frontiersman than it was of the Indian. In war both manifested a deep sense of tribal loyalty. James Smith apparently retained the allegiance of his "old black boys" from the early 1760s to the Revolution. After Pontiac's uprising he assembled them to prevent traders from doing business with the Indians. When Smith was arrested on a murder charge, they offered to storm the jail and release him. While serving in the Pennsylvania assembly in 1777, he met a number of his old companions in Philadelphia on their way to join Washington's army. The old ties were irresistible. He petitioned the assembly for leave, and led a scouting party into New Jersey.[57] A similar sort of tribal identity united the frontiersmen from the Nolichucky settlements led by John Sevier. His son James referred to the group that caught Ferguson at King's Mountain as "our little band of warriors." His father knew every man personally. "They were but few in number, but that few so often called together, that they were like a band of brothers raised in the same family." As with the Indians, the officers were the best fighters, and they tended to be leaders rather than commanders.[58]

Yet for all their camaraderie among themselves, the westerners were violent men. In his attack on the Paxton Boys, Franklin had called them "CHRISTIAN WHITE SAVAGES." Americans identified violence with savagism, and they could be no less violent than the savages. But Franklin expressed little sympathy for the Indians who warred against the white man. On the contrary, the crime of the Paxton Boys was precisely that they behaved the way Indians

[56]"Journal of Sergeant Thomas Roberts," June 29, 1779, ibid., p. 241.

[57]Smith, *An Account of the Remarkable Occurrences in the Life and Travels of Col. James Smith,* Darlington, ed., pp. 108-10, 119-23, 131.

[58]James Sevier, "A Memoir of John Sevier," *American Historical Magazine,* 6 (1900): 41, 43; Brown, *Old Frontiers,* p. 202.

behaved.[59] During the Revolution this tendency of the Americans to slip into savagery seemed more real. After Lexington and Concord, Lord Percy was not surprised to discover "the cruelty and barbarity of the Rebels, who scalped & cut off the ears of some of the wounded that fell into their hands."[60] The story that the South Carolina whigs had encouraged the Indians to kill anyone who would not sign the Continental Association appeared every bit as plausible.[61] And when patriots near Augusta, Georgia, tortured one Thomas Brown by applying flaming wood splinters to the soles of his feet because he refused to join the association of the provincial congress, savagerism seemed to have triumphed.[62]

The Seneca war chief Sayenqueraghta said of his white enemies that "the title Savages wou'd with much greater justice be applied to them than to us."[63] One of the more noted candidates for the title was Timothy Murphy, a rifleman who came from Virginia with Daniel Morgan to halt Burgoyne's advance. He first gained notoriety by picking off General Simon Fraser at Bemis Heights. Murphy liked New York well enough to settle at Schoharie, and in 1779 he joined Sullivan's drive against the Iroquois. His life seemed to be charmed, in part because he carried a double-barreled rifle which invariably gave him an advantage over his native enemies. Among the tribesmen he was legend. The Iroquois came close to catching him at the Groveland ambush where they captured Lieutenant Boyd and Captain Parker. Murphy and one other soldier escaped; Boyd and Parker were tortured to death. If the story that went the rounds among the Indians was correct, thirty-three Indian scalps hung from Murphy's belt at Groveland. He boasted that he had killed forty Indians during the war and scalped half of them.[64]

During the colonial period all of the colonies at one time or another paid bounties for scalps. By the time of the Revolution

[59]Franklin, "Narrative of the Late Massacres . . . ," *The Writings of Benjamin Franklin,* Smyth, ed. 4: 298-310.

[60]Graymont, *Iroquois in the American Revolution,* p. 62.

[61]Philip Davidson, *Propaganda and the American Revolution, 1763-1783* (Chapel Hill, 1941), p. 297.

[62]James H. O'Donnell, ed., "A Loyalist View of the Drayton-Tennent-Hart Mission to the Upcountry," *South Carolina Historical Magazine,* 67 (1966): 16.

[63]Graymont, *Iroquois in the American Revolution,* p. 256.

[64]William L. Stone, *The Campaign of Lieut. Gen. John Burgoyne, and the Expedition of Lieut. Col. Barry St. Leger* (Albany, 1877), pp. 249-51 and note; Parker, "Indian Interpretation of the Sullivan-Clinton Campaign," p. 55.

New York and Massachusetts had recently abandoned the practice.[65] But South Carolina offered £75 for a Cherokee scalp and £100 for a prisoner.[66] In 1777 the North Carolina assembly lowered the rate to £15 for an Indian prisoner and £10 for a scalp.[67] The bounty system also worked in the opposite direction. Washington recommended in 1776 that Congress offer the Indians £5 for every British prisoner they might take at Niagara. Actually, the congressional resolves proposed $100 for an officer and $30 for a common soldier.[68] Neither the Congress nor the British government paid bounties for scalps, though both sides accused the other of doing so. What lesser functionaries in the field may have done cannot be said with assurance. Henry Hamilton probably did not pay for scalps directly, but he did engage in the traditional practice of gift giving very soon after his native allies returned from their forays against the American settlements. Of course, he also paid the Indians for the Kentucky prisoners taken at Blue Licks. He offered £100 for Daniel Boone but was refused. Money changed hands for both scalps and prisoners during the Revolution.[69]

Frontier warriors needed no encouragement to scalp. For the tribesmen the practice held deep totemic meaning. For white men scalping had long been acceptable behavior in fighting Indians. Whites did not scalp other whites. Whether a reversion to some deep atavistic impulse or simply revenge visited upon a savage enemy, white men in the border conflict of the Revolution looked on scalps as perfectly acceptable symbols of the triumph of civilization. In the southern attacks on the Cherokees in 1776 and 1782[70] and on Sullivan's campaign against the Iroquois, the militia and the Continental army took scalps as a matter of course.[71] Sullivan made much

[65]Andrew McFarland Davis, "The Indians and the Border Warfare of the Revolution," *Narrative and Critical History of America*, Justin Winsor, ed., 8 vols. (Boston, 1884-89), 6: 682.

[66]Brown, *Old Frontiers*, p. 154.

[67]Higginbotham, *The War of American Independence*, p. 347n.

[68]Washington to President of Congress, June 9, 1776, *Writings of George Washington*, Fitzpatrick, ed., 5: 114; Washington to Philip Schuyler, June 2, 1776, ibid., p. 162 and note.

[69]Davis, "The Indians and the Border Warfare of the Revolution," pp. 682-84; Withers, *Chronicles of Border Warfare*, Thwaites, ed., p. 266n.

[70]Brown, *Old Frontiers*, p. 156.

[71]"Journal of Lieut.-Col. Henry Dearborn," August 29, 1779, *Journals of the Military Expedition of Major General John Sullivan*, Cook, ed., p. 72; "Journal of Lieut.-Col. Adam Hubley," August 29, 1779, ibid., p. 156.

of his gentle treatment of an elderly squaw found at one of the abandoned Indian towns. But he could not control his men. A younger native woman came in to help her when assurances were spread about that the women would not be hurt. On the return march the body of the younger woman was found in a ditch.[72] There may have been some reluctance to kill and scalp women and children (at least John Sevier's men mocked one of their comrades who scalped an old squaw)[73], but such humane behavior was exceptional. During the Revolution frontier troops made free use of the scalping knife, and it remained part of their equipment in later years.

The Indians could be blamed for originating scalping, but white savagery made its own contribution to the violence of life on the frontier. While planning an attack on Onondaga in 1779, Governor James Clinton cautioned Colonel Goose Van Shaick to be sure that his men refrained from violating any of the native women taken prisoners. He assured Van Shaick that he knew the troops would not commit such crimes, but he also took the trouble to recall the Indian practice in the same circumstances. They never violated women sexually. As it turned out the Americans seized a number of women prisoners, and the Indians claimed they were raped.[74] During Sullivan's campaign an officer in command of a raid toward Lake Cayuga found an old squaw and a crippled boy. He left a house standing for them. But he could not account for the behavior of his men. They locked the two Indians in the house and burned it to the ground.[75]

Although the torture of prisoners and the mutilation of bodies occupied an important place in the culture of the eastern tribes, the Indians did not skin and tan the hides of their victims. White men did. The day following the battle of Newtown one of Sullivan's officers recorded the following incident: "At the request of Maj. Piatt, sent out a small party to look for some of the dead Indians — returned without finding them. Toward noon they found them and skinned two of them from their hips down for boot legs; one pair for the Major the other for myself."[76] The spring before, near Picketts

[72]"Journal of Lieut. William Barton," September 23, 1779, ibid., pp. 9, 12; "Journal of Lieut.-Col. Adam Hubley," September 23, 1779, ibid., p. 164.
[73]Brown, *Old Frontiers,* p. 201.
[74]Graymont, *Iroquois in the American Revolution,* p. 196.
[75]"Journal of Lieut. William Barton," September 26, 1779, *Journals of the Military Expedition of Major General John Sullivan,* Cook, ed., p. 13.
[76]Ibid., August 30, 1779, p. 8.

fort in West Virginia, David Morgan, a sixty-year-old relative of Daniel Morgan, killed two Indians who had attempted to capture his children. Both Indians were skinned to make drum heads.[77] In the years following, skinning happened often enough to become a common mode of defiling the savage enemy.[78]

The irony of Indian-white relations during the Revolution lay in the apparent determination of the white man to draw the sharpest distinction between civilization and savagery and at the same time to conquer the Indian by becoming more like him. The white man's belief in ignoble savagism no doubt increased the bitterness and brutality of the struggle. Moreover, it held profound meaning for the formation of American culture. Yet it is questionable that it revealed a great deal about the actual relations between white and Indian. Not only was the concept untenable anthropologically, but it failed to account for the process of acculturation by which the native tribes adapted to a new situation on the American continent. Perhaps certain white men increased their proficiency in the forest by becoming more like Indians, but the new American government did not triumph over the tribes in the Revolution because it resorted to savage war. Victory came first over the British and only incidentally over the Indians. They succumbed not to military power, but to the gradual process of disintegration that had begun long before the Revolution and would continue long after.

If the soldiers who marched into the Iroquois country with Sullivan in 1779 used the language of *savagism* to describe native society, they also perceived much that was not easily reconciled with the savage state. By the middle of the eighteenth century, the traditional longhouse had begun to fall into disuse among the Iroquois. The Indians built cabins in imitation of white settlers and with consequences for the communal order that centered around the life of the longhouse.[79] Sullivan's men found a variety of structures. One of his

---

[77]Letter dated Westmoreland, April 26, 1779, *Affecting History of the Dreadful Distresses of Frederick Manheim's Family* . . . (Exeter, N. H., 1793), pp. 11-14.

[78]For later incidents, see Thomas S. Woodward, *Woodward's Reminiscences of the Creek, or Muscogee Indians* . . . (Tuscaloosa, Alabama, 1939), p. 85; Thurman Wilkins, *Cherokee Tragedy: The Story of the Ridge Family and the Decimation of a People* (New York, 1970), p. 77.

[79]Anthony F. C. Wallace, *The Death and Rebirth of the Seneca* . . . (New York, 1970), p. 23.

officers described Onoquaga as "one of the Neatest of the Indian towns on the Susquehanna, it was built on each side of the River with good Log houses with Stone Chimneys and glass windows[.] it likewise had a Church & burying ground and a great number of apple trees. . . ."[80] Some of the structures had yet to make the transition from the old to the new. They were built of log frames and covered with bark. But the whites saw buildings of hewn logs and others of plank.[81] Clearly, important developments had taken place in the physical character of native culture.

The Iroquois had blocked the expansion of the New York frontier for more than a century and when finally the Continental army forced its way into the Indian territory, the soldiers looked upon the land with covetous eyes. But they did not see virgin territory. "The land exceeds any that I have ever seen," wrote Major John Burrowes in his diary, "some corn stalks measured eighteen feet, and a cob one foot and a half long. Beans, cucumbers, watermelons, much-melons, cimblens are in great plenty."[82] Sullivan's soldiers lived off the agricultural prosperity they discovered.[83] Many of the Indian towns were surrounded by orchards. Though domestic animals were few, the whites found chickens and pigs and a few horses and cows.[84] By the late eighteenth century, the Seneca alone raised as many as a million bushels of corn each year.[85]

The eastern Indians had long subsisted on agriculture, though doubtless not on the scale reached by the major tribes in the late eighteenth century. The consequence when war came was to make them more vulnerable to attack by the whites. Washington seemed to sense this, though nothing he or any of his officers wrote ranked the Indians above the savage state. "The immediate objects," he told Sullivan, "are the total destruction and devastation of their settle-ments. . . . It will be essential to ruin their crops now in the ground

---

[80]"Journal of Lieut. Erkuries Beatty," August 14, 1779, *Journals of the Military Expedition of Major General John Sullivan,* Cook, ed., p. 23.

[81]"Journal of Lieut. William McKendry," September 7, 1779, ibid., p. 205; "Journal of Lieut.-Col. Adam Hubley," September 10, 1779, ibid. p. 160.

[82]"Journal of Major John Burrowes," August 30, 1779, ibid., p. 45.

[83]"Journal of Lieut.-Col. Adam Hubley," September 27, 1779, ibid., p. 165; "Journal of Lieut. John Jenkins," September 11, 1779, ibid., p. 174.

[84]"Journal of Major Jeremiah Fogg," September 7, 1779, ibid., p. 97; "Journal of Serg't Major George Grant," September 6, 1779, ibid., p. 111.

[85]Wallace, *Death and Rebirth of the Seneca,* p. 24.

& prevent their planting more." He added that the Iroquois territory should "not be merely overrun, but destroyed." No wonder
then that in later years the Iroquois called Washington the "Town
Destroyer."[86] Sullivan burned forty villages, numerous isolated cabins,
160,000 bushels of corn, and an unaccountable quantity of crops.[87]
The southern militia followed similar tactics in attacking the Cherokees. As the Virginians approached the Cherokee towns in 1776, the
Indians fled leaving crops and domestic animals behind. The frontiersmen burned forty or fifty thousand bushels of corn and ten or fifteen
thousand of potatoes. In 1780 they repeated the performance. This
time a thousand houses perished.[88]

If white men believed that they fought wily savages who lived
on what the virgin wilderness would yield, they designed their tactics
for the destruction of a socety with a substantial investment in civilized
improvements. The destruction was considerable and cost the Indians
dearly, but it did not utterly cripple the tribes as many in the new
government hoped. "The nests are destroyed," wrote one of Sullivan's
officers, "but the birds are still on the wing."[89] It was a tribute to the
resiliency and adaptability of the eastern tribes that they survived the
Revolutionary onslaught.

Washington thought frontier fighters did better against Indians
than recruits from the more settled regions, but this did not mean
that he favored the creation of an American army fashioned according
to the Indian mode. He knew that the British would have to be
opposed by regular forces using regular tactics. In fact, the reason for
the promotion of indianization in the army, as far as it went, was
precisely the widespread feeling that Americans were not particularly
adept as forest warriors.[90] Washington sent Morgan to New York in
1777 because "the people in the Northern Army seem so intimidated

[86]Washington to John Sullivan, May 31, 1779, *Sullivan-Clinton Campaign,*
pp. 90-91; Parker, "Indian Interpretation of the Sullivan-Clinton Campaign,"
p. 58.
[87]Graymont, *Iroquois in the American Revolution,* p. 218.
[88]O'Donnell, *Southern Indians in the American Revolution,* pp. 48, 107,
111.
[89]"Journal of Major Jeremiah Fogg," September 30, 1779, *Journals of the
Military Expedition of Major General John Sullivan,* Cook, ed., p. 101.
[90]Washington to Patrick Henry, October 5, 1776, *Writings of George Washington,* Fitzpatrick, ed., 6: 166.
[91]Washington to Israel Putnam, August 16, 1777, ibid., 9: 70.

by the Indians. . . ."[91] Although Sullivan did his best to raise a competent force to chastise the Iroquois, he admitted that he had scarcely an officer acquainted with the Iroquois region. At times he seemed on the point of dispair when he contemplated an attack upon the Iroquois. He thought three thousand American troops against fourteen hundred Indians risky odds.[92] A prisoner told Washington that the British estimated the fifteen hundred Indians and rangers that could be mustered to oppose Sullivan equal to twice their number. Washington thought the estimate sound.[93]

In 1778, at a time when war had settled into a stalemate, Washington was pressed to turn his forces on the Iroquois. For a year and a half they had harassed the out-settlements unchecked. But he resisted, and for good reason. He reported to the Board of War that no matter how much the activities of the Indians may be deplored, they could not be considered more than evils of a "partial nature" that would have to await the settlement of "matters of higher moment."[94] The situation changed in 1779 and he dispatched Sullivan to conclude affairs with the Iroquois. It was a question of perspective. The main conflict took place between the Americans and the British. The Indians became important only when they could affect that contest. To Washington, indianization was significant in about the same proportion.

Much has been made of the tendency of Americans to behave as Indians because many Americans made a great deal of it. Yet that fact obscures a simple truth. Americans won their war for independence by using trained soldiery in formal combat, and the Indians were defeated by the same means. Much informal fighting took place, but the frontiersman did not break the power of the Indians. That task was left to the regular army and the militia organized in the traditional way.[95]

Even the formal treatises, written to support the creation of a distinctly American military force attuned to the tactics of the Indian

[91]Washington to Israel Putnam, August 16, 1777, ibid., 9: 70.

[92]Sullivan to George Washington, April 16, 1779, *Sullivan-Clinton Campaign,* pp. 79-80; Sullivan to John Jay, September 30, 1779, *Journals of the Military Expedition of Major General John Sullivan,* Cook, ed., p. 304.

[93]Washington to John Sullivan, August 1, 1779, *Writings of George Washington,* Fitzpatrick, ed., 16: 30.

[94]Washington to Board of War, August 3, 1778, ibid., 12: 264.

[95]Mahon, "Anglo-American Methods of Indian Warfare, p. 254.

tribes, are ambiguous. The treatment by Thomas Hutchins, the most ambitious effort, called for certain modifications in cumbersome European methods, but it did so with all the formality of a European handbook on tactics. And he supported his argument with a short description of the success of the Romans against the light troops they fought in Africa. The author balanced praise for the freedom and initiative of the native warriors with plans for the maintenance of discipline on the march, the placing and protection of baggage, and the construction of fortified camps. The object was as much to counter the menace of savage tactics as to imitate them. Hutchins taught caution, vigilence, and discipline, virtues fully consistent with European methods of war.[96] James Smith's rough and ready advice also contained an element of formality. Troops on the march in Indian country should be organized in three columns, one rod separating the ranks and forty rods between columns. Each column should have its own flankers. When the battle began the soldiers were to face out and take trees (the one concession to native custom). The center column should be prepared to support either flank if the enemy threatened attack. At the close of the day, camp should be arranged in a hollow square with sentries well placed. Both writers attended to the peculiar needs of war in the wilderness, but neither showed any signs of abandoning the traditional organization of an army.[97]

Conflict with the Indians in the later years of the eighteenth century testified to the success of formal tactics. The white man's fort remained invulnerable to Indian attack, though not of much use in protecting the frontier. Unless they were taken by surprise or surrendered by an incompetent or weak garrison, they remained as an abiding symbol of the white men's presence in the Indians' world. Even in the most spectacular defeat of a European force by the Indians — Braddock's disaster of 1755 — the outcome was caused not so much by the genius of the Indians and French as by the failure of Braddock to enforce the rules of European war.[98] In the battle at Bushy Run during Pontiac's uprising, General Bouquet was victorious

---

[96][William Smith], *Historical Account of Bouquet's Expedition against the Ohio Indians,* p. 127.

[97]Smith, *An Account of the Remarkable Occurrences in the Life and Travels of Col. James Smith,* pp. 135-37.

[98]Stanley Pargellis, "Braddock's Defeat," *American Historical Review,* 41 (1936): 253-69.

because he moved quickly without the encumbrance of baggage, held his men together when they were attacked, and finally enticed the Indians into an ambush and out-flanked them. He brought his European training to the New World, and with slight concessions to circumstances, he found it effective against the Indians.[99]

During the Revolutionary War Washington stressed America's formal military power by inviting native delegations whenever possible to view contingents of the army on parade.[100] And when he resolved to attack the Iroquois, he sent Sullivan with a well supplied and trained military force. Sullivan agreed to the need for careful preparation. More so than Washington, for he was woefully late in moving. Take, for example, these orders for an attack on an Indian town:

> The infantry and the artillery, to push on in front; General Maxwell's brigade, with the left flanking division, to endeavour to gain the enemy's right; General Poor's brigade to move and gain their left; the right flanking division, and two regiments from General Clinton's brigade to move round Poor's right flank; the infantry to rush on in front. . . .[101]

Hardly the stuff of savage war. At Newton, the one notable battle in the campaign, both sides lined up their forces, the British and Indians behind barracades; the Americans raked the line with artillery, made a flanking movement to the right, and charged with the bayonet. The Indians panicked at the artillery and the rest of the British force broke at the charge. Sullivan worried about the Indians, but when the battle came the old methods worked.[102]

The Indian tribes were no less flexible in selecting the proper mix of new and traditional methods to fight their enemies. Their adaptation of tactics scarcely resembled the undifferentiated frenzy of the ignoble savage. Very early in the relations between white and Indian,

[99][William Smith], *Historical Account of Bouquet's Expedition against the Ohio Indians*, pp. 16-24; Mahon, "Anglo-American Methods of Indian Warfare," p. 270.

[100]Thacher, *Military Journal of the American Revolution*, pp. 213-14; Washington to Philip Schuyler, October 16, 1776, *Writings of George Washington*, Fitzpatrick, ed., 6: 192.

[101]"Journal of Lieut. Col. Adam Hubley," September 13, 1779, *Journals of the Military Expedition of Major General John Sullivan*, Cook, ed., p. 162.

[102]John Butler to Lieut. Col. Bolton, August 31, 1779, *Sullivan-Clinton Campaign*, p. 137; "Journal of Lieutenant Robert Parker," August 29, 1779, ibid., p. 197.

the warriors had made significant revisions in their military methods. Sir William Johnson noted in 1772 that before the white man came the Iroquois had fought in larger groups under the direction of a chief. It was the introduction of firearms that led them to break up into smaller contingents.[103] In fact, the fighting had been even more formal. In those days the Iroquois wore body armor and the opposing sides lined up in the open and exchanged arrows. Guns made this obsolete.[104] The Indians absorbed European technology; some of the New England tribes learned blacksmithing and how to build European fortifications. And, finally, the coming of the Europeans reoriented the object of native hostility. Henceforth it would be directed predominantly against the white man rather than other native groupings.[105]

The tribes felt the consequences of the European invasion of the new continent almost immediately. The fur trade, for example, increased the number of permanent Indian settlements in the interior regions. The tribes staked out hunting territories with sharper boundaries than pre-Columbian existence had required. This tendency affected family relationships. The village became a center for hunting, a male occupation, and hence patrilocal. Land more strictly bounded could be sold and inherited through the male line.[106] The matrilineal society of aboriginal days came under profound stress. Disease, war, and alcohol reduced the population.[107] Wholesale acquisition of the white man's artifacts in many ways increased the proficiency of the Indians, but it diminished their autonomy. The major effect of relations between white and Indian was the creation of dependent native societies. The appearance of prophets among the eastern tribes in the late eighteenth century revealed the deep malaise that had settled on native life.[108] Neither the independence of the noble savage

---

[103]Johnson to Arthur Lee, March 28, 1772, *The Papers of Sir William Johnson*, Milton W. Hamilton, ed. (Albany, 1957), 12: 952.

[104]Keith Otterbein, "Why the Iroquois Won: An Analysis of Iroquois Military Tactics," *Ethnohistory*, 11 (1964): 57.

[105]Wilcomb E. Washburn, *The Indian in America* (New York, 1975), pp. 134-35, 139-40; Sherburne F. Cook, "Interracial Warfare and Population Decline among the New England Indians," *Ethnohistory*, 20 (1973): 3.

[106]Washburn, *Indians in America*, pp. 73-74.

[107]Cook, "Interracial Warfare and Population Decline among the New England Indians," p. 24, claims that between 1620 and 1720 the tribes of New England and lower New York lost a quarter of their population through war.

[108]Wallace, *Death and Rebirth of the Seneca*, p. 120.

nor the viciousness of his ignoble cousin could be reconciled with the dependent Indian of the revolutionary period.

When the war broke out the Indians' ties with the whites were so close that they could not avoid becoming embroiled in the conflict. The Creeks told George Galphin in 1777 that "we have been used so long to wrap our Children up as soon as they are born in Goods procured of the white People that we cannot do without [them]...."[109] American and British agents in the South made extensive use of trade goods in order to obtain the loyalty of the tribes. When the Chickasaws sued for peace with the Americans in 1782, they claimed that the British had "put the Bloody Tomahawk into our hands, telling us that we should have no Goods if we did not Exert ourselves to the greatest point of Resentment against you. . . ."[110] And once the fighting began Ethan Allen's observation was proved true. "It is impossible," he wrote, "for [the Indians] to carry on a war, except they are supported by the trade and commerce of some civilized nation. . . ."[111] The war made it increasingly difficult for any of the tribes to exercise autonomy.

The long period in which the Iroquois had maintained their independence by playing off the British and French came to an end in the 1760s. After the departure of the French, the Iroquois faced the problem of controlling the tribes to the west and south that had been subject to league power for a hundred years or more. After 1768, when they bargained away the land south of the Ohio without asking the Shawnees or Delawares, these tribes began to make their own settlements with the whites. By the time of the Revolution the Iroquois grip on political independence had been much weakened.[112]

Factionalism among all the tribes accelerated the decline of independence. Whites exploited the factions for their own purposes. The two major tribes involved in the Revolution — the Iroquois and Cherokees — were both rent by factions. In 1777 Dragging Canoe split the Cherokees by establishing the Chicamauga towns and supporting the British.[113] Largely because of the influence of the mis-

---

[109]O'Donnell, *Southern Indians in the Revolution,* p. 60.

[110]Ibid., pp. 69, 125.

[111]Allen, *A Narrative of Colonel Ethan Allen's Captivity,* p. 5.

[112]Iroquois Conference with Guy Johnson, January 23, 1775, *Documents Relative to New-York,* O'Callaghan, ed., 8: 537.

[113]Brown, *Old Frontiers,* pp. 161-64; O'Donnell, *Southern Indians in the Revolution,* p. 137.

sionary Samuel Kirkland, the Oneida and Tuscarora broke with the Iroquois League and fought against the British.[114] Such factionalism had always been part of native life and had always been a hindrance to political unity. During the Revolution factionalism and the growing dependence of the tribes were major symptoms of the decline of native society.

The Indians entered the Revolution because two centuries of contact with Europeans had enmeshed them inextricably in the white man's world. But the persistence of the warrior culture also conspired to bring them in. The Cherokees attacked the American settlements in 1776 long before John Stuart had planned to bring them into the conflict.[115] Provoked by the invasion of other lands by Virginia and North Carolina settlers, the warriors retaliated. Every rational interest should have kept the Iroquois out, but the British played on the tribesmen's need for the white man's goods and exploited the warriors' inclination to engage in war.[116] The Americans followed the same policy.

The Indians who took part in the Revolution were not ignoble savages bent upon the destruction of civilization. On the contrary, they entered the war because they had already moved dangerously close to the white man's ways, because they had learned to depend on his goods and even to feel loyalties similar to those that moved Englishmen and Americans. This did them little good in the outcome of the conflict. White men found it virtually impossible to think about Indian-white relations outside the categories of civilization and savagery, though they found it entirely possible to exploit the actual attachments of the tribes to the white man's world. The whites fought ignoble savages and believed they had defeated them. In fact, American independence merely created a situation in which the tribes became more dependent on the white man's society. The ignoble savage survived the Revolution as did the dependent Indian. In the years following, Americans invoked either image as might fit the occasion.

---

[114]Guy Johnson to the Earl of Dartmouth, February 13, 1775, *Documents Relative to New-York,* O'Callaghan, ed., 8:533; Kirkland to Philip Schuyler, March 12, 1776, Lothrop, *Life of Samuel Kirkland,* p. 24; Graymont, *Iroquois in the American Revolution,* p. 33-40.

[115]O'Donnell, *Southern Indians in the American Revolution,* p. 14.

[116]Seaver, *Narrative of the Life of Mary Jemison,* p. 66; Wallace, *Death and Rebirth of the Seneca,* p. 45; Fenton, "The Iroquois in History," p. 142.

Ignoble savagism periodically reared its head and white men went to war to destroy it. In the dependent Indian, Americans increasingly saw an object of pity and philanthropy.

THE IMPACT OF THE AMERICAN REVOLUTION ON THE BLACK POPULATION

BY WILLIE LEE ROSE

When I was first asked to give my impressions of the impact of the American Revolution on the black population, I must admit that I wondered what might be said, silently confessing to myself the doubts implied by an editor of a prominent black magazine who recently asked me, bluntly, whether there was any good reason why blacks should celebrate this Bicentennial. I reflected that once, long ago, in 1852 to be precise, the famous black abolitionist, Frederick Douglass, had been asked to speak on the Fourth of July in Rochester, New York, and that he had mused aloud why he, of all men, should have been asked to do any such thing. "Fellow citizens, pardon me," he begged, "are the great principles of political freedom and justice, embodied in that Declaration of Independence, extended to us?"[1] Speaking as an escaped slave, in a period when slavery was still alive and thriving, Douglass in asking the question was suggesting the answer.

Considering the intervening 200 years, the slow development of the promise of the Declaration, and the incomplete realization, even now, of that promise for black America, the editor's question of me seemed not unreasonable, and Douglass's answer of 1852 not entirely inappropriate, even these 124 years later. But it then occurred to me that if this were true, that blacks still had no reason to celebrate, then perhaps nobody has a reason to celebrate. By such a standard American liberty would have failed the test of twentieth-century problems.

Laying that question aside for a moment, I began to think further about the meaning of the entire Revolutionary epoch for slaves, and

---

[1] Oration, delivered at Corinthian Hall, Rochester, by Frederick Douglass, July 5, 1852 as reprinted in Benjamin Quarles, ed., *Frederick Douglass* (Englewood Cliffs, N.J., 1968), pp. 45-46.

indeed for all those left out on the first round of freedom. In the most general terms, the answer is simple: ideas long circulating in the western world were given a concrete reality in a new government, ideas that moved slowly but very surely toward a great enlargement of human freedom, at first for a few, later for many, as our ideas of the relationship between freedom and property slowly changed. But that would be to defer too much to the future, beyond doubt, and my task is to assess the more immediate effects of the Revolution.

What convinced me that something might be said to good effect was the sudden thought that this was really the question Chief Justice Roger Brooke Taney felt obliged to answer back in 1857, in the famous Dred Scott case, whether a black man, even if free, could really be a citizen of the United States, endowed with the right to bring his case into federal court. It must be believed that Justice Taney thought he understood the frame of mind of the Founders and their world when he came out with a thumping "no," and declared that our government was formed by white men, for whites only, and that such rights as even free blacks enjoyed were mere courtesies, and further, in the line that angered so many of his contemporaries, that "They had no rights which the white man was bound to respect" and further yet, that "this opinion was at that time . . . universal in the civilized portion of the white race. . . ."[2] He spoke less than a 100 years after the Declaration of Independence, and sixty-nine years after the Constitution was formed. Although he was, of course, interpreting the Constitution, his generalizations apparently refer to the dominant attitudes of the entire Revolutionary generation, and it has not been hard for historians now, or indeed for lawyers then, to show that the Chief Justice was mistaken in so summarily dismissing the impact of Enlightenment ideas, natural law, the concept of the essential worth of man, on both whites and blacks in the late eighteenth century.

Justice Taney lived in a period when a reaction against natural rights had affixed to Southern blacks a more difficult legal position than they had had in the Revolutionary period. There were restrictions on free blacks that had not existed earlier, and for slaves the chances of becoming free had become much dimmer. It is true that there were also laws requiring masters to provide decently for their chattels, and restraining them from cruel punishments and other

[2]*Dred Scott* v. *Sanford*, 19, Howard 393. See pp. 406-7.

barbarisms that marred the laws of the eighteenth century. No doubt these laws were frequently ignored, but the owner who did so was scouting public opinion, and there seems little doubt that life in a physical sense was becoming more bearable for most slaves in the nineteenth century. A new position for slaves was crystallizing, so that a slave might be regarded with more benign paternalism, almost *because* he could no longer hope for eventual emancipation.[3]

Ironically, an age of expanded liberties for whites had witnessed the rationalization of the slave system, making it harder for slaves to become free (even if their masters desired to emancipate), to learn to read, or open their minds in any way. It would almost appear to be an historical trade-off, in which the society-at-large indicates by law a will to secure decent order and some humanity on the plantations in return for some assurance that slaves would not become free men and trouble society-at-large. Roger B. Taney, victim of his own time-frame, failed as an historian in sensing the very different spirit of Revolutionary times, no matter how ambivalent attitudes on race in that earlier period can be proven to have been. Might not the passage of another century, with new views of property and freedom, allow a clearer perspective on how blacks were involved in the Age of Revolution, and what it meant to them?

This might be an appropriate place to recite the exploits of black men and women in the Revolution — of Crispus Attucks and the Boston Massacre, Phyllis Wheatley's poems about liberty, the black soldiers who served in various sectors of the war, to tell of the black men who served as spies, scouts, pilots, sailors, laborers for the patriot's cause, or perhaps to tell of the Battle of Rhode Island in August of 1778, where a black regiment figured prominently and served bravely.[4] No. We shall hear a lot about these matters, no doubt, in the coming months, and much that we hear will of necessity be speculative, perhaps pious and therapeutic. Black partici-

---

[3]I have attempted an exploration of this paradox in an unpublished paper called "The Domestication of Domestic Slavery." Since I first turned my thoughts to this subject, two recent works have appeared that deeply probe the subject of freedom and bondage in the colonial and revolutionary periods respectively. They are David Brion Davis, *Slavery in the Age of Revolution* (Ithaca, 1975), and Edmund S. Morgan, *American Slavery American Freedom: The Ordeal of Colonial Virginia* (New York, 1975).

[4]Benjamin Quarles, *The Negro in the American Revolution* (Chapel Hill, 1961) is a fine survey of black participation.

pation is hard to assess, for a reason that indicates why Justice Taney's period is so very different from that of the Revolutionary era. In the Revolution blacks were for the most part integrated into white units, because they were freely accepted as substitutes, and accepted by many of the colonial governments as volunteers on the same basis as whites, and also, one supposes, because blacks were less alarming to the whites of that period when not concentrated in units.

No, the real meaning of the Revolution for America's black people was more subtle, and rests more on the vigorous circulation of the idea of freedom, the new opportunities the general disruption of society afforded, and most particularly in the important social and demographic changes that came out of the struggle between the British and their obstreperous colonials. Yet it is interesting to note in passing that just as the combatants did eighty-five years later in the Civil War, both the British and the Americans were increasingly ready to call on blacks as soldiers, and hazard the possibility of an insurrection, as the going got rough. By Taney's time men apparently had forgotten what part black soldiers played in the Revolution, and three years after the Dred Scott decision a war began in which black men were ultimately asked to prove themselves as fighting men in special separate units, sometimes, alas, as cannon fodder. The black man of the Revolutionary era was at least dignified by the assumption that he would be a regular fighting man. Reflecting on how poor a conception Taney had of the difference between the 1850s and the spirit of '76 has caused me to appreciate more the advantage of a 200-year perspective on the earlier period.

The most immediate and significant consequence of the Revolution for blacks was the formation during the Revolutionary epoch of a large free black community.[5] How New England, under the impulse of revolutionary zeal provided for emancipation is a well-known and praiseworthy chapter of our history. With only a blush or two for the hesitations of Connecticut and Rhode Island, where slavery was a larger economic factor than in the others, New England had by 1790 only 3,763 slaves to report to the new federal census, out of a population of 16,882 blacks. By 1810 the number of slaves remaining was just 418, in Rhode Island and Connecticut, which had

---

[5]Ira Berlin, *Slaves without Masters: The Free Negro in the Ante-bellum South* (New York, 1974). The judgment is my own, based on the excellent accounting of the process given in the early chapters of Berlin's book.

taken gradual measures.[6] The urgings of blacks themselves, the interpretations of courts favorable to freedom, the new constitutions — all these contributed to the success of the cause now actively pursued by an increasingly vigorous new antislavery movement. The Middle Atlantic states proved more hesitant to act, with New York and New Jersey entirely resistant to emancipation through the Revolutionary period. Pennsylvania joined Rhode Island and Connecticut as a gradualist state. There seems no reason to doubt that the great thrust of this movement owed its main impulse to the workings of the ideals of the Revolution on the minds of both black men and women and their owners.

But the black population of the North was numerically of small significance when compared to the thousands who lived and worked to the south in the tobacco colonies. Therefore it is to Maryland and Virginia that we must look to see the ideals of the Revolution in contact with the most stubborn economic facts of life. In these states the most important accomplishment of the Revolutionary era was the formation of a large free black community in the midst of slavery. Before the Revolution the numbers of free blacks in these states was negligible, and most of them were the mulatto offspring of mixed unions; surprisingly often they were the children of white mothers and black fathers, and therefore born free. The children of white fathers who disliked seeing their children growing up as slaves also contributed to this population, but less than one might imagine on the eve of the Revolution because a law of Virginia in force for sixty years prior to its reversal in 1782 made manumission by will or deed illegal. Maryland, the only colony with a conveniently dated (1755) pre-Revolutionary census, had then only 1817 free blacks, constituting only 4 per cent of the black population. Eighty per cent of those 1817 were mulattoes. This picture would serve reasonably well for other Southern states. Ira Berlin, in his excellent new book on the subject, produces convincing evidence that the numbers of free blacks were small in each state and that of these a very few were of purely African extraction.[7]

---

[6]Arthur Zilversmit, *The First Emancipation: The Abolition of Slavery in the North* (Chicago, 1967), p. 124.

[7]Berlin, *Slaves Without Masters,* pp. 46-47 for tables, text pp. 48-50. For slavery in 18th century Virginia, see Gerald Mullin, *Flight and Rebellion: Slave Resistance in Eighteenth Century Virginia* (New York, 1972).

Over the three decades from 1770 to the end of the eighteenth century, the free black population increased at a remarkable rate, not only in New England, where we have seen general emancipations, but in the Middle Atlantic states, where the pattern of gradual emancipation prevailed, but even more remarkably in the Upper South where the black population was actually concentrated. Virginia and Maryland, the tobacco colonies, accounted for well over half of all the slaves owned before the Revolution. Feeling the impulses of the Revolution early, they showed an increase in manumissions before the war started, and showed approximate percentage increases in free blacks before 1790 of 609 per cent and 340 per cent respectively. By 1810 over 23 per cent of Maryland's blacks were free. Virginia, holding so many thousands of slaves, could count only 7 per cent increase of free blacks by that time, but this per cent amounted to a larger number of free blacks than any other Southern state except Maryland, and came numerically to 30,500 souls; Maryland had over 33,000. This growth represented in Virginia, in the overwhelmingly largest slave state, a surging growth in the free black population, rising from the year 1782 when the liberalized manumission law was passed (overturning a law and a policy of fifty-nine years' duration) prohibiting private manumisson. Free persons of color increased by 1790 to 12,766, to 20,124 by the end of the century, and to 30,570 in 1810.[8]

Leaving aside for the moment the circumstances, and by whose volition these blacks became free, it should be mentioned that these figures cannot include the tens of thousands of slaves who fled to the British, many thousands of them never returning. When the center of the war shifted to the South after 1778 the British systematically took off slaves in groups of hundreds at a time. Benjamin Quarles estimates that the British carried away in their final evacuation perhaps 4,000 or more from New York, the same number from Savannah, from Charleston 6,000, and from Yorktown, before the surrender, 5,000. He estimates that as many as 5,000 had already been carried away during the fighting.[9] The fate of the evacuees was various, some going to Nova Scotia, many freed, some sold without conscience in the

[8]Berlin, *Slaves Without Masters,* tables, pp. 46-47.
[9]Quarles, *Negro in the American Revolution,* pp. 171-172.

West Indies. Some remained the slaves of their loyalist masters who departed at the same time.

It is difficult to assess the full reaction of a largely illiterate black population to the ideas of the Revolution, but the actions of the slaves who seized their opportunities to escape were speaking with their heels. Their vigorous response to Lord Dunmore's policy of offering freedom to those who would defect and join the British spoke reams, especially when the Americans began to counter with proposals to emancipate slaves who bore arms for the patriots. Those who took their chances with the colonials may have reasoned as did a slave named Saul, who had served as a double spy, and asked the legislature for his freedom after the war. He was, he said, "taught to know that the war was levied upon America, not for the emancipation of Blacks, but for the subjugation of Whites, and he thought the number of Bond-ment ought not to be augmented."[10] To their credit, most petitioners received their freedom. By a Virginia law of 1783 "all who had served in the late war" were liberated, the law itself being tacit admission that many slaves had served the American armies in spite of Virginia laws restricting service to free blacks.[11]

Perhaps more important than the struggle between the British and the colonials was the general disruption of the times, which permitted slaves to escape their owners and declare themselves free at some distance from home. The depressed condition of agriculture worked hand-in-glove with the ideas of the Revolution, making many masters who were disposed by conscience to free their slaves more willing to do so. When Richard Randolph freed his slaves by will in the wake of the Revolution, he did so, as he wrote, "To make restitution, as far as I am able, to an unfortunate race of bond-men, over whom my ancestors have usurped and exercised the most lawless and monstrous tyranny, and in whom my countrymen (by their iniquitous laws, in contradiction of their own declaration of rights, and in violation of every sacred law of nature, of the inherent, inalienable and imprescriptible rights of man, and of every principle of moral and

---

[10]General Assembly, Petitions from Norfolk, August - October 1792, Virginia State Library, Richmond.
[11]William W. Hening, comp., *Statutes at Large; Being a Collection of All the Laws of Virginia, from . . . 1619,* 13 vols. (Richmond, 1809-1823), v. 8.

political honesty) have vested me with absolute property. . . ."[12]
Estimating the extent of the Enlightenment upon the emancipators
when counting up the expansion of freedom in the Revolutionary era
is just as puzzling as understanding how much the slaves understood
about the same ideas. Yet the problems are quite different. With the
black population one has to distinguish between the urge, which must
have been present always, to break free, and the special form it would
take under the impulse of new ideas of natural right; with the slave-
owning class, one would have to distinguish between stated motives
and economic facilitators. Exploring this point would extend beyond
the scope of this paper, but it seems reasonable to assume that the
greatly enlarged free black population resulted from impulses from
both sides of the color line, eased by the economic fact of reduced
value, as it proved, a temporarily reduced value, of slave labor, and
the enlarged possibility of an escaped slave's escaping detection, once
there were more free blacks with whom to merge one's identity.

Not only was that free black community enlarged, but in the
Upper South, where it was growing so fast, it was also changing
significantly in color composition. Ira Berlin has recently pointed to
the significance of the non-discriminatory nature of the emancipation
of the period: where owners had once chosen to emancipate only a
few light-colored blood relatives, for special reasons, they now emancipated wholesale on grounds of conscience, which meant that the
free black community began to receive large numbers of blacks with
pure African ancestry, and the free black community began to reflect
more perfectly the entire range of the black population.[13] He regards
this condition in the Upper South as being an important difference
between the free black communities of the Upper South and the
Lower South, particularly Louisiana, where lightness of color remained
a distinguishing feature.

After the Revolution, in Maryland and Virginia, one could
no longer use blackness of complexion as prima facie indication of
slave status, which greatly increased the probabilities of escaping
detection for such slaves of any shade of complexion as decided to
run off the plantation. These circumstances generated a wholesome

---

[12]Will of Richard Randolph, Clerk's Office, Prince Edward County, Va.,
Will Book of 1797.
[13]Berlin, *Slaves Without Masters,* p. 50.

restlessness on the slave population, and there is considerable evidence that the advertisements for runaways register a marked increase in the 1790s of those who are described as being black or African.[14] The talented, skilled, light-colored population that Gerald Mullin describes so well in *Fight and Rebellion*,[15] were now joined in flight by those who were black, and not particularly skilled. With the development of towns in the post-Revolutionary period blacks had an increasingly improved chance of escaping detection, and the seaport cities became a favored target.

The attitudes of blacks who sought freedom is best registered in words through the petitions they made for freedom. These petitions often pointed to the inconsistency of the ideals of the Revolution and the maintenance of slavery. Freedom suits were "invariably won" according to Benjamin Quarles, who appears in this instance to be referring primarily to cases arising in Massachusetts. Petitions were also a favored means. There one group presented themselves as "a Grate number of Blacks . . . who . . . are held in a state of slavery within the bowels of a free and christian Country" . . . they were a free-born people who had never forfeited that natural right, but "were stolen from the bosoms of our tender Parents, . . . to be made slaves for Life in a christian land." A group of blacks in New Hampshire urged a law be passed to free them (1779) "that the name of slave may not more be heard in a land gloriously contending for the sweets of freedom."[16]

Liberal decisions in some key court cases also contributed to the expansion of freedom. In many instances blacks petitioned for freedom, especially in Maryland, on grounds of descent from a white woman. The famous case in that state of the Butler family illustrates the point, and its multiplier effect. William and Mary Butler claimed descent from a white woman's union with a slave. They had produced mulatto offspring sometime between 1664 and 1681, when a law operated to enslave the woman along with her children in such instances. The object was to discourage such alleged "shameful matches." Although the Butlers did not win their suit in 1771 when

---

[14]Unpublished statistics accumulated by Martin Lee Grey at the Johns Hopkins University.

[15]See Footnote 6, above.

[16]Quarles, *Negro in the American Revolution*, pp. 39, 44.

they opened litigation, their daughter, Mary, was more successful sixteen years later. Soon the name of Butler appears regularly in such suits, and for the same reason that Shorter and Toogood family names appear.[17]

Sometimes slaves bought their freedom, but larger numbers gained it by flight, suits for freedom and general emancipations. Thus the free black community emerged, and its importance through the entire slave era would be hard to exaggerate. Not only did its existence inspire flight in slaves, but also it became a center for the development of institutions very important to the entire black population after 1863 and the Emancipation Proclamation. Here the black church experienced its first vigorous semi-independent growth, and in the free black communities the fraternal organizations flourished. The African church became the significant social unit, beyond the home, of the free black community, and at least one able scholar has concluded that blacks had a higher proportion of church membership in the ante-bellum period than whites did.[18] One function of the church was educational, for nearly all the churches conducted Sunday Schools, and through the churches came the largest cadre of black leadership that was to become so significant a resource in the Reconstruction that followed the Civil War. Had there been no substantial free black community the transition in 1863 from slave to freedman, to free men and women, would have been infinitely more difficult.

Almost as significant in its consequences for the condition of the slave population was a second result of the Revolution, the suppression of the African slave trade. The origin of the movement that culminated in the prohibition of 1807 came with the pre-Revolutionary non-importation agreements among the colonial legislatures. Massachusetts acted in 1774, as did Connecticut. Rhode Island, the colony most heavily involved economically in slave-trading, restricted the traffic sharply, stating that "those who are desirous of enjoying all the advantage of liberty themselves, should be willing to extend personal liberty to others."[19] The Middle Atlantic states worked

---

[17]Berlin, *Slaves Without Masters,* pp. 33-35, 39.

[18]Ibid., 287-303.

[19]Zilversmit, *First Emancipation,* p. 106. The process is summarized on pages 105-108, and 156-167. The cynicism of the Rhode Island law, matched to a considerable extent by New Jersey's similar action, is revealed in the provisions that permitted the Rhode Island slavetraders to continue to bring slaves from Africa to the West Indies, and even hold them over in Rhode Island, provided

variously to the same end. As in the case of emancipation, economic circumstances eased the course of Revolutionary rhetoric and idealism. Glutted slave markets and overstocked underpaying plantations in the Middle colonies and the Upper South and the need to hurt British commerce, eased the path of conscience. Virginia, North Carolina and Georgia acted in 1774 and 1775, and three months ahead of the Declaration of Independence the Continental Congress acted in the name of the thirteen united colonies to end the international slave trade to America.[20]

The limited nature of this commitment is a familiar story to all students of American history. How Jefferson's harsh and uncompromising charge against King George for allegedly forcing the colonies to participate in this "piratical warfare" was struck from the Declaration of Independence at the insistence of the Deep South representatives is part of a predictable back-down. Later, in the Constitutional Convention at Philadephia, South Carolina could easily point out that Virginia had more slaves than she needed, while South Carolina had fewer, and suggested that economic motives prompted this liberal view on the part of Upper South representatives who were anticipating a rise in the value of their property. This intra-South debate marked subsequent discussions through the constitution-making era.[21] And yet the magic words were out, that men, all men, were endowed with "inalienable rights" that included "Life, Liberty, and the pursuit of Happiness." As Bernard Bailyn has pointed out, such ideas are weapons. The inconsistency pervading the American fight for liberty and its denial forced itself forward at every turn.[22] The British were, of course, prompt in their derisive reminders; but England's continued status as a slaveholding polity limited the effect of her laughter to embarassment only. The most telling thrusts came

---

they were not sold there. And yet, these limitations not withstanding, by 1787 all the new states from New England south to Virginia had prohibited the importation of slaves as merchandizable property into their own jurisdictions. Donald L. Robinson, *Slavery in the Structure of American Politics, 1765-1820* (New York, 1971), pp. 296-299.

[20]Quarles, *Negro in the American Revolution,* pp. 40-42, 195.

[21]Ibid., p. 42; Robinson, *Slavery in the Structure of American Politics,* p. 82. Robert McColley, *Slavery and Jeffersonian Virginia* (2nd ed., Urbana, 1973), p. 170; Winthrop D. Jordan, *White Over Black: American Attitudes toward the Negro, 1550-1812* (Chapel Hill, 1968), p. 301.

[22]Bernard Bailyn, *The Ideological Origins of the American Revolution* (Cambridge, Mass., 1967), pp. 239-245.

from within, with the development of the first serious attacks not only on the slave trade, but on slavery itself.

Levi Hart in 1775 cried that it was now "high time for this colony to wake up and put an effectual stop to the cruel business of stealing and selling our fellow men," and asked "what inconsistence and self-contradiction is this! . . . When, O when shall the happy day come, that Americans shall be *consistently* engaged in the cause of liberty?"[23] The Amercans' use of the word "slavery" to sum up their position in the British empire was bound to have the result of associating the Revolution with the slavery question where it meant *most,* and for that reason it seems altogether natural that the first organized activities for emancipation began with the Revolution. The work of Anthony Benezet and John Woolman and others like them, the Quakers and other religious sects, did not bear the fruit in their own lives that they could have wished, though they doubtless inspired many to free their slaves in the interest of a clear conscience and consistency.[24] But their work was remembered past the time of reaction against what they had stood for, and inspired a new generation of abolitionists in the next century. The ideas of the Declaration moved blacks deeply, focusing their thoughts on their own emancipation. Truly, they held themselves to be in Quarles' very appropriate phrase, "heirs of the same promise."[25]

A generation of black and white abolitionists taunted slaveholders and their abettors among the politicians with the language of the Declaration, eventually forcing the most ardent defenders of slavery to denounce the document altogether. The abolitionists claimed blacks were included in the promise of the Declaration, and made a fierce distinction between the grandeur of its faith in mankind, when contrasted with the United States Constitution, which many of them ritually burned for its wordless but real sanction of slavery in feudal law. When John Brown organized blacks in Canada for his coming push on Harper's Ferry in 1859 the congress made their own constitution and endorsed the Declaration.[26]

[23]Ibid., p. 243.

[24]The outstanding study of the intellectual roots of the early antislavery movement is David Brion Davis, *The Problem of Slavery in Western Culture* (Ithaca, 1965). See especially Chapter 10.

[25]Quarles, *Negro in the American Revolution,* noting title of Chapter 8.

[26]Joseph C. Robert, *The Road from Monticello* ("Historical Society Papers of the Trinity College Historical Society," XXIV [Durham, 1941]), *passim;*

One final act of the Revolutionary generation should be mentioned because of its ultimate significance in the sectional struggle. When the individual states ceded their western land claims to the new Confederation, they invested the government with the responsibility of determining the laws that would govern it. The Northwest Ordinance of 1787, devised for the purpose, prohibited the introduction of slavery in the territories north of the Ohio River, and became the first positive articulation in law of the policy of containing slavery. It also became the most significant legal precedent for the free-soilers after 1848, and later for the new Republican party in the 1850s when they argued that Congress itself had the duty and right to prohibit slavery in the territories acquired from Mexico. As William W. Freehling has recently pointed out, "containment" was the road that ultimately led to the end of slavery in the United States, and he places Thomas Jefferson, the author of the Ordinance, very close to Abraham Lincoln in his thinking on the subject.[27]

These, to conclude, are my notions of the impact of the Revolution on Black Americans: the development of a free black community of size and strength to become a guardian of cherished institutions and an aid in the struggle for general emancipation and to provide leadership; the suppression of the African slave trade, an event that meant better physical conditions in the nineteenth century for the enslaved population; the rise of the first abolition movement; and the emergence of a policy of containment of slavery in the Confederation period, a policy that had its ups and downs, to be sure, but eventually became the rallying point for the emergent free soil movement and the Republican party, and the sticking point for Lincoln's government in the secession crisis. Containment in time became the precipitating cause of the Civil War and emancipation.

In all this the gains surely were greater than the detrimental side-effects, but these last should be mentioned, for they are thickly entangled with the reaction that followed the passing of the Revolutionary generation. The rise of the free black population in the crucial Upper South region, where the course of the first emancipation stopped

Clement C. Eaton, *Freedom of Thought in the Old South* (Durham, 1940); Stephen B. Oates, *To Purge This Land with Blood; A Biography of John Brown* (New York, 1970), pp. 243-247.

[27]William W. Freehling, "The Founding Fathers and Slavery," *American Historical Review*, 77 (1972): 81-93.

in its tracks, frightened a vulnerable slave-holding society who recognized it as a threat, especially after the black revolution in St. Domingue in 1794 and even more after the disruption of Gabriel Prosser's attempted revolt in Virginia in 1800. Virginia's black population was over 40 per cent of the whole at this period, and heavily concentrated in the eastern counties. The suppression of the African slave trade created a stronger determination to retain in bondage those who were slaves, and contributed in some measure to the restrictive laws on manumission appearing in the early nineteenth century. No doubt some of the cruel strength and vigor of the interstate slave traffic is owing to the rise in value of slave property, which also owes something to reviving agricultural profits. Attempting to answer the unanswerable arguments of the first abolitionists readied the defenders of slavery for the greater onslaught to come. They learned to do better than Patrick Henry, who when asked why he kept slaves, said he would not, could not defend it, and held as his only, very limp excuse "ye general inconvenience" of doing without them.[28] The policy of containment wobbled badly before it struck the iron resistance of the white South, in deep dread of being contained *with* the blacks as a race along with the institution, and then brought on a great war over the question, a war that exacted one life for every five slaves emancipated by the conflict. Surely this was a costly emancipation, even when one joins in the noble meaning of Lincoln's words, who asked in the Second Inaugural, just on this very point:

> Shall we discern . . . [in "this terrible war"] any departure from the divine attributes which the believers in a Living God always ascribe to Him? Fondly do we hope — fervently we pray — that this mighty scourge of war may speedily pass away. Yet, if God wills that it continue, until all the wealth piled [up] by the bond-man's two hundred and fifty years of unrequited toil shall be sunk, and until every drop of blood drawn with the lash, shall be paid with another drawn with the sword, as was said three thousand years ago, so still it must be said 'the judgments of the Lord, are true and righteous altogether'.[29]

Lincoln had God; moderns have Marx. Explaining such costs

---

[28]Quoted in Robert Douthat Meade, *Patrick Henry: Patriot in the Making* (Philadelphia, 1957), p. 300.

[29]Roy P. Basler, ed., *The Collected Works of Abraham Lincoln*, 9 vols. (New Brunswick, 1953), 8: 333.

and the nature of social change is never easy. But who could criticize Lincoln at such a moment for failing to mention the less exalted forces of sectional economic interest and partisan political requirements that had accompanied the spirit of the Declaration of Independence so much cherished by the Republican party down the long road to war?

Lincoln's sense of America's mission, and its derivation from the spirit of the Declaration, justify him, as does the burning sense of suffering in the process of learning that suffused his words. Perhaps for this reason more than for all others the suffering nation could identify with their leader. In all events, his humility contrasts most agreeably with Chief Justice Taney's God-like confidence in his own understanding of the literal nature and the historical background of the Revolution and the Constitution. And who can doubt that Lincoln would have been most pleased had he lived to read the opening clause of the Fourteenth Amendment to the Constitution, designed most specifically to set right the omission that had eased Justice Taney's decision that Dred Scott could *not* be a citizen, a new clause extending the blessing and protection of citizenship to *all* persons born in the United States?

As all men know, setting things right in law does not accomplish all it ought, and the road to realization of the full meaning of the Revolution is far from its goal. That thought might lead to pessimism, but might it not lead as easily to renewed understanding of a generation who had a view of the relationship of property to freedom at considerable variance from our own, and to gratitude for the words they articulated but only partially implemented in their time? All things considered, I take heart, and vote for the words. Their promise though imperfectly fulfilled, is no longer denied. If Frederick Douglass could conclude his Fourth of July oration to the Rochester Ladies' Anti-Slavery Society by drawing encouragement from "the great principles" of the Declaration, "cheered by the obvious tendencies" of his own age, then surely we may, after this long journey and the developments of our own time, do as well.

THE AMERICAN REVOLUTION AND THE RIGHTS OF WOMEN: THE FEMINIST THEORY OF ABIGAIL ADAMS

BY LINDA GRANT DE PAUW

On the eve of the American Revolution, women in British North America enjoyed remarkably high status. They not only exercised economic and social independence that would have shocked their nineteenth-century granddaughters (had they known anything about women's history) but also had rights that were extensive enough to impress women striving for "liberation" in our own times.[1] Indeed, those learning of the life style of colonial women for the first time often leap to the conclusion that the Revolutionary era was a time of rampant feminism.

All women, even the very wealthy, worked in eighteenth-century America. Homemaking in the preindustrial era involved a variety of specialized tasks including producing, preserving and preparing food-stuffs, tending kitchen gardens and raising livestock, processing raw linen and wool, knitting, spinning and sewing, and serving as nurse, midwife, and doctor for family units that averaged about six persons[2] but could run to over a hundred for large plantations with many servants and slaves. The economic value of such "housework" was obvious. It was skilled work and it was hard physical work. Consequently, despite the theoretical restrictions on the property rights of married women, husbands and wives alike considered the wife to have a financial interest in the family estate because of her economic contributions to it. An illustration of this attitude is found in the correspondence of a shoemaker named Joseph Hodgkins who wrote

---

[1]The author has discussed the role and status of women in Revolutionary America in detail in *Founding Mothers: Women of America in the Revolutionary Era* (Boston ,1975) and in *Remember the Ladies: Women of America 1750-1815* [co-authored with Conover Hunt] (New York, 1976).

[2]Robert V. Wells, *The Population of the British Colonies in America before 1776: A Survey of Census Data* (Princeton, 1975), p. 301.

home to his wife while he was serving as a company officer during the Revolution. He assumed that his wife was entitled to one-third of his pay. He apologized when, because his pay was in arrears, he fell behind in his payments to her. He promised to send extra cash when he requested extra shirts or special services from her. And when he wanted her to advance some money to his elderly father, he asked that she "Charge the same." She, in turn, took it for granted that she had a right to her "thirds."[3]

In addition to housework, colonial women routinely took part in some business enterprise designed to make a profit. Usually they worked in partnership with a husband, but many ran businesses independently. During the colonial era women are found in virtually every occupation open to men from apothecary and blacksmith to printer, ropemaker, and shipwright. Furthermore, before the Revolution, equal pay appears to have been the rule. It cost as much to have a woman shoe a horse as to have a man do it. A gill of rum cost as much in a woman's tavern as in a man's. There was no reduction in price if one purchased corn from a woman's farm rather than a man's. It is particularly interesting to note that before the industrialization of cloth manufacturing, which created low paying "women's" jobs outside the home, women even made equal pay in the field of cloth production. A woman who owned an early twisting mill in Pennsylvania was eagerly employed "on the best Terms."[4]

The knowledge that they were not economically dependent on a husband may partially explain the considerable degree of social freedom that colonial women enjoyed. Newspaper announcements reveal that substantial numbers of women deserted their husbands, unilaterally dissolving their marriages. Sometimes they left to live with other men, but others went to escape harsh treatment, in resentment over a husband's adultery, or for various other reasons. Elizabeth Moore left because her husband had "publickly said his Mother would sooner live in a hollow Tree" than with her.[5] Mary Simmons

---

[3]Herbert T. Wade and Robert A. Lively, *This Glorious Cause: The Adventures of Two Company Officers in Washington's Army* (Princeton, 1958), pp. 54, 175, 179, 182, 188, 224, 230.

[4]Joan Hoff Wilson, "The Illusion of Change: Women and the American Revolution," in Alfred F. Young, ed., *The American Revolution: Explorations in the History of American Radicalism* (DeKalb, 1976), pp. 398-399.

[5]*Virginia Gazette,* May 9, 1771.

left her husband to become an actress in the playhouse at Charlestown.[6] In addition, some couples negotiated divorces by mutual consent. For instance, Mary and Joseph M'Gehe published a notice in the *North Carolina Gazette* by which Joseph gave Mary property worth £120 in division of the estate, each promised to make no further claims on the other, and finally "solemnly agreed before God and the World, to be no longer Man and Wife, but for ever hereafter, be as if we had never been married."[7] Divorces such as this were not strictly legal, but the parties and their neighbors considered them to be so and remarriage following such a divorce was not uncommon. At the time the M'Gehes negotiated their separation, Mary was living with another man and expecting his child. She may well have married him.

The tolerance of society toward fornication and premarital pregnancy was greater in the Revolutionary era than it would be again until the 1960s. Precise statistical data on such subjects is, of course, impossible to obtain. Not all extramarital sex relations result in babies and such factors as birth control, abortion, and infanticide — all of which were practiced two hundred years ago — tend to distort statistical conclusions. What statistics do show is that there was a peak in so-called "short term" babies born to white American women in the years just before and just after the Revolution that was not approximated again until the last decade. Thirty per cent of all first babies were born before nine months of marriage.[8] Such events were tolerated and, even encouraged indirectly, by courtship practices such as bundling which only came under attack in the last decades of the century.

Nineteenth-century ladies would have blushed at the freedom with which their grandmothers discussed and enjoyed the physical pleasures of love. They would have been horrified to learn of the freedom with which their grandmothers used physical force to express their opinions. While women of the nineteenth century had to overcome great obstacles even to speak at public meetings, eighteenth-century women organized mob demonstrations and when circum-

[6]*Maryland Journal,* October 26, 1774.
[7]April 7, 1775.
[8]Daniel Scott Smith and Michael S. Hindus, "Premarital Pregnancy in America 1640-1971: An Overview and Interpretation," *Journal of Interdisciplinary History,* 5 (1975) 1:537.

stances called for it attacked their opponents with guns, hatchets, hoes, pots of boiling lye, or, in less extreme cases, chamber pots filled with what was euphemistically called "night soil." Daughters of Liberty as well as Sons of Liberty were known to coat a Loyalist victim with hot tar and feathers.

Modern readers who consider the activities of these strong-minded, self-reliant women are strongly tempted to believe that this generaltion of Founding Mothers must have produced a feminist ideology. And, in fact, one woman, Abigail Adams, is commonly singled out and identified as the first important thinker in the history of American feminism. Professor Richard B. Morris decribes Adams as "a committed feminist [who] often baited her husband about the undue subordination of women. . . ."[9] Ann Forfreedom lists Abigail Adams with Victoria Woodhull and Emmeline Pankhurst in a section of her book entitled "Feminist Movements Through the Ages."[10] In the 1973 edition of his well-known text, *A History of Colonial America,* colonialist Max Savelle declares that Abigail Adams exempli-fied "a new feminism,"[11] while June Sochen notes with regret in her women's history textbook that Abigail Adams's "threat" to rebel against male dominance was "unfortunately never acted upon."[12] Anne F. and Andrew M. Scott describe Adams as "an early feminist" in their recent study of the woman's suffrage movement.[13] A recent brochure from a textbook publisher used a portrait of Abigail Adams and quoted her out of context saying "We are determined to foment a rebellion" to illustrate their women's studies offerings, and columnist Mary McGrory unequivocally labelled Adams as a "feminist" in her nationally syndicated column on April 25, 1976. The author of this paper cheerfully confesses to having listed Abigail Adams in a discussion of "feminists" in her first published writing on Revolutionary women, which appeared in *MS* Magazine.[14]

Abigail Adams herself, I am now convinced, would have been

---

[9]*Seven Who Shaped Our Destiny: The Founding Fathers as Revolutionaries* (New York, 1973), p. 84.

[10]*Women Out of History: A Herstory Anthology* (Los Angeles, 1972), p. 226.

[11](Hinsdale, Illinois, 1973), p. 744.

[12]*Herstory: A Woman's View of American History* (New York, 1974), pp. 73-75.

[13]*One Half the People: The Fight for Woman Suffrage* (Philadelphia, 1975), p. 54.

[14]"The Forgotten Spirit of '76", *MS* 3 (1974): 56.

mortified to learn of the meaning that has been read into some of her private — and not entirely serious — correspondence with her husband. The raw materials for the development of a feminist ideology were unquestionably present in the Revolutionary era. But they were not, in fact, developed, and certainly not by Abigail Adams.

It is safe to assume that Thomas Jefferson was not thinking about women when he penned the famous phrase "We hold these truths to be self-evident, that all men are created equal, that they are endowed by their Creator with certain unalienable Rights . . ." Nevertheless, as the words were understood in the eighteenth century, women were included. In that period, the *Oxford English Dictionary* tells us, the word "man" was understood to mean "a human being (irrespective of sex or age)." The *Dictionary* goes on to explain that the use of the word has changed over the years so that today the older sense, in which it was equivalent to the word "person" appears "only in general or indefinite applications . . . in modern apprehension *man* as thus used primarily denotes the male sex." But in an earlier age, the word was used as Samuel Sewall used it when arguing with a young man about his hair style: "Men were men before they had hair of their faces, (half of mankind have never any)."[15] Thus, when Americans of 1776 read the words "all men are created equal," they understood them to be making an extreme and universal claim. In a sense, the fact that Thomas Jefferson was probably not thinking of women — or blacks or Jews or Irish Catholics or Chicanos for that matter — is merely an academic point. The influence of his statement lies in its absolute nature. Virtually every American reform movement in the past two hundred years has found the principles of the Declaration of Independence relevant to its cause.

As applied to the status of women in America during the lifetime of Abigail Adams — who lived from 1744 to 1818 — the Revolutionary doctrine of equality might have been applied in four ways. First, it might have been applied as a demand for political equality, for the right to vote and consent to the laws that governed women as well as men. Second, it might have been applied as a demand for legal equality, for the abolition of all legal distinctions based on sex,

---

[15]June 10, 1701, *Samuel Sewall's Diary*, Mark Van Doren, ed., (New York, 1927), p. 161. See also uses of the word by Hume in 1752 and Burke in 1793 cited in the *Oxford English Dictionary*.

particularly those in the common law which made married men masters of their wives. Third, it might have been applied as a demand for equal educational opportunity, for recognition of women's brains as equal in quality to those of men and for equal encouragement to daughters and sons to cultivate their intelligence. Finally, however, the doctrine of equality might be applied to American women in a way that ignored sex — and therefore feminism — entirely. It might be applied as a demand that American women of the upper class be recognized as the equals of European women of the upper class.

Abigail Adams was a woman of active intelligence,[16] a keen observer of life, and a prolific writer who, unlike most of her female contemporaries, had descendants who thought her letters worth preserving. She considered all four of the positions respecting women's equality that I have just described, but she firmly embraced only the last. I intend to argue that identifying Abigail Adams as a feminist oversimplifies her views and associates her with a type of egalitarian theory that she would have abhorred. Since I admire Abigail Adams immensely, I rather think that were she alive today she could be argued into more "liberated" positions very easily. Nevertheless, she lived in her times, not in ours, and it is a disservice to history if we refuse to recognize the difference that makes.

Should women have the right to vote since "all men are created equal"? The principle "No taxation without representation" was fundamental to the Patriot ideology from the earliest days of the pre-Revolutionary crisis. The conclusion was inescapable that women who paid taxes should have the right to vote. Of course, very few women in colonial America paid taxes. Married women, under the common law, could not hold title to property. Any taxes due were paid by their husbands. That unmarried group ridiculed as "old maids" rarely included women of wealth. As for widows, the wealthy ones commonly remarried so quickly that few of them were taxpayers on more than one election day. Nevertheless, the principle requiring that taxpayers have the right to consent to legislation affecting their

---

[16]Although Abigail Adams often complained of deficiencies in her education, she was far better educated than the average American man of her time. In addition to the English writers she could read French and had enough basic Latin and Greek to get her children started on those subjects. In addition to advanced training in the classics she lacked the "accomplishments" of music, elegant penmanship, and the ability to spell "correctly."

pocketbooks was so firmly established in America during the Revolutionary era that only three states — Pennsylvania, Delaware, and South Carolina — had laws disfranchising women who otherwise met the property and residence requirements for voters.[17]

Although women were theoretically entitled to vote, there are only isolated instances of them casting ballots in America before the Revolution. Even among the tiny number of females whose ownership of property and absence of a marital tie qualified them, the right to vote was seldom exercised. Of course, the practice of deference to the "natural leaders" of the community resulted in very low rates of political participation even among men who were qualified to vote. Because it was so uncommon for women to go to the polls, it is probable that most women who qualified were unaware that voting was their legal right. In 1777 Hannah Lee Corbin of Virginia wrote to her brother Richard Henry Lee urging him to support giving the suffrage to widows. She pointed out that such women did pay taxes and that it was unfair to impose taxation without representation. He replied that he "would at any time give my consent to establish their right of voting" but in fact they already had "as legal a right to vote as any other person."[18] Nevertheless, there are a mere handful of examples of women voting in Virginia and obviously none of them were acquaintances of Mrs. Corbin.

A year before Hannah Lee Corbin wrote her letter claiming the right to vote, Abigail Adams's husband, John Adams, had discussed the claims of women to the franchise not with his wife, but with his friend James Sullivan. The two men, like Mrs. Corbin, seem to have been unaware that New England women who had property and did not have husbands theoretically could demand voting rights and that a small number had actually exercised them. "It is certain, in theory, that the only moral foundation of government is, the consent of the people," John Adams wrote. "But to what extent shall we carry this principle? Shall we say that every individual of the community, old and young, male and female, as well as rich and poor, must consent . . . Depend upon it, Sir, it is dangerous to open so fruitful a source of controversy and altercation . . . there will be no end of it. New claims

[17]Chilton Williamson, *American Suffrage from Property to Democracy, 1760-1860* (Princeton, 1960), p. 15.

[18]*The Letters of Richard Henry Lee,* James Curtis Ballagh, ed., 2 vols. (New York, 1914), 1: 392-394.

will arise; women will demand a vote; lads from twelve to twenty-one will think their rights not enough attended to; and every man who has not a farthing, will demand an equal voice with any other, in all acts of state."[19] Adams seems to have understood the implications of the Revolutionary ideology very well, little as they may have pleased him.

Political equality for women as a consequence of Patriot principles found expression in the state of New Jersey. Two days before the Continental Congress adopted Jefferson's Declaration, the state of New Jersey adopted a new constitution that put the doctrine of consent into practice. "All inhabitants of this Colony, of full age, who are worth fifty pounds proclamation money, clear estate in the same and have resided within the county in which they claim their vote, for twelve months immediately preceding the election, shall be entitled to vote . . ." In case there was any doubt that the word "inhabitants" included women, the New Jersey legislature adopted an election law in 1797 that explicitly referred to voters by the words "he and she." Unmarried women, now fully aware of their rights, then went to the polls in New Jersey in significant numbers. In some townships it was said they cast a quarter of the votes.[20] A Newark newspaper celebrated this political egalitarianism in a song entitled "The Freedom of Election" published in 1797, which included this verse:

> What we read, in days of yore,
>   the woman's occupation,
> Was to direct the wheel and loom,
>   Not to direct the nation.
> This narrow minded policy
>   by us hath met detection;
> While woman's bound, man can't be free,
>   nor have a fair election.[21]

The entire electoral process in New Jersey, however, was extremely corrupt in the last years of the eighteenth century. Those in charge at the polling places decided whom to admit or exclude according to their own political views. In order to win an election wives as well as single women and an assortment of black slaves, servants, and young boys were allowed to register votes. Under these

---

[19]*The Works of John Adams,* Charles Francis Adams, ed., 10 vols. (Boston, 1850-56), 9: 375-378.

[20]"Friend to the Ladies" in *True American* (Trenton), October 18, 1802.

[21]*Centinel of Freedom* (Newark), October 18, 1797.

circumstances, the women voters were not exercizing any significant right; they were merely exploited. The abuses finally became so scandalous that the New Jersey Legislature acted in 1807 to restrict suffrage to "free, white, male citizens" as was the practice in most of the other states. Free blacks as well as unmarried women thus lost the rights that had been theirs under the original Constitution of 1776.[22]

Abigail Adams was aware that women were voting in New Jersey after the Revolution. Like most people outside New Jersey, she seems to have found the notion of women voting amusing. The closest she ever came to suggesting she would like to have the vote herself was when she referred to the New Jersey practice in an attempt to pay a compliment to a Quincy minister who was seeking the post of assistant to the Reverend Anthony Wibird. "Present my compliment[s] to Mr. Whitman," she wrote to her sister Mary Cranch, "& tell him if our State constitution had been equally liberal with that of New Jersey and admitted the females to a vote, I should certainly have exercised it in his behalf. As it is, he may be sure both of the Presidents and my good wishes for him, with a sincere desire for his settlement."[23]

It is true, of course, that Abigail Adams dearly loved her "dish of politics." Nevertheless, she had firm views as to how far it was seemly for her to involve herself in activity that most moral writers of the time insisted was unsuitable for ladies. She became quite deeply involved not merely in such local political activities as choosing an assistant minister but also in high affairs of state. All her life she considered herself free to discuss political questions and offer advice to her husband, John, and to her son, John Quincy, as well as to other American statesmen with whom she corresponded. She was always careful, however, to keep her political activity behind the scenes and to avoid getting her name into the newspapers.[24] She was outraged when she discovered that she had been cited as an authority by a speaker in the Quincy town meeting. "I could not believe that any Gentleman would have had so little delicacy or so small a sense of

[22]Mary Philbrook, "Woman's Suffrage in New Jersey Prior to 1807," *Proceedings New Jersey Historical Society*, 57, (1939): 87-98.
[23]November 15, 1797, *New Letters of Abigail Adams, 1788-1801*, Stewart Mitchell, ed., (Boston, 1947), p. 112.
[24]See, for instance, Abigail Adams to Mary Cranch [July 4, 1797], ibid., p. 103; Abigail Adams to Mary Cranch, December 12, 1797, ibid., pp. 116-117.

propriety as to have written a mere vague opinion, and that of a Lady too, to be read in a publick assembly as an authority," she wrote to her sister. "The Man must have lost his senses."[25] Much as she enjoyed reading her husband's government documents and influencing political events from behind the scenes, she never expressed an ambition to play an active role in her own right. In 1796 she stated flatly, "Government of States and Kingdoms, tho' God knows badly enough managed, I am willing should be solely administered by the lords of creation. I should only contend for Domestic government, and think that best administered by the female."[26]

When Abigail Adams felt uneasy about the possible impropriety of her passionate involvement in politics, John Adams hastened to reassure her. His background was less aristocratic than hers, he did not study the moral writers who discussed what was proper conduct for ladies so closely as she did, and one of the things he most adored about his Abigail was her ability to share his love of politics. When his mother-in-law died, he wrote to his wife expressing his personal opinion that ladies ought to engage in such outside activities:

> Were not her Talents, and Virtues too much confined, to private social and domestic Life. My Opinion of the Duties of Religion and Morality, comprehends a very extensive Connection with society at large, and the great Interest of the public. . . . The Benevolence, Charity, Capacity and Industry which exerted in private Life, would make a family, a Parish or a Town Happy, employed upon a larger Scale, in Support of the great Principles of Virtue and Freedom of political Regulations might secure whole Nations and Generations from Misery, Want and Contempt.[27]

John Adams was always ready to praise his wife's political ability not only to her directly, but also to his male friends. On her side, she could always blame her husband for leadng her into unladylike activities when her political actions became especially bold. In 1780 she was deeply involved in the Massachusetts elections. Since, as she wrote to him, "I cannot be a voter upon this occasion, I will be a

---

[25]Abigail Adams to Mary Cranch, June 6, 1797, ibid., p. 96.

[26]Quoted in Janet Whitney, *Abigail Adams* (Boston, 1947), p. 290.

[27]John Adams to Abigail Adams, October 29, 1775, *Adams Family Correspondence,* L. H. Butterfield, ed., 4 vols. to date (Cambridge, Mass., 1963-) 1: 316-317. Hereafter AFC.

writer of votes. I can do something in that way." And she added after a paragraph of political comment "What a politician you have made me."[28]

Although political equality became an important goal for the nineteenth-century woman's rights movement, the issue was insignificant for women of the Revolutionary generation. So long as most women married and the common law put wives under the absolute dominion of their husbands, reform of the common law was a far more pressing need than suffrage. Legal equality was more important than political equality. The equality of women under the law was deliberately repudiated by the English legal tradition, and it was rarely proposed by anyone as a desirable goal in the eighteenth century. The anonymous poet in the *Virginia Gazette* of October 15, 1736 met no response when he or she suggested:

> Then Equal Laws let Custom find,
> And neither sex oppress;
> More freedom to Womankind
> Or give to Mankind less.

Those writers who did criticize the common law generally did not suggest anything so extreme as equality for wives. They asked only for some moderation of the virtually unlimited power the law allowed to husbands. Such writers might be described as humanitarians, even as liberals, but not as egalitarians and certainly not as feminists. It would be equally appropriate to describe a person who argued for modifications in the slave code in order to prevent cruelty to black servants as an abolitionist.

The common law of England had been relaxed considerably in America during the seventeenth century. Furthermore, pioneer conditions and the absence of courts and trained lawyers in many places made it possible for women to exercise considerably more freedom than they were legally entitled to. In the eighteenth century, however, a reaction set in which reached its culmination with the publication of William Blackstone's *Commentaries*. This work was published in four volumes between 1765 and 1769. It was such a convenient summary of the law of England and America that lawyers eagerly embraced it. In the colonies particularly, where books were scarce,

---

[28]July 5, 1780, ibid., 3:372.

every lawyer was soon using Blackstone as the final authority on every question. Unfortunately, Blackstone was very unkind to women. "By marriage, the husband and wife are one person in law: that is, the very being or legal existence of the woman is suspended during the marriage," he declared. Since a wife was not a person she could not be a witness in court, control her property, chose where she would live, or claim her own wages. Her husband was entitled to beat her if she disobeyed him. She herself was the property of her husband. He could hire her out as a servant to anyone he chose without her consent. If she ran away from him with the clothes she was wearing she was guilty of steading — stealing both her person and the clothing, for both belonged to her husband. The power of husbands over wives was virtually absolute.[29]

Abigail Adams thought that this was a bit extreme. While she never suggested that wives should be equal to husbands or questioned the propriety of patriarchal families, she did feel some moderation of husbands' rights would be in order. In March of 1776 she dropped a hint to John Adams who was busily discussing liberty, equality, and independence with his fellow members of the Continental Congress: "By the way in the new Code of Laws which I suppose it will be necessary for you to make I desire you would Remember the Ladies, and be more generous and favourable to them than your ancestors. Do not put such unlimited power into the hands of the Husbands. Remember all Men would be tyrants if they could." Abigail Adams was aware that her husband accepted the maxim "power corrupts" and believed that it was inadequately limited power that had made a tyrant of King George III. She drew the parallel closer as she continued her letter: "If perticular care and attention is not paid to the Laidies we are determined to foment a Rebelion, and will not hold ourselves bound by any Laws in which we have no voice, or Representation." She was not disturbed by the legal superiority of husbands, only by the lack of limitation on their power. "That your Sex are Naturally Tyrannical is a Truth so thoroughly established as to admit of no dispute," she went on, "but such of you as wish to be happy willingly give up the harsh title of Master for the more tender and

---

[29]Linda Grant De Pauw, "Land of the Unfree: Legal Limitations on Liberty in Pre-Revolutionary America," *Maryland Historical Magazine,* 68 (1973): 360.

endearing one of Friend. Why then, not put it out of the power of
the vicious and the Lawless to use us with cruelty and indignity with
impunity. Men of Sense in all Ages abhor those customs which treat
us only as the vassals of your Sex. Regard us then as Beings placed by
providence under your protection and in immitation of the Supreem
Being make use of that power only for our happiness."[30]

The Continental Congress, however, had no plans to overhaul
the common law and Abigail Adams's plea for the ladies was so
unexpected that it made her husband laugh. As she had mentioned in
her letter that her "heart" was "gay" as she wrote it, he did not think
she would mind if he carried on the joke. "As to your extraordinary
Code of Laws," he replied, "I cannot but laugh. We have been told
that our Struggle has loosened the bands of Government every where.
That Children and Apprentices were disobedient — that schools and
Colledges were grown turbulent — that Indians slighted their Guard-
ians and Negroes grew insolent to their Masters. But your letter was
the first Intimation that another Tribe more numerous and powerfull
than all the rest were grown discontented. . . . Depend upon it,
We know better than to repeal our Masculine systems. Altho they are
in full force, you know they are little more than Theory. We dare not
exert our Power in its full Latitude. We are obliged to go fair, and
softly, and in Practice you know We are the subjects. We have only
the Name of Masters, and rather than give up this, which would
compleatly subject Us to the Despotism of the Peticoat, I hope
General Washington, and all our brave Heroes would fight. I am
sure every good Politician would plot."[31]

Abigail Adams was not too pleased by this response, which she
characterized as "very sausy."[32] She replied to him saying, "I can not
say that I think you are very generous to the Ladies, for whilst you
are proclaiming peace and good will to Men, Emancipating all
Nations, you insist upon retaining an absolute power over Wives."
But she did not press the point. The question was only academic for
her. Her husband did, indeed, treat her as friend not as master, and
their marriage, as Lyman Butterfield has said, was "as perfect as any
recorded in the annals of matrimony, and theirs happens to be particu-

[30]Abigail Adams to John Adams, March 31, 1776, *AFC*, 1: 370.
[31]John Adams to Abigail Adams, April 14, 1776, ibid., 382.
[32]Abigail Adams to Mercy Warren, April 27, 1776, ibid., 397.

larly well recorded."³³ Furthermore, she knew that ladies who had disagreements with their husbands would do best sweetly to acknowledge the male's superior authority. Accordingly she ended this exchange with her husband by quoting a bit of ladylike verse from one of her books of moral essays: "Charm by accepting, by submitting sway/ Yet have our Humor most when we obey."³⁴ As far as is known she never mentioned the reform of the common law to him or anyone else after the spring of 1776.³⁵ Indeed, before the war was over she was citing the legal inferiority of her position as proof of the superior patriotism of American women. In June 1782 she wrote, "Patriotism in the female Sex is the most disinterested of all virtues. Excluded from honours and from offices, we cannot attach ourselves to the State or Government from having held a place of Eminence. Even in the freeest [sic] countrys our property is subject to the controul and disposal of our partners, to whom the Laws have given a sovereign Authority. Deprived of a voice in Legislation, obliged to submit to those Laws which are imposed upon us, is it not sufficient to make us indifferent to the publick Welfare? Yet all History and every age exhibit Instances of patriotick virtue in the female Sex; which considering our situation equals the most Heroick of yours. . . . I will take praise to myself. I feel that it is my due. . . ."³⁶

When Abigail Adams and others like her accepted the principle of male domination in the family and in society, they necessarily accepted the idea that boys and girls should receive different educations even when they were convinced that women were intellectually equal to men. It is clear from the quotations with which Abigail Adams sprinkles her letters, that she had read a good many books that discussed proper education for ladies. One that she particularly admired was Dr. James Fordyce's *Sermons to Young Women*. When she first read the *Sermons*, in 1767, she wrote to her sister, "I cannot say how much I admire them, and should I attempt to say how worthy

³³Lyman H. Butterfield, "Abigail Adams," in Edward T. James et al., eds., *Notable American Women, 1607-1950: A Biographical Dictionary,* 3 vols. (Cambridge, Mass., 1971) 1: 6.

³⁴Abigail Adams to John Adams, May 7, 1776, *AFC,* 1: 402-403.

³⁵Of course, she may have. In addition to private conversations which can never be recovered, we have lost most of the letters written to Abigail Adams by women unrelated to the family; Charles Francis Adams destroyed them.

³⁶Abigail Adams to John Adams, June 17, 1782, *AFC,* 4: 328.

they are of admiration I fear I should not do justice to this most Excellent performance."[37] Dr. Fordyce was certainly no feminist. "Be even careful," he warned young women, "in displaying your *good sense*. It will be thought you assume a superiority over the rest of the company. But if you happen to have any learning, keep it a profound secret, especially from the men, who generally look with a jealous and malignant eye on a woman of great parts and a cultivated understanding."[38] Abigail Adams agreed that ladies should not display their learning. She admired the accomplishments of the French ladies of the salons, but disapproved of women like Madame de Staël whom, she thought, sought to steal the center of attention from their husbands.[39] She no doubt seconded the advice John Adams gave their daughter "Nabby" when she began to study Latin grammar under her mother's tutelage: "I learned in a letter from your mamma, that you was learning the accidence. This will do you no hurt, my dear, though you must not tell many people of it, for it is scarcely reputable for young ladies to understand Latin and Greek."[40]

Abigail Adams, and others like her, agreed that women should keep their learning a secret yet justified educating their daughters more broadly than the English did by citing the special demands made on American mothers. Good schools were scarce in America so mothers must be teachers. Furthermore, America's republican form of government made well-educated male citizens essential to the survival of the nation. Therefore the intellectual development of women was justified because it would be useful to their husbands and children. It was never considered as a means to elevate women to a status of equality within the family. For instance Thomas Jefferson, whom no one would ever call a feminist, described the education he wanted for his daughter Patsy. He explained what he planned was "considerably different from what I think would be most proper for her sex in any other country than America. I am obliged in it to extend my views beyond herself, and consider her as possibly at the head of a little family of her own. The chance that in marriage she will draw a blockhead I calculate at about fourteen to one, and of course that the

---

[37]Abigil Adams to Mary Cranch, January 31, 1767, AFC, 1: 61.

[38]Quoted in Julia Cherry Spruill, *Women's Life and Work in the Southern Colonies* (Chapel Hill, 1938), p. 220.

[39]Whitney, *Abigail Adams*, p. 189.

[40]April 18, 1776, *AFC*, 1: 388.

education of her family will probably rest on her own ideas and direction without assistance. With the best poets and prosewriters I shall therefore combine a certain extent of reading in the graver sciences."[41] Abigail Adams's argument in favor of advanced education for women is almost identical. In an often-quoted letter to her husband she wrote, "if you complain of neglect of Education in sons, What shall I say with regard to daughters, who every day experience the want of it? With regard to the Education of my own children, I find myself soon out of my debth, and destitute and deficient in every part of Education. . . . If we mean to have Heroes, Statesmen and Philosophers, we should have learned women. . . . If as much depends as is allowed upon the early Education of youth and the first principals which are instilld take the deepest root, great benefit must arise from the litirary accomplishments in women."[42] Even Mercy Otis Warren, who is generally acknowledged to be the leading woman intellectual of Revolutionary America, did not presume to question the inequality of the sexes even as she insisted on the equality of male and female brains. She emphasized that "we own the appointed subordination (perhaps for the sake of order in families)" even as she encouraged women not to "acknowledge such an inferiority as would check the ardour of our endeavors to equal in all mental accomplishments the most masculine heights."[43]

Toward the close of the eighteenth century, as the United States prospered, educational opportunities for upper class girls expanded rapidly. This education, was not intended, however, to obilterate the differences between the sexes. Advanced education, after all, had little practical value in the eighteenth century. With the possible exception of the ministry, no occupation required advanced book-learning. Reading, writing, and simple aritthmetic were sufficient for most occupations. Boys and girls often studied these subjects in school together. Lack of advanced education barred women from no profes-

---

[41]Jefferson to Marbois, December 5, 1783, *The Papers of Thomas Jefferson,* Julian P. Boyd, ed., 18 vols. to date (Princeton, 1950-) VI, 374.

[42]August 14, 1776, *AFL,* 2: 94. See also her letter of June 30 [1778], ibid., 3:53, in which she approvingly quotes a male author who says "Nor need we fear to loose our Empire over them [women] by thus improveing their native ability since where there is most Learning, Sence and knowledge there is always observed to be the most modesty and Rectitude of manners."

[43]Quoted in Katharine Anthony, *First Lady of the Revolution: The Life of Mercy Otis Warren* (New York, 1958), p. 188.

sion. There are examples of women drafting wills and other legal documents and even appearing in court. The practice of medicine was dominated by women who diagnosed and treated disease with the aid of experience and medical books they studied without supervision. All education beyond the basics, then, was desirable only because it gave pleasure to the student or, more commonly, because it was a sign of high social status. So-called "accomplishments," which included the ability to dance, to read music, to write an elegant hand, and to spell according to upperclass conventions as well as acquaintance with the classics of English and French literature were acquired in order to move to a higher social rank. A Pennsylvania teacher advertising the advantages of his school pointed out that he had taught "several of the reputed fine accomplished ladies in New York, some of which were married within two, three, or four years afterwards."[44] The parents who purchased such educational advantages for their daughters sought thereby to make them equal to English ladies, not to make them the intellectual equals of men.

Abigail Adams was better acquainted than most American mothers with the standard of aristocratic feminine behavior that was respected abroad. She had the opportunity to live and mingle in high society both on the Continent and in England. When she bemoaned her own lack of education, it was the lack of "accomplishments" she missed. There is not the slightest hint anywhere in her writings that she would have liked to have gone to Harvard. She educated her own daughter to be a lady. Nabby Adams grew up preferring social activities to her mother's "dish of politics." She learned to adopt the fashions and manners of European aristocrats. She married a man for whom she felt no passion after her parents discouraged a match with a man to whom she was strongly attracted. And when the approved husband proved to be inconsiderate and generally worthless, Abigail Adams prided herself in not encouraging Nabby to criticize her husband. "I make no reflections but in my own Breast," she told her sister. "It is some comfort, to know that she has not been the cause, and that she could not prevent the misfortunes to which she is brought."[45]

---

[44]Quoted in Eugenie Andruss Leonard, *The Dear-Bought Heritage* (Philadelphia, 1965), p. 277.

[45]October 22, 1797, *New Letters*, p. 109.

Abigail Adams's son, John Quincy Adams, was also prevented by his parents from marrying the girl he loved. Instead he married a woman toward whom he appears to have been emotionally indifferent and whose chief attributes, according to Lyman Butterfield, were "endurance, wifely loyalty, and submission."[46] Before he married, John Quincy Adams noted in a letter to his mother the new-fashioned ladylike behaviour of the American girls he met. Certainly it was nearly impossible for him to have found an upper-class girl in 1790 who resembled "the girl who married dear old Dad." Abigail Adams was not very unlike other women of her rank in Massachusetts in the first half of the eigtheenth century. But increasing wealth, the disappearance of the hardships of pioneer days, and the desire to prove American society equal to that of England persuaded upper-class American women to cultivate the passivity and gentility of English ladies in place of the strength, independence, and bravery that they had valued in an earlier period. All the girls John Quincy Adams met were "simpering" and "superficial" and did nothing but "dance and talk scandal."[47] His mother sharply rebuked him for making such observations. If girls were frivolous she said it was because men liked them that way. Women were "like clay in the hands of the artist — and may be molded to whatever form [men] please."[48] Although Abigail Adams did not approve of the idleness and frivolity of the "lady of fashion," she did believe women should be pious, sexually pure, delicate, genteel, attentive to their homes and families, and submissive to their husbands. In other words, if Abigail Adams had had her way, the aristocracy ideal of the "lady of fashion" would have been replaced by the middle-class ideal of the "true woman," which did, in fact, become the dominant image in American society in the nineteenth century. The ideal she championed was precisely that which leaders of the nineteenth-century woman's movement attacked. She would have been pleased at the tribute to her and other wives of the Founding Fathers published in 1854: "Women unhesitatingly evinced their sympathies with whatever was generous and honorable in public conduct, but rarely if ever in forgetfulness of the require-

---

46*Diary and Autobiography of John Adams,* Lyman H. Butterfield, ed., 4 vols. (New York, 1964), 1: *xx.*

47Quoted in Page Smith, *John Adams,* 2 vols. (New York, 1962) 2: 657.

48Ibid., p. 658.

ments of feminine propriety. Though patriotic they were content to be women still, and were anxious for the distinctions of delicacy and grace. They perceived that it was their nobility not to be men, but to be women worthy of men. In possession of every right with which they were endowed by nature, they had no desire to exercise men's prerogatives. There were indeed some shameless females, not unwilling to exhibit mortification at having been created of a sex whose finer attributes were beyond their emulation . . . but these creatures were not in society; they were regarded only as curious monsters. Such wives as those of Washington, Adams, Jay, Wolcott, Bradford, and King, had no desire, as Montaigne expresses it, 'to cover their beauties under others that were none of theirs.' "[49]

Abigail Adams can properly be called a "feminist" only if the words is defined very loosely. The term itself is anachronistic. According to Alice S. Rossi, the first use of the word in print occurred in 1895. It was only at the beginning of the present century that the terms "feminist" or "feminism" were familiar enough to be used by writers without quotation marks. In her book entitled *The Feminist Papers From Adams to de Beauvoir* (which shows her opinion on the feminism of Abigail Adams), Dr. Rossi employs this definition of the term: "opinions and principles of the advocates of the extended recognition of the achievements and claims of women."[50] To my minds, this is much too broad. It seems clear to me that not everyone who claims to like and respect women is a feminist. Rossi's definition would embrace writers who advocate extended recognition for such "achievements" as successfully breast feeding a dozen children and support such "claims" as those to protective legislation deemed necessary because of assumed inability of women to compete on equal footing with men. I prefer the definition in Webster's *Dictionary:* "the theory of the political, economic, and social equality of the sexes." The emphasis is on the word "equality." Equality of rights is a central theme of the American Revolutionary ideology. It was not, however, applied to women in America until many years after Abigail Adams's death. Even the radical suffrage experiment in New Jersey did not

<hr>

[49]Rufus Wilmot Griswold, *The Republican Court* (New York, 1854), pp. 369-370.
[50]Alice S. Rossi, *The Feminist Papers From Adams to de Beauvoir* (New York, 1973), pp. xii-xiii.

give women equal political rights since it deprived married women but not married men of the right to cast a ballot.

The failure of the Revolutionary generation to apply the doctrine of equal rights that it claimed for "all men" to those "men" who happened to be female, did not mean that the doctrine was inapplicable. As Bernard Bailyn has pointed out, the doctrine was "contagious." "The movement of thought was rapid, irreversible, and irresistible. It swept past boundaries few had set out to cross, into regions few had wished to enter. . . . Institutions were brought into question and condemned that appeared to have little if any direct bearing on the immediate issues of the Anglo-American struggle."[51] Indeed, it might be reasonably argued that the entire history of reform in America has involved a working out of the implications of our Revolutionary ideology. In the short run, however, the decades immediately following the Revolution reflected a retreat from egalitarian principles. Inequalities of wealth increased, the slave system hardened into a more rigorous pattern, and the status of women declined so precipitously that it is difficult to realize that scarcely a generation separated the strong, self-reliant women of the Revolution from the "true women" of the Jacksonian age. The Revolution itself was not responsible for the retreat from egalitarian ideals. Powerful forces including the Industrial Revolution and shifting demographic patterns created strains in American society that prevented uninterrupted progress toward the absolute goals implicit in the Revolutionary doctrines. But the tide turned again. Although no one had intended it, the principles of the Revolution became the basis of an attack on the patriarchal family only thirty years after Abigail Adams's death.

In 1848 the first woman's rights convention at Seneca Falls adopted a Declaration of Sentiments, which has been called "the most famous document in the history of feminism."[52] It took the Declaration of Independence as its inspiration and as its literary model. It attacked women's inequality in politics, marriage, religion, property laws, sexual moral conventions, and concluded with a blast at the "tyrant Man" for endeavoring "in every way that he could, to destroy

[51]Bernard Bailyn, *The Ideological Origins of the American Revolution* (Cambridge, Mass., 1967), pp. 231-232.
[52]Aileen S. Kraditor, ed., *Up From the Pedestal: Selected Writings in the History of American Feminism* (Chicago, 1968), p. 183.

her confidence in her own powers, to lessen her self-respect, and to make her willing to lead a dependent and abject life."[53] This sounds much more like what we mean by the word "feminism." It is a long way from Abigail Adams's now famous "plea for the ladies." She had quietly penned a few teasing lines to her husband asking for some limitations on the "tyrant"; the women of Seneca Falls called for the overthrow of the "tyrant" and declared their sentiments publicly "to a candid world." Most probably, Abigail Adams would have disapproved.

---

[53]Ibid., p. 186.

THE AMERICAN REVOLUTION AND
THE MODERN WORLD

BY SUNG BOK KIM*

On November 25, 1783, when the British troops under Sir Guy Carleton completed their withdrawal from New York City, Governor George Clinton of New York gave a public dinner at Fraunce's Tavern at which George Washington and his generals were present. After dinner, they raised thirteen toasts, three of which touched on the cause of liberty in the world: "the Vindicators of the Rights of Mankind in every Quarter of the Globe," "May America be an Asylum to the Persecuted of the Earth," and "May the Remembrance of This be a Lesson to Princes (of the World)."[1] The international character of the Revolution which the toasts invoked was underscored by other Revolutionary Americans as well. Thomas Paine declared in *Common Sense,* that "the cause of America is in a great measure the cause of all mankind" and that "we . . . have it in our power to begin the world over again."[2] Thomas Jefferson struck much the same note: "We feel that we are acting under obligations not confined to the limits of our own society. It is impossible not to be sensible that we are acting for all mankind."[3] John Adams opined that the Revolution was fought

*The author wishes to thank his colleagues, especially Professors Kendall Birr and Lawrence Wittner, and his research assistant, Mr. Jon S. Guttman, of the History Department, State University of New York at Albany, for their assistance and suggestions in the preparation of this essay.

[1]Hugh Hastings, ed., *Public Papers of George Clinton, First Governor of New York, 1777-1795, 1801-1804,* 10 vols. (New York and Albany, 1899-1914), 8:300.

[2]*The Complete Writings of Thomas Paine,* Philip S. Foner, ed., 2 vols. (New York, 1945), 1:3, 4.

[3]Jefferson to Joseph Priestly, June 19, 1802, Andrew A. Lipscomb and A. L. Bergh, eds., *The Writings of Thomas Jefferson,* 20 vols. (Washington, D.C., 1904), 10:324-25. See also Jefferson to John Adams, September 12, 1821, ibid., p. 334.

"for future millions, and millions of millions," and hoped that it would "spread liberty and Enlightenment everywhere in the world."[4]

Underlying these declarations were the profound beliefs that the entire world was "overrun with oppression" and that "freedom hath been hunted round the globe."[5] Nurtured on ideas of the Enlightenment that presupposed the unity of mankind in reason, impulses, and natural laws, the Revolutionary Americans were optimistic that oppressed people abroad would be inspired by their examples and would eventually rise up against repressive regimes. This optimism was not mere wishful thinking, but had been consecrated by their own experience in the last decade of the colonial period. The colonists regarded their campaign against British imperial policies as an episode in a world-wide struggle then under way — in Ireland, Scotland, Spain, France, Turkey, Poland, Corsica, England, and Russia — between liberty and tyranny. It was this sene of camaraderie with international freedom fighters and "absorption in affairs outside their continent" which "played a central role in the colonists' own conversion to active revolution."[6] The American Revolution was a chapter of what Robert R. Palmer has called a "great" Atlantic revolution.[7]

For the Revolutionary generation, the independence of America from Britain would have been "a matter but of little importance, had it not been accompanied by a revolution in the principles and practices of governments"; the struggle for liberation should be merely a pre-condition for building a new foundation of freedom.[8] The outbreak of the War for Independence was followed rapidly by the making of new constitutions in the states based on republican principles. Republicanism as a theory was nothing new; it was as old as the Roman Republic. What was new and revolutionary is that the Americans took theoretical republican ideas out of the ivory tower and salon and turned them into an effective revolutionary instrument and a workable governmental institution. Speaking of the ideas contained

---

[4]Adams to the Congress, October 25, 1781, quoted in Page Smith, *John Adams,* 2 vols. (New York, 1962), 1:504.

[5]Paine, *Common Sense,* Foner, ed., *Writings of Thomas Paine,* 1:30, 435.

[6]Pauline Maier, *From Resistance to Revolution: Colonial Radicals and Development of American Opposition to Britain, 1765-1776* (New York, 1972), p. 162.

[7]*The Age of Democratic Revolution: A Political History of Europe and America, 1760-1800,* 2 vols. (Princeton, 1959-64).

[8]Paine, *The Rights of Man,* Foner, ed., *Writings of Thomas Paine,* 1:354.

in the Declaration of Independence, Thomas Jefferson refused to make even a modest claim to originality: [I did not] "try to find out new principles, or new arguments, never thought of . . . , but to place before mankind the common sense of the subject."[9] John Adams, the author of the Massachusetts Constitution of 1780, said of the document: "It is Locke, Sidney, Rousseau, and de Mably reduced to practice." On another occasion, when talking about the American system of government, he said "the principles of Aristotle and Plato, of Livy and Cicero, and Sidney, Harrington and Locke; the principles of nature and eternal reason; [are] the principles on which the whole government over us now stands."[10]

Nevertheless, it would be terribly wrong to imagine that the Founding Fathers merely borrowed ideas from others. There were a number of areas in which the Founders made distinct contributions to political theory and procedure. The most important was the invention of the "constitutional convention" as the means of making, unmaking, and remaking a written constitution, a method which had never before been tried by any other nation. The resultant constitution, embodying the sovereignty of the people, created and defined the powers of government and spelled out the "inalienable" rights of the people. The governments emerging from the constitutional conventions were hamstrung with checks, balances, restrictions, and prohibitions, while the rights and liberty of the people were jealously guarded. Having escaped from "a long train of abuses and usurpations" by the British government and impressed with the prevalence of European autocracy, the Americans were determined to make their government limited and moderate. They feared power regardless of where it was located and who wielded it because they understood the inevitable tendency of its possessor to abuse it.[11]

The most dramatic illustration of this fear of power was the incorporation into the new state constitutions of various bills of rights — giving such things as religious toleration, freedom of press and

---

[9]Gilbert Chinard, *Thomas Jefferson: The Apostle of Americanism* (Boston, 1929; Ann Arbor Paperback edition, 1962), pp. 71-73.

[10]*The Works of John Adams,* Charles Francis Adams, ed., 10 vols. (Boston, 1850-1856), 4:193, 216.

[11]*The Federalist,* Henry Cabot Lodge, ed., (New York, 1902), No. 51, p. 323. In general, see Wood, *The Creation of the American Republic, 1776-1787* (Chapel Hill, 1969).

assembly, freedom of person under the protection of habeas corpus, and trial by juries, and subordination of the military to the civilian authority — with the view to placing permanent restraints on the government of their own creation. The Revolutionaries seem to have agreed with James Lovell, a Massachusetts orator, that free people were not those who merely had escaped from oppression "but those who have a constitutional check upon the power to oppress."[12] The process of adopting bills of rights began, it will be remembered, at the very time the United States was engaged in a war with mighty Britain and the state governments needed power and vigor to cope with both internal and external enemies. The significance of this unremitting concern for personal freedom takes on special meaning given the suspension of basic civil rights in such subsequent national emergencies as the Civil War and the First and Second World Wars. It was this institutionalization of liberty during the Revolution that probably prompted Lord Acton to declare: "In the strictest sense the history of liberty dated from 1776 'for never till then had men sought liberty knowing what they sought.' "[13]

At the very inception of the nation, then, Americans were committed to a government whose supreme goal was to secure the fundamental liberties of the people — a truly revolutionary doctrine. They had no intention of replacing a monarchical tyranny with an elective tyranny whether exercised by a majority or a minority. Nowhere was this attitude revealed better than in the movement to create a new federal system of government. The critical problems during the Confederation period were numerous, but the seeming majoritarian licentiousness and accompanying social and economic disorder in various states which led to the impairment of minority rights particularly distressed the Founding Fathers. Seasoned in what John Adams called "the divine science of politics — the art of discovering the forms and combinations of power in republics,"[14] the Founders distributed the power among the different branches of the government so that neither the majoritarian interest nor the minority interest would predominate. This arrangement may seem undemocratic to the

---

[12]"An Oration Delivered April 2, 1771: . . ." (Boston, 1771), in Hezekiah Niles, ed., *Principles and Acts of the Revolution in America* (New York, 1876), p. 18.

[13]Gertrude Himmelfarb, *Lord Acton* (London, 1952), p. 141.

[14]Niles, ed., *Principles and Acts,* p. 402.

modern citizen long accustomed to a majoritarian democracy. But the Founders thought otherwise. James Madison, a chief architect of the Constitution, was convinced that "if *all* power be suffered to slide" into either party "liberty will be subverted" and that "it is of great importance in a republic not only to guard the society against the oppression of its rulers; but to guard one part of the society against the injustice of other parts."[15]

Indeed, the uniqueness of the American brand of federalism lies in the fact that it not only allowed for the rise and interplay of the divergent political, social, and economic forces or factions that were inevitable in such a heterogeneous society as America, but also made such diversity the essential guarantor of equilibrium and liberty for all members of the society. In the United States federalism was not the tool of a class or estate or order as it had been for the corporate localities dominated by oligarchic or privileged families in Switzerland and Holland,[16] but a representative process in which every class, faction, and local jurisdiction was supposed to have a meaningful voice. For this democratic imperative, federalism did not presuppose the destruction of the states as intermediate political units, although it did subordinate and bypass them to derive its power directly from the people. That Americans did not establish a powerful unitary or national form of government but instead created a federal form encumbered by an intricate network of checks and balances and limited by a bill of rights was another measure of the people's fear of power and preoccupation with civil liberty.

Fear is inherently a negative force. It makes a man timid, immobile, blind, desperate, mad, and even worse, brutally destructive — the traits which Aristotle spelled out in detail twenty-five centuries ago. Harold Laski, a distinguished English political scientist and a laborite, noted that "a government built upon fear is driven into tyranny."[17] The American Revolutionary experience, however, pro-

---

[15]Madison, "The North American No. 1," September 17, 1783, in Marvin Meyers, ed., *The Mind of the Founder: Sources of the Political Thought of James Madison* (Indianapolis, 1973), p. 59; *The Federalist*, Lodge, ed., No. 51, p. 325, and No. 10, pp. 54-56.

[16]R. R. Palmer, "The World Revolution of the West: 1763-1801," *Political Science Quarterly*, 69 (1954): 1-14.

[17]The negative manifestations of fear in human behavior were long ago detailed by *Aristotle in his Politics and Plato in the Republic;* Laski, *Reflections on the Revolutin of our Time* (New York, 1943), pp. 26-27.

vides a convincing rebuff to this time-honored pattern of human behavior. Though gripped with fear of the British oppression, the colonists did not lash out against their internal subversives (Tories) with blind fury. Nor did they wholly destroy the inherited institutions: the die-hard republicans in Connecticut and Rhode Island retained their colonial charters as state constitutions well into the nineteenth century. When Americans became dissastified with the existing state-dominated system of the Confederation, they built another system on top of it rather than on its extinction. The aggrieved states rightists, known as Antifederalists, though fearful of the extension of the central power, willingly submitted to the new national political settlement. In the hands of the Revolutionary generation, the fear of power, cushioned by "the wisdom of their greatest men," was made into an innovative force of liberty with the result that the transformation from British rule to independence, from the state constitutions to the federal system, in Alexis de Tocqueville's words, "proceeded hand in hand with a love of order and legality."[18]

The Founding Fathers were hopeful that the political achievements of the Revolution — namely, the doctrine of national independence, the constitutional convention, the limited constitutional government, republican federalism, and the bills of rights — would awaken every nation in the world and that a spirit and blessings of liberty would gain ground everywhere. They were certain that their government was the finest, "the world's best hope," and, being derived from and supported by the people, was the "strongest Government on earth."[19] These were the achievements, hopes, and convictions which our forefathers bequeathed to us all.

What kind of reception did modern history accord to the legacies of the American Revolution? Let us for a moment look around the globe. To me, most of its living space looks like a graveyard for liberty. In the Western Hemisphere authoritarian regimes, whether military or civilian, are in the majority. The same is true in Africa, Asia, Eastern and Central Europe, and Asia Minor. Some countries, like the Philippines, may have constitutions patterned after the American or British model, but they are no more than paper declarations without

---

[18]Alexis de Tocqueville, *Democracy in America* (New York, Vintage edition, 1945), Book I, pp. 117-118.

[19]Thomas Jefferson's First Inaugural Address in Merryn Williams, ed., *Revolutions, 1775-1830* (Middlesex, England, 1971), p. 180.

any bearing on actual practice. Some leaders, like Indira Gandhi of India, invoke the "inspiring words" of the Founding Fathers, but do so only for public relations on ceremonious occasions or during press conferences.[20] Countries like monarchical Spain may call themselves "free nations," but the language is meaningful only in relation to the Communist nations. In these countries the government, by means of the most advanced techniques of thought and social control, systematically suppress dissenters. It is only in a handful of countries on both sides of the North Atlantic, in Japan, and in Australia and New Zealand that freedom maintains its lonely existence. Even there, the future of democracy seems uncertain.

To be sure, some leaders of the emerging nations seem to have been inspired by the principles of national self-determination embodied in the Declaration of Independence. For instance, Ho Chi Minh, who had been trained primarily in Marxism-Leninism, "knew more" about the historic document than a young American officer operating in Indochina in 1945, and was "deadly serious about it." In August of that year, when the Vietminh seized power, Ho read to 500,000 people assembled in Hanoi the Declaration of Independence of the Democratic Republic. Its opening words were: "All men are created equal. They are endowed by their Creator with certain inalienable Rights . . ."[21] These words are, of course, Jefferson's. Yet, a national aspiration for independence was the only thing he had in common with the American Revolution. In the Third World, the securing of independence has not developed simultaneously with the equally arduous — and probably more difficult — task of securing and practicing constitutional guarantees of civil liberties as it had in America's revolutionary experience. It may be, as will be argued later, that other priorities existed there. From the contemporary perspective, we can therefore state that the legacies of the American Revolution are rejected by most people and linger on in only a few countries.

The picture, however, changes when we turn our attention to the dawn of modern history. The American Revolutionaries' successful efforts to put politics on an entirely different plateau and their bold

---

[20]See Indira Gandhi's statement, *Saturday Review,* December 13, 1975, p. 6.
[21]David Halberstam, *Ho* (New York, 1971), p. 74; Edward Hotaling, "The Ho Chi Minh Story: Making of a President," *The Village Voice,* July 17, 1969, pp. 5-6.

republican language enthralled the discontented in the Old Society, heightened their hope for a new political order, and fortified their faith in the infinite progress of humanity. Richard Price, a nonconformist minister in England, wrote in 1776 that he would turn to the United States "as now the hope and likely soon to become the refuge of mankind" and that Americans were "inspired by the noblest of all passions, the passions for being free."[22] A few years later Price observed that the American example already had liberated one country (by which in 1785 he probably meant Holland or Ireland) and would soon liberate others.[23] Henry Grattan, a leading Irish Parliamentary reformer, urged his countrymen that "before you decide on the practicability of being slaves forever, look to America." One observer of the Irish situation noted in 1776 that "all Ireland is America mad" and three years later that "It is now too publicly known to be disguised any longer, that Ireland has much the air of Americanizing."[24] Aleksandr Nikolaevich Radischev, a Russian reformer, addressing the American people sometime during the years 1781-1783, wrote "Thou were and art invincible: Thy leader, Washington, is Liberty" and "your example has set a goal for us — we all wish for the same. I have no part in your glory, but since the soul is subject to no one, allow at least my ashes to rest in your soil!"[25] In 1777, Benjamin Franklin, United States emissary in France, wrote home that "all Europe is on our side of the question, as far as Applause and good Wish can carry them. Those who live under arbitrary Power do nevertheless approve of Liberty, and wish for it; they almost despair of recovering it in Europe; they read the Transactions of our separate Colony Constitutions with Rapture. . . . Hence 'tis a common observation here, that our Cause is the cause of all Mankind, and that we are fighting for their Liberty in defending our own."[26] Many European

[22]Price, *Observations on the Nature of Civil Liberty and the Justice and Policy of the War with America* (London, 1778, first pub. 1776), pp. 3-4.

[23]Palmer, *The Age of Democratic Revolution*, 1:264.

[24]Michael Kraus, "America and the Irish Revolutionary Movement in the Eighteenth Century," in Richard B. Morris, ed., *The Era of the American Revolution* (New York, 1939), pp. 335-336.

[25]Aleksandr Nikolaevich Radischev, *A Journey From St. Petersburg to Moscow*, trans. by Leo Wiener, Roderick Page Thaler, ed., (Cambridge, Mass., 1958), pp. 8-9.

[26]Quoted in Halvdan Koht, *The American Spirit in Europe: A Survey of Transatlantic Influences* (Philadelphia, 1949), p. 18.

writers voiced their idealization of America so frequently that the repetition of their examples would be tedious.

If the Irish became "America mad," a host of French philosophers became American enthusiasts. The Marquis de Condorcet, in his prize-winning essay *"The Influence of the American Revolution in Europe,* asserted: "it is not enough that the rights of man be written in the books of philosophers and inscribed in the hearts of virtuous men; the weak and ignorant must be able to read them in the example of a great people. America has given us this example." On another occasion, he said that Thomas Jefferson was "entitled to the eternal gratitude of mankind" for his authorship of the Virginia Bill of Rights.[27] Curiosity, excitement, and debate about the American constitutional ideas were more intense in France than anywhere else. The American state constitutions were published there not once but on at least five different occasions between 1776 and 1786.[28] Thomas Paine's *Common Sense* was quickly translated into French.[29] This is understandable, since France was an ally of the United States and, more important, was the most vibrant center of the Enlightenment despite having the most absolute of the ancient regimes. The frequency of publications of American books and the avid reading of them, as reported by Franklin, may tell us about the popularity of the writings but not necessarily reveal their influence on French opinion.[30]

However, the initial course of the French Revolution is a concrete manifestation of that influence. When the Estates-General was about to be convened, Brissot, a future Girondist leader who had just returned from an American tour, published *A Plan of Conduct* for the deputies. In this tract, he called for a special constitutional convention for the purpose of drawing up a constitution for France, denying the Estates-General the power to do so on the grounds that the body did not represent the people. He admitted that "we owe [the idea of a constitutional convention] to the Free Americans . . .

---

[27]For an excellent discussion of the American influence, see in addition to Koht, *The American Spirit in Europe,* see also Durand *Mirage in the West: A history of the French Image of American Society to 1815* (Princeton, 1957), esp. pp. 173-174.

[28]Condorcet, *The Influence of the American Revolution in Europe,* trans. and ed. by Durand Echeverria, in *William and Mary Quarterly,* 3rd ser., 25(1968): 91, 99-100.

[29]Palmer, *The Age of Democratic Revolution,* 1:263.

[30]Koht, *The American Spirit,* p. 16.

and this device . . . of the Free Americans can perhaps be very easily adapted to the circumstances in which France now finds itself."[31] Another example of the American influence is the Marquis de Lafayette, who led the revolt of the Estates-General against the aristocracy and the king. Lafayette first participated in the American war not from a love of liberty but from a venturesome spirit and desire to weaken England. Then, during his service in the Revolution as a Continental army officer and through his close association with George Washington, he developed an incurable affection for the "American principles." The very day he was elected vice-president of the National Assembly of France (July 11, 1789), he proposed to the adoption of a declaration of the rights of man which he hoped would imitate the American model. The committee charged with drafting the declaration obliged his wishes. The committee explained before the Assembly the philosophical genesis of the draft declaration:

> This noble idea, conceived in another hemisphere, should by preference, be transplanted among us at once. We have cooperated in the events which have established liberty in North America; she shows us on what principles we should base the conservation of our own; and the New World into which hitherto we have borne only a sword, teaches us today to guard ourselves from the dangers of carrying it to our own hurt.

It should also be noted that during the hectic summer and fall of 1789 the so-called "American party" under the leadership of Lafayette held their meetings at Thomas Jefferson's house in Paris to discuss a new constitution for France and consulted the American minister about the various forms of a parliamentary system. Finally, Condorcet's advocacy of unicameralism for the French legislature was directly "inspired" by the Constitution of Pennsylvania of 1776.[32]

With these observations I am not suggesting that the American Revolution and its revolutionary legacies led directly to the French Revolution, as one French historian argued sometime ago.[33] Such an argument is as absurd as saying that the old ideas of the Enlightenment and the English opposition to them caused the American Revolution.

[31]Palmer, *The Age of Democratic Revolution,* 1:262, 472.
[32]Koht, *The American Spirit,* pp. 16-18.
[33]Condorcet so argued in *The Influence of the American Revolution,* trans. Echeverria, p. 86.

The basic and immediate causes of the French Revolution were French in origin, relating to serious financial and other domestic political problems excerbated by the American War for Independence. The effect of the American Revolution upon the French Revolution was contributory at best. The successful implementation of the Enlightenment in the United States brought into sharper relief the anarchronisms of the absolute monarchy and the resurgence of aristocracy and encouraged the French intellectuals to re-examine their ideas and assumptions in terms of practicability.[34] Condorcet was emphatic: "America has proved that a country can prosper even though it harbors neither persecutors nor hypocrites."[35]

Nonetheless, once the French Revolution came under the sway of Jacobin leadership, it began to lose almost every trace of the American ideological flavor. It ceased to be the search for constitutional system and even Maximilien Robespierre's "despotism of liberty" and of "Republican virtue." The Jacobin dictatorship of Public Safety (1793-1794) represented the transformation of the Revolution into a mass social movement primarily directed against France's traditional social hierarchy and for liberation from abject poverty and acute human misery. The poor are always under the crushing weight of necessity. Robespierre, overwhelmed by the poor's cry for vengeance upon the nobility and scarcity, subjected his revolutionary government to "the most sacred of all laws, the welfare of the people, the most irrefragable of all titles, necessity," that is, necessity of "dress, food and reproduction of their species." Meanwhile, dissenters were crushed in the name of all absorbing *General Will* which, in actuality, meant nothing but the will of the republican sans-culottes. Thus, the "Rights of Man" became the class rights of the dispossessed.[36] Ironically, however, the fury of the proletariat unleashed the reign of terror and soon made the Revolution to devour its own children. Equally ironic is that the Revolution, from the Jacobins to Napoleon Bonaparte, far from changing the political spirit of the old state, made the new

[34]Palmer, *The Age of Democratic Revolution,* 1:239; Echeverria, *Mirage in the West,* pp. 116, 140.
    [35]Condorcet, *The Influence of the American Revolution,* trans. by Echeverria, pp. 94-95.
    [36]Hannah Arendt, *On Revolution* (New York, 1963), pp. 54-55, 129; Albert Soboul, *The Sans Culottes,* trans. by Rémy Inglis Hall (Garden City, N.Y., 1972), pp. xvii-xxxiv, 6, 10, 14, 15, 44, 48-49, 52, 56-57, 59, 256.

state more absolute and the exercise of its power more arbitrary than ever before.[37]

The French Revolution, as far as its Jacobin phase was concerned, constituted the antithesis of everything the American Revolution promoted except for the abolition of monarchy. The Jacobins promised an instant happiness through the expropriation of the aristocratic estates and were obsessed with such social questions as poverty, scarcity, and inequality of wealth. The American Revolution promised no such socioeconomic program, but guaranteed to citizens only the right to engage in the "pursuit of happiness."[38] The French created an absolute and unitary state in the place of the old regime, while the Americans worked to preserve the foundation of civil freedom and limit government.

It was the Jacobin model of the French Revolution with its preoccupation with the social questions, not the American model with its preoccupation with civil liberties, which inspired and affected almost all subsequent revolutions. To be sure, the American Revolutionary creed, particularly its constitutional formulations, would be adopted by many countries. The Belgium revolt against the Hapsburg monarchy invoked some phrases of the American Revolution, and some democratic elements in Belgium in 1790 even considered molding their government in the image of certain American state constitutions.[39] The abortive Polish Constitution of May 3, 1791, reflected the attempts by the Polish gentry to reorganize the government in the spirit of the Federal Constitution of the United States and the French Declaration of the Rights of Man and Citizen. Thaddeus Kosciusko must have perceived his leading an insurrection against Russia for the independence of Poland in 1794 in the light of the American Revolution in which he had participated side-by-side with Washington and his dear friend Jefferson.[40] The American idea of a written constitution as the basis of public law would have a continuing impact on the

[37]Lionel Kochan, *Acton on History* (London, 1954), p. 123.

[38]Irving Kristol, "The American Revolution As A Successful Revolution," in *The American Revolution: Three Views* (New York, 1975), p. 42; G. D. Lillibridge, *Beacon of Freedom: The Impact of American Democracy upon Great Britain, 1830-1870* (Philadelphia, 1955) pp. 55-56.

[39]Palmer, *The Age of Democratic Revolution,* 1:265.

[40]Manfred Kridl et al., eds., *For Your Freedom and Ours: Polish Progressive Spirit Through the Centuries* (New York, 1943), pp. 75-76.

constitutional history of Switzerland.[41] In Russia, the Northern Society, a moderate wing of the Decembrist Movement of 1825 advocated a constitutional scheme similar to the American Federal Constitution.[42] In the 1830s and 1840s the English reformers and the radical Chartists attacked the suppression of freedom and the corruption of the nobility, monarch, and church by invoking the principles of the American Revolution. Henry Hetherington, the publisher of the popular but illegal *Poor Man's Guardian,* soon after the House of Lords rejected the Reform Bill in 1831, reminded his readers that the American Revolution was "the best precedent and guide to the oppressed and enslaved people of England in their struggle for the RIGHT OF REPRESENTATION FOR EVERY MAN."[43] The American Declaration of Independence appeared on the English political scene again and again. The Chartists warned of the American example of dealing with tyranny. The English Chartist Circular, dated November 6, 1841, observed: "America is not only a phenomenon in the history of the nation, but an example worthy of emulation of all who invoke the sacred name of liberty — who long to see her blessings diffused and her cause triumphant over the dark friends of despotism, vice, and wretchedness."[44] Of all the revolutionary movements of 1848, the Hungarian uprising seems to have been very much stirred by the principles in the American Declaration of Independence which Louis Kossuth, one of the Hungarian patriots, characterized as the "noblest, happiest page of mankind's history."[45]

But the importance of the message of the American Revolution, which is fundamentally bourgeois and political in character, waned as modern history became afflicted more and more with the social questions of poverty and scarcity. We cannot blame the Founding Fathers for not addressing themselves to these questions because plentiful land and benign civil constitutions in the American colonies had overcome poverty and because American colonial society had been spared from the entrenched feudal nobility and privileged class. As Tocqueville

---

[41]Palmer, *The Age of Democratic Revolution,* 1:265.
[42]Marc Raeff, ed., *The Decembrist Movement* (Englewood Cliffs, N.J., 1966), pp. 100-118.
[43]Lillibridge, *Beacon of Freedom,* p. 28.
[44]Quoted ibid., p. 43.
[45]*Selected Speeches of Kossuth,* condensed and abridged by F. W. Newnian (London, 1853), pp. 144-145.

perceptively put it, "The great advantage of the Americans is that they have arrived at a state of democracy without having to endure a democratic revolution, and they are born equal instead of becoming so."[46] This was precisely the reason why Americans with Jefferson could hold as "self-evident" the notion that "men are created equal," a notion which eighteenth-century Europeans could not accept so easily.

The non-social American Revolution could not be an example for many Eastern and Central European countries to follow, for they had yet to liberate themselves from such feudal oppression as serfdom and racking landlords. The French model, therefore, became the blueprint for social revolutionaries. Furthermore, the spread of the French influence to most of Latin Europe, the Low Countries, Switzerland, and West Germany, was accelerated with the march of the French conquering armies proclaiming in the name of the French nation "the abolition of tithes, feudality, and seigneureal rights." Through direct or indirect agency of the French Revolution, feudalism was abolished from 1789 to 1848 from Gibraltar to East Prussia, and from the Baltic to Sicily.[47] The persistent influence of the Gallic revolution is suggested by the fact that political organizations like Young Italy, Young Poland, Young Switzerland, Young Germany, Young France, Young Czechs, and Young Turks adopted a tricolor of some kind in the image of the French revolutionary flag. The present Irish, Yugoslav, Rumanian, Syrian, South African, Mexican, and other Latin American tricolors point to the same inspiration.[48]

Indeed, most of the nationalist movements from 1820 on were closely bound up with social struggle. José de San Martin, the Argentinean liberator, fought not only for independence but also for social and economic changes.[49] The Democratic Society of Poland, founded by Polish emigres in Paris after the failure of the November Uprising of 1830-31, declared in 1836 that the elimination of feudal exactions and social injustice in Poland was the precondition for bringing about "a free and harmonious development of national forces."[50] Sun

---

[46]Tocqueville, *Democracy,* 2:109.

[47]E. J. Hobsbawm, *The Age of Revolution, 1789-1848* (New York, 1964), pp. 184-185, 187.

[48]Ibid., pp. 164-165; Palmer, *The Age of Democratic Revolution,* 1:348.

[49]See the classic study, Bartolome Mitré, *The Emancipation of South America,* trans. by William Pilling (New York, 1969).

[50]Kridl, *For Your Freedom and Ours,* pp. 78-79.

Yat-sen, the father of Modern China, upheld the principle of social equality as one of the three major goals of his revolution.[51] Jawaharlal Nehru, the Indian Nationalist leader, believed that a real revolution should affect the "whole fabric of life and society" as did the French and Russian revolutions — and not just political life as did the American Revolution. It was this "real" revolution he tried to apply to his country.[52] In 1954 Gamal Abdel Nasser of Egypt asserted that he had "no alternative" but to carry out political and social [class] revolutions together and at the same time.[53]

In Industrial Europe, too, the social questions continued to occupy the center stage of revolutionary ferment. The industrial development produced a horde of workingmen subject to bourgeois exploitation, which, in turn, deepened their miseries and threw them into despair. Karl Marx, emerging as their spokesman, rejected the entire constitutional, economic, social, and cultural systems based on the sanctity of private property and traditional civil liberties. He preached a class revolution to obtain freedom for the proletariat from the fetters of scarcity.

This ideological scheme, like Jacobinism, posed a serious challenge to the American republicanism. The American system with its worship of private property and its guarantee of free-play of capitalistic interests was anathema to the socialists who worshipped a collective ownership of productive means and the historical inevitability of a revolution in which "one class overthrows another."[54] In 1873, Peter Lavrov, a Russian Populist (Narodnik) writer, while commemorating the centennial of Pugachev's Rebellion, commented on the achievements and influence of the American Revolution. As much as he was impressed with them, he did not seem wholly persuaded with their relevance for American society of the Gilded Age characterized by the rule of money, corruption, and growing social inequality. He believed that the splendid achievements of the "heroic" Revolu-

---

[51]Sun Yat-sen, *San Min Chu I: The Three Principles of the People,* trans. by Frank W. Price (Shanghai, 1928).

[52]Jawaharlal Nehru, *Glimpses of World History* (New York, 1942), pp. 360-362, 377.

[53]Paul E. Sigmund, ed., *The Ideologies of the Developing Nations* (New York, 1972), pp. 124-126, 137, 150-151, 106-111, passim.

[54]*Quotations From Chairman Mao Tse-Tung,* intro. by A. Doak Barnett (New York, 1967), pp. 7, 14, 42; John Gerassi, ed., *Venceremos! The Speeches and Writings of Ernesto Che Guevara* (New York, 1968), chaps. 11, 14.

tion were now "exhausted" due to the emergence of the social evils, for which the American "constitutions and codices" appeared to be impotent and that "the social question smashed, destroyed and buried the political creations of the revolutionary period."[55] Lavrov's view with respect to the American conditions seems to hold true not only of the contemporary European society, but also of the world in the subsequent decades when the social problem aggravated. The irrelevance of the American Revolutionary heritage for the socialistic movement was clearly signalled when American socialists, gathered in the Masonic Hall at Indianapolis one summer day in 1901, sang the "Marsellaise" instead of "Yankee Doodle" or the "Star Spangled Banner" after they had just finished founding the Socialist Party of America.[56]

The political and constitutional practices on the part of the ideological right and center in modern history also seem to have little relationship with the American system of government. All of them were deficient in a balance built on the principle of separation of powers and tempered by the popular sovereignty. These governments were either too strong or unstable at the center. Typical of the former were Imperial Germany and Japan, distinguished for their authoritarianism. Typical of the latter was France, where fourteen constitutions came and went from 1789 to 1875, one constitution for every six years on the average. Such a record would defy an attempt to locate the origin for each of them. The countries of limited monarchy, like Belgium, turned to the British constitutional arrangement for guidance. After the First World War, many of the monarchical constitutions in Europe were replaced by those modelled largely after the American constitution, but the new constitutions were mistrusted by the people living under them. Fifteen years after the fall of the monarchical governments, half of Europe would live under some form of dictatorship.[57]

Modern history has shabbily dealt with the legacies of the American Revolution. The record is due to no fault of the Founders

---

[55]David Hecht, *Russian Radicals Look to America, 1825-1894* (Cambridge, Mass., 1947), pp. 153-55. See also Richard B. Morris, *The Emerging Nations and the American Revolution* (New York, 1970), p. 106.

[56]David A. Shannon, *The Socialist Party of America: A History* (New York, 1955), p. 1.

[57]Arendt, *On Revolution*, p. 144.

of the American Republic. Rather, it was the deeping social and economic malaise of pre-modern and modern society which dulled people's sensitivity for the classical political liberties and enhanced their concern for equality and necessity.

It would be remiss not to say something about the record of the United States regarding its Revolutionary heritage. Americans still live under the Constitution created almost two centuries ago, but no longer live by its original spirit. Local township government, the matrix and mainstay of our democracy, is no longer what it used to be, having badly atrophied under the heavy hand of the state and federal governments. The government in Washington, D.C., has become so powerful that one sensitive historian recently described its executive branch as the "Imperial Presidency."[58] Its huge and expensive bureaucracy seems to have acquired a life of its own unsusceptible to the feelings and opinions of the people. Even the behavior of elected officials has been such as to warrant a loss of faith in representative system.

In the conduct of foreign affairs, the record is no better. America has argued for the principles of open door and national self-determination, but has often failed to live up to those lofty ideals whenever they came into conflict with its own interests and security considerations. It is true that the United States, from Woodrow Wilson to Harry S. Truman, has liberated many people from both domestic and foreign tyrants and given them democratic constitutions. Yet in these instances, America seems to have been motivated by considerations other than its Revolutionary principles. Being the richest nation, enjoying an unprecedented influence in international affairs and holding vast investments abroad, protecting its stakes has become the main obsession of our "security managers" since the Second World War. In 1948, President Truman, disturbed by increasing Communist insurgency in the Mediterranean area, declared: "We cannot allow changes in the Status Quo." This passion for order has often led to intervention, overtly and covertly, in many parts of the world. During our 1965 intervention in the Dominican Republic, the commanding U. S. admiral explained as he took over the Dominican occupation: "our troops will remain until all revolutionary

[58]Arthur M. Schlesinger, Jr., *The Imperial Presidency* (Boston, 1973).

movements have been stamped out."[59] America inflicted terrible pain and destruction on the Vietnamese people in a vain attempt to "save" them from Communism, although they were fighting for their independence. The United States has become the Metternich of the mid-twentieth century, a posture which runs afoul of its Revolutionary heritage.

Yet, no nation has been more critical and scrutinizing of its own conduct in the light of its national creed than has the United States. No nation has tried so hard in reconciling the gap between its creed and the sordid realities of racism and foreign adventurism than the Americans. There have been many Jeffersons and Lincolns who, suffering from heavy guilt feelings about the black Americans' plight, worked for equal justice. There have been many anti-imperialists like Lincoln and Ulysses Grant who vigorously condemned the immorality of the Mexican War, like Mark Twain and Andrew Carnegie who warned of the betrayal of the Revolutionary heritage by the annexation of the Philippines, like William Fulbright and George McGovern who denounced our activities in Vietnam for the same reason. There have also been many Archibald Coxes and John Siricas who displayed courage to defend the Constitution at a critical moment. We are entitled to the comfortable thought that, through these great men, our Revolutionary legacies have been kept alive, affecting our life and modern history alike, and that this country, without a history of social revolution, has provided an asylum for fifty million or more people escaping from that perennial albatross of mankind, scarcity, which all the modern social revolutions have yet to overcome.

America may not have become a place where Hegel's *Geistes-Geschichte* (Spirit-History) of the world lodged, but it has been a nation of an "abounding strength and vitality."[60] Ultimately, the vindication of the American Revolution does not have to be found in its approval or duplication by other nations, but rather in how well it has worked for and how strongly it will continue to inspire the people of the United States of America.

---

[59]Richard J. Barnet, *Intervention and Revolution* (New York, 1968), pp. 8, 81.

[60]James Bryce, *The American Commonwealth*, ed. by Louis Hacker, 2 vols. (New York, 1959), 1:8.

CONTRIBUTORS

RICHARD D. BROWN, Professor of History at the University of Connecticut, is the author of *Revolutionary Politics in Massachusetts: The Boston Committee of Correspondence and the Towns, 1772-1774*, and *Modernization: The Transformation of American Life, 1600-1865*.

RICHARD L. BUSHMAN, Professor of History at University of Delaware, is the author of *From Puritan to Yankee: Character and the Social Order in Connecticut, 1690-1765*, winner of the Bancroft and the Phi Alpha Theta prizes.

JERALD A. COMBS, Professor of History at San Francisco State Univerity, is the author of *The Jay Treaty: Political Battleground of the Founding Fathers*.

LINDA GRANT DePAUW, Professor of History at The George Washington Univerity, is the author of *Founding Mothers: Women of America in the Revolutionary Era*, and *The Eleventh Pillar: New York State and the Federal Constitution*.

JAMES A. DOLPH, Associate Professor of History at Weber State College, is currently studying the career of conservationist William Temple Hornaday.

JOSEPH A. ERNST, Professor of History at York University, Ontario, Canada, is the author of *Money and Politics in America, 1755-1775: A Study in the Currency Act of 1764 and the Political Economy of Revolution*.

LARRY R. GERLACH, Professor of History at the University of Utah, is the author of *Prologue to Independence: New Jersey in the Coming of the American Revolution* and *Connecticut Congressman: Samuel Huntington, 1731-1796*.

MICHAEL KAMMEN, Professor of History and Director of the Society for the Humanities at Cornell University, is the author of *People of Paradox: An Inquiry Concerning the Origins of American Civilization* (winner of the Pulitzer Prize), and *Colonial New York: A History.*

SUNG BOK KIM, Associate Professor of History at the State University of New York at Albany, is the author of *Manors, Landlords, and Tenants in Colonial New York, 1664-1775.*

MICHAEL L. NICHOLLS, Associate Professor of History at Utah State University, is currently engaged in a study of the social and economic development of the Virginia "southside" in the eighteenth-century.

WILLIE LEE ROSE, Professor of Southern and Afro-American History at the Johns Hopkins University, is the author of *Rehearsal For Reconstruction: The Port Royal Experiment* (for which she won the Allan Nevins Prize of the American Historical Association, the Francis Parkman Prize of the Organization of American Historians, and the Charles Sydnor Prize of the Southern Historical Association.

BERNARD W. SHEEHAN, Professor of History at Indiana University is the author of *Seeds of Extinction: Jeffersonian Philanthropy and the American Indian.*

JOHN SHY, Professor of History at the University of Michigan, is the author of *Toward Lexington: The Role of the British Army in the Coming of the American Revolution.* He has received the John H. Dunning Prize from the American Historical Association.